STUDY GUIDE on SHAKESPEARE'S

ROMEO AND JULIET

MADE SUPER SUPER EASY

TEXT EXPLAINED IN GREAT DETAIL

ACHIEVE TOP GRADES
A MUST FOR ALL STUDENTS

EVELYN SAMUEL on Shakespeare

Shakespeare's Romeo and Juliet
Made Super Super Easy
First Edition Published by Evelyn Samuel
Copyright © 2020 Evelyn Samuel

EveMadeSuperEasyBooks
www.EveSuperEasyBooks.com
evesupereasybooks@gmail.com

DEDICATED TO
RAVI MOODLEY

No words I write could ever say
How sad and empty I feel today.
The angels came for you
Much sooner than I planned.
I'll brave the bitter grief that comes,
And I'll try my best to understand.
Why did you have to go away?
Why wasn't it right for you to stay?
In my heart you will always be.
I love you dearly and I know you'll watch over me.

PREFACE

To all students reading my study guide **Romeo and Juliet made super super easy**, I do hope that my wealth of information will assist you to achieve the highest possible grades. I have formulated a unique structure where detailed explanation is next to text to make it super super easy for you to connect and understand the book, and to revise without the need to resort to more than one book.

Each scene in each Act is defined by a detailed explanation next to Shakespeare's text. The detailed explanation is evidenced and highlighted with relevant important quotes. It identifies connotative meaning, imagery, symbolism, and linguistic devices.

Each scene in each Act is summarised to aid in the understanding of the Shakespearean storyline.

A detailed explanation of each main character in the book is provided so that the fabric of their relationships can be better understood.

The themes of fate and love are analysed to reveal the true nature of star-crossed lovers as perceived by society in Shakespeare's era.

Typical exam questions are included to give some idea of the scope sought by the Exam Boards. Further details can be found in the Specification published by the Exam Boards on their websites.

Good Luck with your studies and your exam results on *Romeo and Juliet*.

FOREWARD

What a super super easy way to study and understand Shakespeare's tragedy, 'Romeo and Juliet'. No need to match text with explanation when both are next to each other - with important quotes highlighted.

I really enjoyed looking left at the text and then right at the explanation. The structure and content of this fantastic book is a solid base to get to grips with Shakespeare's tragedy about two young star-crossed lovers whose self-imposed deaths through misunderstanding, ultimately reconciles the feud between their respective families, the Montagues for Romeo and the Capulets for Juliet.

I can, without hesitation, recommend this study guide to all students, and hope they gain as much insight as I did into Shakespeare's tragedy, 'Romeo and Juliet'.

Research Professor of English

CONTENTS

Historical Context and Setting

- William Shakespeare, one of the greatest playwrights of the Elizabethan era, wrote 'Romeo and Juliet' sometime between 1591 and 1596 during the reign of Queen Elizabeth 1 of England.
- The plot stems from an Italian tale translated into verse as 'The Tragical History of Romeo and Juliet' by Arthur Brooke in 1562 and retold in prose in 'Palace of Pleasure' by William Painter in 1567.
- The play is set in Verona, Italy during the Renaissance, the era of rebirth of Ancient Greek and Roman learning, when rivalry between different groups in society, promoted conflict to attain wealth and power.
- During his lifetime, and today, 'Romeo and Juliet', is still one of Shakespeare's most popular plays only matched by 'Hamlet', a tragedy of a different kind written by Shakespeare circa 1602 and set in Denmark.

Tragic Lovers

- Throughout history there have been many events of star-crossed lovers meeting a tragic end: Cleopatra and Mark Anthony in 30 BC; or the Celtic tale of Tristan and Isolde (circa prior to 1200 AD) - both a precursor to Romeo and Juliet, and both pairs of lovers suffering a similar fate to Romeo the Montague and Juliet the Capulet.
- The tragedy occurs because Romeo mistakenly thinks that Juliet has killed herself and wishing to join her in death, takes poison and dies. But, in fact, Juliet had taken a sleeping drug as a ruse to evade marriage to Paris simply because Friar Laurence had secretly married her to Romeo before he was exiled. On awakening, distraught, she refuses to leave the tomb and stabs herself to join Romeo in the afterlife.
- The mantra for true lovers is that they will never be parted in life or death.

The Feud

- Dominance and position in society seem to be the driving force that sets the Montagues and Capulets against each other and any relinquishing of rights or possessions must be denied with the consequence that conflicts are resolved by force of arms not diplomacy.
- Juliet cannot be allowed to marry a Montague because that would violate the feud as would that of Romeo were to marry a Capulet.
- The feud is ended by their tragic deaths.

THE PLAY

CHARACTERS

[House of Montague]

ROMEO	son and heir of Lord and Lady Montague
LORD MONTAGUE	father of Romeo and the patriarch of the family
LADY MONTAGUE	mother of Romeo
BENVOLIO	nephew of Lord Montague, cousin of Romeo
BALTHASAR	dedicated servant of Romeo
ABRAHAM	servant of the House of Montague

[House of Capulet]

JULIET	daughter of Lord and Lady Capulet
LORD CAPULET	father of Juliet and the patriarch of the family
LADY CAPULET	mother of Juliet
NURSE	cared for Juliet her entire life
TYBALT	cousin of Juliet on her mother's side
SAMPSON	servant of the House of Capulet
GREGORY	another servant of the House of Capulet
PETER	servant of the House of Capulet
MUSICIANS	group of 3 musical players

[Franciscans]

FRIAR LAURENCE	friend to both Romeo and Juliet
FRIAR JOHN	colleague of Friar Laurence

[Others]

PRINCE ESCALUS	Prince of Verona
MERCUTIO	kinsman to the Prince and friend of Romeo
PARIS	kinsman to the Prince and the suitor of Juliet
THE APOTHECARY	chemist in Mantua who sales poison and potions
ROSALINE	woman whom Romeo is infatuated with
THE CHORUS	single narrator commenting on plots and themes

ENTRANCES

A list of when each CHARACTER in the play makes their ENTRANCES

ACT	1					2						3					4					5		
SCENE	1	2	3	4	5	1	2	3	4	5	6	1	2	3	4	5	1	2	3	4	5	1	2	3
LOVERS																								
Romeo	■	■		■	■	■	■	■	■		■	■		■		■						■		■
Juliet			■		■		■			■	■		■			■	■	■	■					■
STATE																								
Escalus	■											■												■
Paris		■													■		■				■			■
Mercutio				■		■			■			■												■
Page																								
Watchmen	■																							■
CHURCH																								
Friar Laurence								■			■			■			■		■		■			■
Friar John																							■	
MONTAGUE																								
Lord	■											■												■
Lady	■											■												
Benvolio	■	■		■	■	■			■			■											■	■
Balthasar																						■		■
Abraham	■																							
CAPULET																								
Lord	■	■		■											■	■		■		■				■
Lady	■		■						■				■		■	■		■	■					
Nurse			■		■		■	■		■			■		■		■	■	■					
Tybalt					■	■			■			■												
Peter		■						■	■															
Sampson	■																							
Gregory	■																			■				
Servants	■			■																■				
Musicians																				■				
OTHERS																								
Apothcry																						■		
Rosaline																								
SCENE	1	2	3	4	5	1	2	3	4	5	6	1	2	3	4	5	1	2	3	4	5	1	2	3
ACT	1					2						3					4					5		

TIMELINE

Events in the play take place over **FOUR** days.

Day	ACT	scene	Event
Sunday	**Act 1**	scene 1	Capulets & Montagues Street brawl stopped by Prince
		scene 2	Paris seeks Juliet's hand in marriage
		scene 3	Juliet arrives home and agrees to consider marriage
		scene 4	Romeo, Mercutio & Montagues go to Capulet's feast
		scene 5	At the feast, Romeo & Juliet meet and fall in love
Monday	**Act 2**	scene 1	Benvolio & Mercutio look for Romeo
		scene 2	Romeo below Juliet's window both declaring their love
		scene 3	Friar Laurence agrees to marry Romeo & Juliet
		scene 4	Benvolio tells Mercutio - Tybalt will challenge Romeo
		scene 5	Nurse tells Juliet about the wedding arrangements
		scene 6	Romeo and Juliet are married by Friar Laurence
	Act 3	scene 1	Tybalt kills Mercutio, Romeo kills Tybalt and then flees
		scene 2	Nurse tells Juliet - Romeo is banished for killing Tybalt
		scene 3	Romeo stays with Juliet the night then goes to Mantua
		scene 4	Paris to wed Juliet in 3 days with Capulet's blessing
Tuesday		scene 5	Capulet tells Juliet - she is to marry Paris
	Act 4	scene 1	Juliet rebuffs Paris, Friar tells Juliet to fake her death
		scene 2	Juliet agrees marriage, wedding brought forward
		scene 3	Juliet takes sleeping potion
		scene 4	Capulets make final wedding preparations
Wednesday		scene 5	Nurse finds Juliet dead, wedding turns to funeral
	Act 5	scene 1	Balthasar tells Romeo of Juliet's death, who then visits Apothecary in Mantua to get poison, then returns to Verona
		scene 2	Friar John returns letter Friar Laurence wrote to Romeo
Thursday		scene 3	Romeo kills Paris at Juliet's Tomb, then kills himself on discovering Juliet's lifeless body. Juliet awakes and on finding Romeo dead, kills herself Capulets & Montagues reunite in grief

Shakespeare's Romeo and Juliet is the story of two young people who fall in love but find themselves on opposite sides of a feud between their two families. The Capulets expect their daughter Juliet to marry her suitor, Paris. However, Juliet cannot bear to marry anyone but Romeo of the House of Montague, so they get married in secret with the help of Juliet's Nurse and Friar Laurence.

Unfortunately, because of the ongoing feud, Tybalt of the House of Capulet challenges Romeo to a fight. Instead, Mercutio, a close friend of Romeo, enraged at Romeo's refusal to fight accepts the challenge and is accidentally killed by Tybalt when Romeo intervenes to stop the fight.

Romeo reacts by seeking revenge, fights Tybalt and kills him. In judgement, Prince Escalus banishes Romeo from Verona. Romeo is distraught, as he cannot be now with Juliet, his newlywed wife.

In a desperate attempt to reunite with Romeo, Juliet seeks help from Friar Laurence who persuades her to fake her own death as a ruse to escape her next-day, would-be bigamous marriage to her suitor Paris, chosen by her parents Lord and Lady Capulet. Tragically, Romeo is not aware of the ruse, as a letter sent by Friar Laurence explaining the ruse, fails to reach him in time.

Romeo arrives to find Juliet dead, or so he thinks. Distraught, he drinks poison and dies next to the drugged Juliet. When Juliet awakes, she is devastated to discover Romeo's dead body beside her. Consequently, she stabs herself, so that, as in life, she would be with her true love Romeo in death.

In remorse, at such a loss of two star-crossed lovers, the House of Capulets and the House of Montague end their feud.

SETTING

Shakespeare's play 'Romeo and Juliet' is set mostly in the city of Verona and to a less extent in the town of Mantua. Both places are in the north of Italy, during the latter period of the Renaissance sweeping Europe in the 16th Century.

Although, regarded as an affluent and romantic country, Italy was also regarded as a country where murderous feuds and passionate love affairs took place. However, customs and attitudes in the play are not dissimilar to those exhibited by families in Elizabethan England. The audience at the Globe Theatre in the East End of London on the north bank of the river Thames, would have easily identified with the characters and uncomplicated plots in the play.

The Verona locations used in the story are:

HOUSE of Capulet

HOUSE of Montague
STREETS in Verona
CELL of Friar Laurence
TOMB Capulet Family

The Mantua locations used in the story are:

STREET in Mantua

SHOP of the Apothecary

FORM

Shakespeare's Romeo and Juliet takes the form of a play made up entirely of dialogue where the audience discover through words delivered by actors, the type of characters, their motives, their relationships together with the storyline.

Shakespeare's aim was to educate and entertain ordinary people in an age when few people could read - to draw out the emotions in people. In this case, to elicit empathy and understanding for two young lovers caught up in a world of two feuding families, each young lover belonging to a different opposing feuding family. Such is the tragedy in the play 'Romeo and Juliet', when true love is destroyed by the uncontrollable event of the feud between the House of Capulet and the House of Montague, with the consequence that although the feud is ended, both lovers have died by their own hand.

The dialogue is in three different forms: mainly blank verse, prose and rhyming verse. Each line of blank verse, is made up of roughly ten syllables, organised into five groups of two, where an unstressed syllable is followed by a stressed syllable. This creates an air of authority and identifies higher status characters such as Lord Capulet from lower characters such as servants who speak in ordinary prose. To illustrate this, in Act 4 scene 2:

CAPULET	(to Second Serviceman)	**[blank verse]**
	Sirrah, go hire me twenty cunning cooks.	
Second	You shall have none ill, sir,	**[ordinary prose]**
Serviceman	for I'll try if they can lick their fingers	

Rhyming verse is used by Shakespeare to end lines in a memorable way so that the audience recall it in later scenes; to make characters complete each other's rhymes to emphasise unity in thought, action, ideas and moods between them. To illustrate this,

Act 1 scene 3   **LADY CAPULET**
Verona's summer hath not such a **flower**
Nurse
Nay, he is a **flower**. In faith, a very **flower**

Act 3 scene 1   **PRINCE**
Benvolio, who began this bloody   **fray**?
BENVOLIO
Tybalt here slain; whom Romeo's hand did **slay**.

STRUCTURE

The play 'Romeo and Juliet' is edited into five Acts, each containing several scenes. The storyline is straightforward based on the classical five-part structure:

- an initial incident   - termed **Exposition**
- a growth in tension   - termed **Rising Action**
- a climax to the drama   - termed **Climax**
- an unravelling of the plot   - termed **Falling Action**
- a resolution to the drama   - termed **Denouement**

There are no subplots and therefore the play conforms to the structure of place, action and time. The action moves apace from the opening fight scene to the closing tragic deaths of the young lovers. The short time frame of a few days secures the interest of the audience as events move swift-on leaving no time for the audience to anticipate the next event.

The Prologue is a structure used by Shakespeare to alert the audience to the forthcoming storyline.

The Soliloquy is a structure used by Shakespeare to present a deeper insight into the characters. To illustrate this, in Act 5 scene 1, Romeo speaks directly to the audience as if thinking aloud, revealing his inner thoughts, feeling and intentions about his love for Juliet.

Language Device - Tragedy and Comedy

Shakespeare uses different language devices to create tragedy and comedy in the play. To illustrate this,

Act 1 scene 1 **LORD CAPULET**
What noise is this?
Give me my long sword, ho!
LADY CAPULET
A crutch, a crutch!
Why call you for a sword?

The juxtaposition of tragedy and comedy reveals the turmoil in Veronese society. Shakespeare exploits the class difference present in Veronese society by using the low characters to parody the actions of the higher characters in the play.

This was a typical Elizabethan literary device to promote laughter within the audience. To illustrate this,

Act 1 scene 3 **LADY CAPULET**
Verona's summer hath not such a **flower**.
Nurse
Nay, he is a **flower**. In faith, a very **flower**.

Shakespeare uses wit to rationalise the irony of tragic events as illustrated in Act 3 scene 1 where Mercutio remarks to Romeo just before he dies, killed by Tybalt:

Act 3 scene 1 **MERCUTIO**
Ask for me tomorrow,
and you shall find me a grave man.

Language Device - The Chorus

The Chorus is equivalent to the third-person narrative voice in a novel. Shakespeare makes use of the Chorus to prime the audience as to the forth coming events in the play.

The Prologue spoken by the Chorus prior to an Act is written in sonnet form made up of three quatrains (set of four lines). Each quatrain informs the audience of one aspect of the story. At the end of the three quatrains is a rhyming couplet to remind the audience of their duty.

The Prologue is a literary device used in ancient times by the Greek, to build anticipation within the audience for what is to come.

The Prologue in Act 1 informs the audience of two feuding households, both alike in dignity, whose feud is ended by the tragic deaths of a pair of star-crossed lovers. The Prologue ends with a rhyming couplet.

Act 1 Prologue   The which, if you with patient ears **attend**,
                                 What here shall miss, our toil shall strive to **mend**

The Prologue prior to Act 2 is again in sonnet form made up of three quatrains, but this time informs the audience about Romeo and Juliet's requited love. The Prologue ends with a rhyming couplet

Act 2 Prologue   But passion lends them power, time means, to **meet**
                                 Tempering extremities with extreme **sweet**

Language Device - Verse and Prose

Shakespeare makes use of poetry (verse) and prose (speech) to distinguish between characters of high rank in society and those of low rank - a ploy used in theatrical conventions at the time.

Characters higher in rank speak in verse. For example, Prince Escalus, the Lords and their Ladies, Friar Laurence, Romeo and Juliet. Consequently, this makes their pronouncements sound important and intelligent, as evident in

Act 2 scene 3 -   Friar Laurence speaks in verse (poetry)

However, when danger in, verse (poetry) changes to speech (prose), as evident in

Act 2 scene 4 -   Mercutio speaks in prose stressing his disturbed state of mind
Act 3 scene 1 -   Mercutio fights with Tybalt conveying his agitation

Characters lower in rank speak in speech (prose). For example, the servants, the musicians, and Peter, as evident in

Act 1 scene 1 - Sampson and Gregory speak in prose (speech) about chores **Act 1 scene 5** - the serving men speak in prose about chores
Act 4 scene 5 - the musicians speak in prose to Peter

Language Device - Imagery

Shakespeare makes use of words to create a visual picture of an object or event to enhance its impact.

The 'death' imagery is ever present throughout the play as the feud ensures that death is always present. This is evident in The Prologue in Act 1,

The fearful passage of their death-marked love

Verona is a dangerous place, where the young accept death as a way of life.

Act 1 scene 5 - Romeo senses 'untimely death'

Act 2 scene 6 - Romeo muses 'then love-devouring death' **Act 3 scene 2** - Juliet muses 'than the death-darting eye'

Act 4 scene 5 - Capulet states, 'She was a flower, but death deflowered her' **Act 5 scene 3** - Romeo muses 'that unsubstantial death is amorous'

The 'disease' imagery is used as a negative undertone. This is evident in

Act 1 scene 1 - Romeo feels 'a choking gall, and a preserving sweet'
Act 1 scene 2 - Benvolio states 'take thou some new infection to thy eye'

Juxtaposed to disease is Juliet's beauty:

Act 2 scene 2 - Romeo said:
'Arise, fair sun, and kill the envious moon, Who is already sick and pale with grief'

The 'religious' imagery is used to elevate the purity of their love:

Act 1 scene 5 - Romeo muses to Juliet 'Your hand is like a holy place' **Act 4 scene 2** - Juliet says 'God joined my heart and Romeo's'

The 'light and dark' imagery is used to contrast opposites:

Act 2 scene 2 - Romeo says:
'The brightness of her cheek would shame those stars'
Act 3 scene 5 - Romeo says:
'More light and light, more dark and dark our woes!'
Act 5 scene 3 - Romeo says:
'her beauty makes This vault a feasting presence full of light'

Language Device - Symbolism

Shakespeare makes use of symbolism to express ideas and emotions in the play. The symbolism of birds is used to great effect by Shakespeare to:

[] forecast the future
[] herald the death of former lovers
[] herald the nesting of new lovers
[] herald the separations of lovers

In Shakespeare's era, birds were seen as important auguries (forecasters) of fate, reflecting the superstitious nature of society in Elizabethan times. Benvolio attempts to alleviate Romeo's torment for Rosaline by making him think that she is not a swan but a crow, a bird thought to foreshadow death.

Benvolio in

Act 1 scene 2 - "And I will make thee think thy swan is a crow"

The irony is that it is Romeo's love for Juliet, his new swan, that leads to his death and not his love for Rosaline, his former swan.

Shakespeare continues the idea of bird symbolism by using the practice of Falconry, popular in Elizabethan times, to convey the idea of a lover hunting his prey. Besotted by his new love, Romeo hunts Juliet down to her nest where they exchange messages of undying love. Juliet appears aloft at the window, Romeo is below. She utters the immortal phrase:

Act 2 scene 2 - O Romeo, Romeo! wherefore art thou Romeo?

Later, she calls to the falconer, Romeo, to lure the bird, in this case, herself

Act 2 scene 2 - O for a falconer's voice
To lure this tassel-gentle back again!

Later, Romeo responds to Juliet's wooing,

Act 2 scene 2 - My niess!

the name used for a young hawk, implying her youth.

The bird symbolism continues as Juliet calls out:

Act 2 scene 2 - And yet no further than a wanton's bird
That lets it hop a little from her hand

Romeo responds

Act 2 scene 2 - I would I were thy bird

The exchange between the falconer, Romeo, and the bird, Juliet, reveals the irony that love can and will lead to death, even when Juliet said in jest.

Act 2 scene 2 - Yet I should kill thee with much cherishing

and concludes with the famous phrase

Act 2 scene 2 - Parting is such sweet sorrow

Shakespeare concludes the bird symbolism with the two lovers Romeo and Juliet by heralding the separation of the lovers before the tragic end. Juliet blames the nightingale as the harbinger of dome not the lark. Romeo thinks the lark, not the nightingale is the culprit.

Act 3 scene 5 - Juliet said:
'It was the nightingale, and not the lark'
Romeo replied:
'It was the lark ... . No nightingale'

At the break of day, the lark is a positive omen of hope, but this is rejected by Juliet in favour of the nightingale a negative omen associated with doom.

Language Device - Puns and Innuendos

Shakespeare makes use of crude, uncouth Puns and Innuendos to create humour that supports and makes the play more understandable to the audience. The numerous puns and innuendos create an ambiguity, inviting the audience to laugh.

For example, the Nurse uses bawdy innuendos often when speaking to Juliet

Act 2 scene 5 - I am the drudge, and toil in your delight
But you shall bear the burden soon at night

The crude and uncouth language of love by the servants is juxtaposed with the highly poetic language of love used by Romeo and Juliet, with their love founded more on physical attraction rather than romantic sentiment.

Language Device - Oxymorons and Antithesis

Shakespeare makes use of phrases made of words that contradict (oxymorons), to create emotional turmoil. For example, when Juliet says good night to Romeo

Act 2 scene 2 - Good night, good night!
Parting is such sweet sorrow

Shakespeare makes use of phrases with opposing ideas (antithesis). For example, after preparing for Juliet wedding festival, the family find themselves arranging her funeral. Lord Capulet says

Act 4 scene 5 - All things that we ordained festival
Turn from their office to black funeral

Language Device - Rhyming Couplets

Shakespeare makes use of rhyming couplets to emphasise important points or moments or the end of an action. Romeo ends the action with the rhyming couplet

Act 1 scene 2 - I'll go along, no such sight to be **shown**
But to rejoice in splendour of mine **own**

The play is ended by Prince Escalus with the rhyming couplet

Act 5 scene 3 - For never was a story of more **woe**
Than this of Juliet and her **Romeo**

Language Device - Repetition

Shakespeare makes use of repetition to emphasise ideas and emotions. Juliet repeats Romeo's name more than once, in the famous phrase

Act 2 scene 2 - O **Romeo**, **Romeo**, wherefore art thou **Romeo**?

Benvolio repeats Romeo's to emphasise a tragic event

Act 3 scene 1 - O **Romeo**, **Romeo**, brave Mercutio's dead

Lord Capulet repeats the action stir

Act 4 scene 1 - Come, **stir**, **stir**, **stir**! The second cock hath crowed

Language Device - Dramatic Irony

Shakespeare makes use of dramatic irony to create humour and emotion whenever the actors are clueless, but the audience are not, as to the truth. Paris is unaware that Juliet is already married to Romeo.

Act 4 scene 1 - Paris says:
> 'Happily, met, my lady and my wife!'
- Juliet replies:
> 'That may be, sir, when I may be a wife'

The irony is apparent when Juliet's family mourn her death when the audience knows that Juliet has taken a sleeping potion.

There are many other examples of dramatic irony throughout the play to make the audience muse, laugh, cry and enjoy the humour employed.

Language Device - Metaphors and Similes

Shakespeare makes use of metaphors and similes to create comparisons and heighten awareness of emotions and events.

Romeo makes use of the metaphor, when one thing is described as something different,

Act 2 scene 2 - what light through yonder window breaks?

Juliet is the light, Romeo the window.

Romeo later makes use of the simile, when one thing is not described as something different,

Act 2 scene 2 - ..., for thou art
> As glorious to this night, being o'er my head,
> As is a winged messenger of heaven

Romeo compares Juliet to an angel. Juliet is heavenly and her beauty light.

There are many other examples of metaphors and similes throughout the play to make the audience create vivid pictures in their minds as the play progress.

The Shakespearean text is written in the left column, and the explanation and interpretation, in the right column.

Important quotes and phrases in the text are highlighted and reproduced in the explanation column for discussion, on the same page. Consequently, there is no need to turn pages!

[1st quatrain]

Two households, both alike in dignity
(In fair Verona, where we lay our scene),
From ancient grudge break to new mutiny,
Where civil blood makes civil hands unclean

[2nd quatrain]

From forth the fatal loins of these two foes
A pair of star-crossed lovers take their life;
Whose mis adventured piteous overthrows
Doth with their death bury their parents' strife

[3rd quatrain]

The fearful passage of their death-marked love
And the continuance of their parents' rage,
Which, but their children's end, naught could remove,
Is now the two hours' traffic of our stage

[rhyming couplet]

The which, if you with patient ears **attend**,

What here shall miss, our toil shall strive to **mend**.

[*Exit*]

The prologue sung by the chorus in the Elizabethan Era foreshadows the story of the play in a nutshell and using dramatic irony, the audience is aware of certain events unravelling before the actors do.

Using an AB-AB rhyme scheme, in the 1st quatrain, the prologue spells out the darkness and evil that the unsuspecting audience is about to witness. It tells of two 'alike in dignity' and rich families who harboured an 'ancient grudge' for each other and their fury has once more ignited into strife, 'new mutiny'.

Ironically, Shakespeare's repetitive use of the adjective 'civil' suggests a mocking tone because he expresses his annoyance that people of such high calibre and status should behave in such a disagreeable manner.

In the 2nd quatrain, 'fatal loins' suggests that Romeo and Juliet were offspring of hatred which resulted in fatalities - death and destruction. Since the Elizabethans believed that fate controlled their lives, Shakespeare integrated the motif of fate recurring throughout the play which determined Romeo and Juliet's fate as well.

"A pair of star-crossed lovers take their life"

Their hate for each other was so intense that only their children's death could quell that hate.

In the 3rd quatrains and rhyming couplet, the chorus goes on to say that if the audience didn't grasp the whole story, then they will work hard to ensure that they understand it by watching the play.

"What here shall miss, our toil shall strive to **mend**"

Shakespeare deliberately employed the use of a sonnet here which is generally reserved for a love poem. But it expresses untold hate and untimely deaths as opposed to love and peace.

Public Place in Verona

[*Enter* SAMPSON *and* GREGORY, *of the house of Capulet, with swords and bucklers*]

SAMPSON
Gregory, on my word, we'll not carry coals.
GREGORY
No, for then we should be colliers.
SAMPSON
I mean, if we be in choler, we'll draw.
GREGORY
Ay, while you live,
Draw your neck out of collar.
SAMPSON
I strike quickly, being moved.
GREGORY
But thou art not quickly moved to strike.
SAMPSON
A dog of the house of Montague moves me.
GREGORY
To move is to stir
And to be valiant is to stand, therefore,
If thou art moved, thou runniest away.
SAMPSON
A dog of that house shall move me to stand:
I will take the wall
Of any man or maid of Montague's.
GREGORY
That shows thee a weak slave
For the weakest goes to the wall.
SAMPSON
'Tis true; and therefore women,
Being the weaker vessels,
Are ever thrust to the wall:
Therefore,
I will push Montague's men from the wall
And thrust his maids to the wall.
GREGORY
The quarrel is between our masters
And us their men.
SAMPSON
'Tis all one, I will show myself a tyrant:
When I have fought with the men,
I will be cruel with the maids
And cut off their heads.
GREGORY
The heads of the maids?

In Act 1 Scene 1 Shakespeare sets the mood and the atmosphere of the play because he starts with the servants fighting.

The motif of violence runs throughout the play - fighting, murder and death.

[Enter SAMPSON and GREGORY]

They are in a fighting mood and the use of their alliterative devices and puns can suggest this

'Colliers', 'choler', 'collar'

We note that Samson and Gregory have different temperaments, Shakespeare prepares the audience for Mercutio's fate later in the play where the servants fight and Tybalt kills Mercutio.

Gregory is mild-mannered and he tries to dissuade him. He warns Samson against his actions,

"the weakest goes to the wall"

Suggesting that he will be killed.

Sampson is also portrayed as being sexist, referring to women as,

"the weaker vessel."

and later, he will

"cut off their heads"

Sampson is stirring up trouble by biting his thumb at Abram which is a gross insult.

Here Sampson behaves like Mercutio. Shakespeare portrays him to be all geared up to fight and his aggression is seen in,

"Therefore,
I will push Montague's men from the wall
And thrust his maids to the wall"

SAMPSON
Ay, the heads of the maids,
Or their maidenheads
Take it in what sense thou wilt.
GREGORY
They must take it in sense that feel it.
SAMPSON
Me they shall feel while I am able to stand:
And 'tis known I am a pretty piece of flesh.
GREGORY
'Tis well thou art not fish,
If thou hadst, thou hadst been poor John.
Draw thy tool!
Here comes two
Of the house of the Montagues.

[*Enter* ABRAHAM *and* BALTHASAR]

SAMPSON
My naked weapon is out:
Quarrel, I will back thee.
GREGORY
How! Turn thy back and run?
SAMPSON
Fear me not.
GREGORY
No, marry; I fear thee!
SAMPSON
Let us take the law of our sides
Let them begin.
GREGORY
I will frown as I pass by,
And let them take it as they list.
SAMPSON
Nay, as they dare.
I will bite my thumb at them
Which is a disgrace to them if they bear it.
ABRAHAM
Do you bite your thumb at us, sir?
SAMPSON
I do bite my thumb, sir.
ABRAHAM
Do you bite your thumb at us, sir?
SAMPSON
[*Aside to* GREGORY]
Is the law of our side if I say ay?
GREGORY
No.

Shakespeare builds tension between the two opposing Houses by wit and lewd remarks,

"Draw thy too!
Here comes two
Of the house of the Montagues"

SAMPSON and GREGORY of HOUSE CAPULET

[Enter ABRAHAM and BALTHASAR]

In Shakespeare's time, biting of the thumb is a social symbol of disrespect inevitably leading to conflict. Gregory and Sampson deliberately provoke Abraham and Balthasar with intent to start a fight.

ABRAHAM and BALTHASAR of HOUSE MONTAGUE

SAMPSON
No, sir, I do not bite my thumb at you, sir,
But I bite my thumb, sir.
GREGORY
Do you quarrel, sir?
ABRAHAM
Quarrel sir! No, sir.
SAMPSON
But If you do, sir, I am for you:
I serve as good a man as you.
ABRAHAM
No better.
SAMPSON
Well, sir.

[*Enter* BENVOLIO *on one side public place
Enter* TYBALT *on the other*]

GREGORY
Say 'better:
Here comes one of my master's kinsmen.
SAMPSON
Yes, better, sir.
ABRAHAM
You lie.
SAMPSON
Draw, if you be men.
Gregory, remember thy washing blow.

[ABRAHAM *and* SAMPSON *fight*]

BENVOLIO
Part, fools!
Put up your swords
You know not what you do.
TYBALT
What!
Art thou drawn among these heartless hind?
Turn thee, Benvolio, look upon thy death.
BENVOLIO
I do but keep the peace: put up thy sword
Or manage it to part these men with me.
TYBALT
What, drawn, and talk of peace!
I hate the word,
As I hate hell, all Montagues, and thee:
Have at thee, coward!

[*They fight*]

[Enter BENVOLIO]

BENVOLIO of HOUSE MONTAGUE

[Enter TYBALT]

TYBALT of HOUSE CAPULET

[They Fight]

BENVOLIO forced to fight TYBALT

Sampson and Abram fight, Benvolio enters and tries to stop the fight. Then TYBALT enters and he is just as temperamental as Sampson, and he deliberately challenges innocent Benvolio without any course and forces him to fight.

"What, drawn, and talk of peace!
I hate the word"

[*Enter, several of both houses, who join the fray; then enter Citizens, with clubs*]

First Citizen
Clubs, bills, and partisans!
Strike, beat them down!
Down with the Capulets!
Down with the Montagues!

[*Enter* CAPULET *in his gown, and his wife*]

CAPULET
What noise is this?
Give me my long sword, ho!
LADY CAPULET
A crutch, a crutch!
Why call you for a sword?

[*Enter* MONTAGUE *and* LADY MONTAGUE]

CAPULET
My sword, I say!
Old Montague is come,
And flourishes his blade in spite of me.
MONTAGUE
Thou villain Capulet! —
Hold me not, let me go.
LADY MONTAGUE
Thou shalt not stir a foot to seek a foe.

[*Enter* PRINCE ESCALUS, *with Attendants*]

PRINCE
Rebellious subjects, enemies to peace,
Profaners of this neighbour– stained steel, —
Will they not hear?
What, ho! You men, you beasts,
That quench the fire of your pernicious rage
With purple fountains issuing from your veins,
On pain of torture, from those bloody hands
Throw your mis-tempered weapons
On the ground,
And hear the sentence of your moved Prince. Three civil brawls, bred of an airy word,
By, thee, old Capulet, and Montague,
Have thrice disturbed the quiet of our streets, And made Verona's ancient citizens
Cast by their grave beseeming ornaments,
To wield old partisans, in hands as old,

Shakespeare once again foreshadows Tybalt's fate by his irrational behaviour and his intense hate.

[*Enter* CAPULET *and* LADY CAPULET]

It must be noted that the hatred between these two families is so intense that it spilled onto their servants. Capulet's impulsive behaviour is shocking, and he immediately demands a sword without any reasoning.

"Give me my long sword, ho!"

Shakespeare cuts the tension of this volatile situation by adding a bit of humour when Lady Capulet says,

"A crutch, a crutch!
Why call you for a sword?"

Referring to his old age. Montague enters and he is just as hot-headed as Capulet. Here Shakespeare sets the mood and tone of the play and highlights for us the intense hate that exists between the Capulets and the Montagu es, which has disastrous consequences later in the play.

[*Enter* PRINCE ESCALUS]

Here we can feel the prince's fury in his outburst by using alliterative devices,

"peace, Profaners"

"stained steel"

Accusing them of disturbing the peace and staining their swords with blood. The Prince makes reference to,

"With purple fountains issuing from your veins"

The colour purple is associated with royalty and the prince is furious that people from such high status can behave in such a crass manner and shed

"purple fountains,"

of blood.

PRINCE (*continues*)
Cankered with peace,
To part your cankered hate.
If ever you disturb our streets again,
Your lives shall pay the forfeit of the peace.
For this time, all the rest depart away:
You Capulet, shall go along with me:
And, Montague, come you this afternoon,
To know our further pleasure in this case,
To old Freetown,
Our common judgment–place.
Once more, on pain of death, all men depart.

[*Exeunt all but* LORD & LADY MONTAGUE, *and* BENVOLIO]

MONTAGUE
Who set this ancient quarrel new abroach?
Speak, nephew, were you by when it began?
BENVOLIO
Here were the servants of your adversary,
And yours, close fighting ere I did approach:
I drew to part them: in the instant came
The fiery Tybalt, with his sword prepared,
Which, as he breathed defiance to my ears,
He swung about his head and cut the winds,
Who nothing hurt withal hissed him in scorn:
While we were interchanging
Thrusts and blows,
Came more and more
And fought on part and part,
Till the Prince came, who parted either part.
LADY MONTAGUE
O, where is Romeo?
Saw you him today?
Right glad I am he was not at this fray.
BENVOLIO
Madam, an hour before the worshipped sun
Peered forth the golden window of the east,
A troubled mind drave me to walk abroad,
Where, underneath the grove of sycamore
That westward rooteth from the city's side,
So early walking did I see your son:
Towards him I made, but he was ware of me
And stole into the covert of the wood:
I, measuring his affections by my own,
Which then most sought
Where most might not be found,
Being one too many by my weary self.
And gladly shunned who gladly fled from me.

The prince's repetition of the verb 'cankered' depicts how their intense hate is corrupting their peace.

Lady Montague demands an explanation about the fight from Benvolio and he relays exactly what happened.

She then, as though having a premonition, immediately turns her attention to Romeo and enquires about his whereabouts. Ironically, she says,

"Right glad I am he was not at this fray"

Once again Shakespeare uses foreshadowing to prepare us for later events, because Romeo becomes embroiled in this fight resulting in his banishment and hence Lady Montague's demise.

Shakespeare's Romeo and Juliet is steeped in lots of rich and varied linguistic devices, vocabulary, imagery, sensory imagery, suspense and tension which are prevalent throughout the play and which I will be explaining in full detail for examination purposes.

A classic example of this, right at the outset is Benvolio's speech when he describes Romeo's altered state of mind when Romeo tried to allude him.

'worshipped sun'
'golden window'

He uses natural imagery to describe Romeo's emotions and behaviour

MONTAGUE
Many a morning hath he there been seen,
With tears augmenting the fresh morning dew
Adding to clouds more clouds
With his deep sighs
But all so soon as the all-cheering sun
Should in the furthest east begin to draw
The shady curtains from Aurora's bed,
Away from the light
Steals home my heavy son,
And private in his chamber pens himself,
Shuts up his windows, locks far daylight out
And makes himself an artificial night:
Black and portentous Must this
humour prove,
Unless good counsel may the cause remove.
BENVOLIO
My noble uncle, do you know the cause?
MONTAGUE
I neither know it nor can learn of him.
BENVOLIO
Have you importuned him by any means?
MONTAGUE
Both by myself and many other friends:
But he, his own affections' counsellor,
Is to himself
I will not say how true —
But to himself so secret and so close,
So far from sounding and discovery,
As is the bud bit with an envious worm,
Ere he can spread his sweet leaves to the air,
Or dedicate his beauty to the sun.
Could we but learn
From whence his sorrows grow.
We would as willingly give cure as know.

[*Enter* ROMEO]

BENVOLIO
See, where he comes:
So please you, step aside,
I'll know his grievance or be much denied.
MONTAGUE
I would thou wert so happy by thy stay,
To hear true shrift. Come, madam, let's away.

Lord Montague also uses sensory imagery to describe Romeo's romantic blues,

With tears augmenting the fresh morning dew

And he,

"Shuts up his windows, locks fair daylight out

Romeo's gloomy surroundings matches his gloomy mood.

PRINCE ESCALUS and Attendants

**LADY CAPULET, BENVOLIO and
LORD CAPULET**

LORD and LADY MONTAGUE

[*Exeunt* MONTAGUE *and* Lady MONTAGUE]

BENVOLIO
Good morrow, cousin.
ROMEO
Is the day so young?
BENVOLIO
But new struck nine.
ROMEO
Ay me! Sad hours seem long.
Was that my father that went hence so fast?
BENVOLIO
It was.
What sadness lengthens Romeo's hours?
ROMEO
Not having that,
Which, having, makes them short.
BENVOLIO
In love?
ROMEO
Out —
BENVOLIO
Of love?
ROMEO
Out of her favour, where I am in love.
BENVOLIO
Alas, that love, so gentle in his view,
Should be so tyrannous and rough in proof!
ROMEO
Alas, that love, whose view is muffled still,
Should, without eyes,
See pathways to his will!
Where shall we dine?
O me! What fray was here?
Yet tell me not, for I have heard it all.
Here's much to do with hate,
But more with love.
Why, then, O brawling love! O loving hate!
O anything, of nothing first create!
O heavy lightness! Serious vanity!
Mis-shaped chaos of well–seeming forms!
Feather of lead, bright smoke,
Cold fire, sick health!
Still–waking sleep, that is not what it is!
This love feel I, that feel no love in this.
Dost thou not laugh?

ROMEO

Shakespeare yet again foreshadows Romeo's morose state of mind later when he is banished and has to depart from Juliet.

Romeo expresses his heartbreak by using several oxymorons,

"Feather of lead, bright smoke,
Cold fire, sick health!"

BENVOLIO talking to ROMEO about love

BENVOLIO
No, coz, I rather weep.
ROMEO
Good heart, at what?
BENVOLIO
At thy good heart's oppression.
ROMEO
Why, such is love's transgression.
Griefs of mine own lie heavy in my breast,
Which thou wilt propagate, to have it prest
With more of thine:
This love that thou hast shown
Doth add more grief to
Too much of mine own.
Love is a smoke raised
With the fume of sighs,
Being purged, a fire sparkling in lovers' eyes,
Being vexed a sea nourished with lovers' tears
What is it else? A madness most discreet,
A choking gall and a preserving sweet.
Farewell, my coz.
BENVOLIO
Soft! I will go along,
And if you leave me so, you do me wrong.
ROMEO
Tut, I have lost myself, am not here,
This is not Romeo, he's some other where.
BENVOLIO
Tell me in sadness, who is that you love?
ROMEO
What, shall I groan and tell thee?
BENVOLIO
Groan! Why, no.
But sadly, tell me, who?
ROMEO
Bid a sick man in sadness make his will:
A word ill urged to one that is so ill!
In sadness, cousin, I do love a woman.
BENVOLIO
I aimed so near when I supposed you loved.
ROMEO
A right good mark-man!
And she's fair I love.
BENVOLIO
A right fair mark, fair coz, is soonest hit.

Romeo views love as

"A madness most discreet"

Benvolio wishes to go with Romeo, telling him

"And if you leave me so, you do me wrong"

In response, Romeo confesses that

"I have lost myself"

ROMEO sculptures ROSALINE

ROMEO
Well, in that hit you miss, she'll not be hit
With Cupid's arrow; she hath Dian's wit,
And, in strong proof of chastity well-armed,
From love's weak childish bow
She lives unharmed.
She will not stay the siege of loving terms,
Nor bide the encounter of assailing eyes,
Nor ope her lap to saint–seducing gold:
O, she is rich in beauty, only poor,
That when she dies
With beauty dies her store.

BENVOLIO
Then she hath sworn
That she will still live chaste?

ROMEO
She hath, and in that
Sparing makes huge waste,
For beauty starved with her severity
Cuts beauty off from all posterity.
She is too fair, too wise, wisely too fair,
To merit bliss by making me despair:
She hath forsworn to love, and in that vow
Do I live dead that live to tell it now

BENVOLIO
Be ruled by me, forget to think of her.

ROMEO
O teach me how I should forget to think.

BENVOLIO
By giving liberty unto thine eyes,
Examine other beauties.

ROMEO
'Tis the way
To call hers exquisite, in question more:
These happy masks
That kiss fair ladies' brows
Being black put us in mind they hide the fair,
He that is strucken blind cannot forget
The precious treasure of his eyesight lost:
Show me a mistress that is passing fair,
What doth her beauty serve but as a note
Where I may read
Who passed that passing fair?
Farewell: thou canst not teach me to forget.

BENVOLIO
I'll pay that doctrine, or else die in debt.

[*Exeunt*]

Romeo's unrequited love for Rosaline has sent him into the depths of great despair.

"she'll not be hit
 With Cupid's arrow"

He describes her qualities,

"She is too fair, too wise, wisely too fair"

Benvolio then urges Romeo to

"Be ruled by me, forget to think of her"

and to

"Examine other beauties"

Romeo is besotted with Rosaline, and tells Benvolio,

"thou canst not teach me to forget"

but Benvolio is adamant that he will be proved right, Romeo will forget,

"I'll pay that doctrine, or else die in debt"

A Street, later in the day

[*Enter* CAPULET, PARIS, *and* PETER]

CAPULET
But Montague is bound as well as I,
In penalty alike, and 'tis not hard, I think,
For men so old as we to keep the peace.
PARIS
Of honourable reckoning are you both,
And pity 'tis you lived at odds so long.
But now, my lord, what say you to my suit?
CAPULET
But saying over what I have said before:
My child is yet a stranger in the world,
She hath not seen
The change of fourteen years,
Let two more summers wither in their pride,
Ere we may think her ripe to be a bride.
PARIS
Younger than she are happy mothers made.
CAPULET
And too soon marred are those so early made
Earth hath swallowed all my hopes but she,
She is the hopeful lady of my earth:
But woo her, gentle Paris, get her heart,
My will to her consent is but a part,
And she agreed, within her scope of choice
Lies my consent and fair, according voice.
This night I hold an old-accustomed feast,
Whereto I have invited many a guest,
Such as I love; and you, among the store,
One more, most welcome,
Makes my number more.
At my poor house look to behold this night Earth–
treading stars
That make dark heaven light:
Such comfort as do lusty young men feel
When well–apparelled April on the heel
Of limping winter treads, even such delight
Among fresh female buds shall you this night
Inherit at my house; hear all, all see,
And like her most whose merit most shall be:
Which on more view, of many mine being one
May stand in number,
Though in reckoning none,
Come, go with me.

[Enter Capulet, PARIS and PETER]

Paris asks Capulet for Juliet's hand in marriage. The Elizabethan era was a patriarchal society and women had no status and could not voice their opinions about who

they should marry. They had to marry whoever their father chose for them to marry as is the case of Juliet's forced marriage to Paris.

Although Capulet acknowledges that Juliet was too young to marry, he nevertheless agrees to the marriage despite not having Juliet's consent at all.

Capulet tells Paris that he must attend his party where he will be delighted to meet beautiful young women like,

"fresh female buds"

And that he wouldn't think that Juliet is the most beautiful to take his fancy.

CAPULET conversing with PARIS

[CAPULET *gives* PETER *a wedding list*]

Go, sirrah, trudge about through fair Verona
Find those persons out
Whose names are written there,
And to them say:
My house and welcome
On their pleasure stay

[*Exeunt* CAPULET *and* PARIS]

PETER
Find them out whose names are written here!
It is written that the shoemaker
Should meddle with his yard,
And the tailor with his last,
The fisher with his pencil,
And the painter with his nets,
But I am sent to find those persons
Whose names are here writ,
And can never find what names
The writing person hath here writ.
I must to the learned. - In good time.

[*Enter* BENVOLIO *and* ROMEO]

BENVOLIO
Tut, man,
One fire burns out another's burning,
One pain is lessened by another's anguish,
Turn giddy, and be holp by backward turning,
One desperate grief
Cures with another's languish:
Take thou some new infection to thy eye,
And the rank poison of the old will die.
ROMEO
Your plantain leaf is excellent for that.
BENVOLIO
For what, I pray thee?
ROMEO
For your broken shin.
BENVOLIO
Why, Romeo, art thou mad?
ROMEO
Not mad,
But bound more than a madman is,
Shut up in prison, kept without my food,
Whipped and tormented
And— God–den, good fellow.

COUNTY PARIS

CAPULET, PARIS, PETER with paper

[Exit CAPULET and PARIS]

[Enter BENVOLIO and ROMEO]

BENVOLIO conversing with ROMEO

Benvolio is trying to persuade Romeo to try and forget Rosaline and find someone new.

"one fire burns out another's burning"

PETER
God gi' god–den. I pray, sir, can you read?
ROMEO
Ay, mine own fortune in my misery.
PETER
Perhaps you have learned it without book:
But I pray, can you read anything you see?
ROMEO
Ay, if I know the letters and the language.
PETER
Ye say honestly: rest you merry!
ROMEO
Stay, fellow; I can read.

[ROMEO *reads the list*]

'Signior Martino and his wife and daughters,
County Anselme and his beauteous sisters,
The lady widow of Vitruvio,
Signior Placentio and his lovely nieces,
Mercutio and his brother Valentine,
Mine uncle Capulet, his wife and daughters,
My fair niece Rosaline and Livia,
Signior Valentio and his cousin Tybalt,
Lucio and the lively Helena.'
A fair assembly: whither should they come?
PETER
Up
ROMEO
Whither?
PETER
To supper; to our house.
ROMEO
Whose house?
PETER
My master's.
ROMEO
Indeed, I should have asked you that before.
PETER
Now I'll tell you without asking:
My master is the great rich Capulet,
And if you be not of the house of Montagues,
I pray, come and crush a cup of wine.
Rest you merry!

[*Exit* PETER]

PETER gives ROMEO the paper to read

[ROMEO reads]

Shakespeare highlights the fact that most citizens were illiterate. Peter cannot read and so he asks Romeo to read for him. At first, Romeo makes out he cannot read, but as Peter walks away,

"Stay, fellow, I can read"

PETER with ROMEO who reads paper

BENVOLIO

At this same ancient feast of Capulet's
Sups the fair Rosaline whom thou so loves'
With all the admired beauties of Verona:
Go thither; and, with unattainted eye,
Compare her face with some that I shall show
And I will make thee think thy swan a crow.

ROMEO

When the devout religion of mine eye
Maintains such falsehood,
Then turn tears to fires,
And these who,
Often drowned, could never die,
Transparent heretics be burnt for liars!
One fairer than my love!
The all–seeing sun never saw her match
Since first the world begun.

BENVOLIO

Tut, you saw her fair, none else being by,
Herself poised with herself in either eye:
But in that crystal scales let there be weighed
Your lady's love against some other maid
That I will show you shining at this feast,
And she shall scant
Show well that now shows best.

ROMEO

I'll go along, no such sight to be shown,
But to rejoice in splendour of mine own.

[*Exeunt*]

Benvolio tells Romeo that Rosaline will be at the Capulet's ball, and he challenges Romeo to compare her to the other beautiful women.

Rosaline, he says, will prove to be a 'crow' rather than a 'swan',

"I will make thee think thy swan a crow"

But Romeo is adamant that Rosaline,

"never saw her match
Since first the world began"

And to him she is the most beautiful woman ever. Finally, he agrees to go to the ball to see Rosaline.

A Room in Capulet's House

[*Enter* LADY CAPULET *and* Nurse]

LADY CAPULET
Nurse, where's my daughter?
Call her forth to me.
Nurse
Now, by my maidenhead, at twelve-year-old,
I bade her come:
What, lamb! What, ladybird!
God forbid, where's this girl?
What, Juliet!

[*Enter* JULIET]

JULIET
How now! Who calls?
Nurse
Your mother.
JULIET
Madam, I am here.
What is your will?
LADY CAPULET
This is the matter: —
Nurse, give leave awhile,
We must talk in secret: —
Nurse, come back again,
I have remembered me,
Thou's hear our counsel.
Thou know'st my daughter is of a pretty age.
Nurse
Faith, I can tell her age unto an hour.
LADY CAPULET
She's not fourteen.
Nurse
I'll lay fourteen of my teeth —
And yet, to my teeth be it spoken,
I have but four —
She is not fourteen.
How long is it now
To Lammas–tide?
LADY CAPULET
A fortnight and odd days.

[Enter LADY CAPULET and NURSE]

Lady Capulet summons Juliet in a rather formal way in the opening scene. There is a marked contrast in the relationship between the Nurse and Lady Capulet to Juliet.

We can sense a certain detachment here in Lady Capulet towards Juliet's wellbeing. Lady Capulet addresses Juliet very formally without even mentioning her name.

"Nurse, where's my daughter?"

Whereas, the nurse, on the other hand is very endearing to Juliet and addresses her very cordially,

"What, lamb! What, ladybird!"

Note also that Juliet addresses her mother very formally and calls her 'Madam' hence a clear depiction of the detachment that exists between Juliet and her mother.

We see that the nurse was more clued up than Lady Capulet about Juliet's age because the nurse remembered her exact age, but her mother didn't.

"Faith, I can tell her age unto an hour"

JULIET, NURSE and LADY CAPULET
discussing Juliet's age.

Nurse
Even or odd, of all days in the year,
Come Lammas–Eve at night
Shall she be fourteen.
Susan and she —
God rest all Christian souls! —
Were of an age:
Well, Susan is with God; She was
too good for me:
But, as I said,
On Lammas–Eve at night
Shall she be fourteen,
That shall she, marry,
I remember it well.
'Tis since the earthquake now eleven years,
And she was weaned —
I never shall forget it —
Of all the days of the year, upon that day,
For I had then laid wormwood to my dug
Sitting in the sun under the dove–house wall,
My lord and you were then at Mantua —
Nay, I do bear a brain: But, as I said,
When it did taste the wormwood on the nipple
Of my dug, and felt it bitter, pretty fool,
To see it tetchy and fall out with the dug!
'Shake' quoth the dove–house:
'twas no need, I trow, to bid me trudge:
And since that time, it is eleven years,
For then she could stand high-lone,
Nay, by the rood,
She could have run and waddled all about,
For even the day before, she broke her brow:
And then my husband - God be with his soul!
A was a merry man - took up the child:
'Yea', quoth he, 'dost thou fall upon thy face?
Thou wilt fall backward
When thou hast more wit,
Wilt thou not, Jule?' And, by my holidam,
The pretty wretch left crying and said 'Ay.'
To see, now, how a jest shall come about!
I warrant, an I should live a thousand years,
I never should forget it:
'Wilt thou not, Jule?', quoth he,
And, pretty fool, it stinted and said 'Ay.'

LADY CAPULET
Enough of this, I pray thee, hold thy peace.

NURSE

JULIET

LADY CAPULET

Nurse
Yes, madam: yet I cannot choose but laugh,
To think it should leave crying and say 'Ay.'
And yet, I warrant, it had upon its brow
A bump as big as a young cockerel's stone,
A parlous knock, and it cried bitterly:
'Yea' quoth my husband, 'fallst upon thy face?
Thou wilt fall backward
When thou comest to age:
Wilt thou not, Jule?' It stinted and said 'Ay.'
JULIET
And stint thou too, I pray thee, Nurse, say I.
Nurse
Peace, I have done.
God mark thee to his grace!
Thou wast the prettiest babe
That ever I nursed
An I might live to see thee married once,
I have my wish.
LADY CAPULET
Marry, that 'marry' is the very theme
I came to talk of.
Tell me, daughter Juliet,
How stands your disposition to be married?
JULIET
It is an honour that I dream not of.
Nurse
An honour! Were not I thine only nurse,
I would say thou hadst sucked
Wisdom from thy teat.
LADY CAPULET
Well, think of marriage now,
Younger than you
Here in Verona, ladies of esteem,
Are made already mothers, by my count,
I was your mother much upon these years
That you are now a maid.
Thus then in brief:
The valiant Paris seeks you for his love.
Nurse
A man, young lady!
Lady, such a man as all the world —
Why, he's a man of wax.
LADY CAPULET
Verona's summer hath not such a flower.
Nurse
Nay, he's a flower,
In faith, a very flower.

Servant dressing JULIET with JULIET talking to NURSE and LADY CAPULET

Lady Capulet asks Juliet if she wants to marry Paris,

"How stands your disposition to be married?"

Juliet is forthright in her answer about her marriage to Paris.

"It is an honour that I dream not of"

Juliet's response to her mother is not one that we would expect from a girl of the Elizabethan period because children were expected to obey their parents and marry who they choose.

Lady Capulet tells Juliet that she was married at her age and that Paris wants to marry her.

"I was your mother much upon these years"

Lady Capulet tells Juliet that she is marry Paris and the nurse adds that,

"he's a man of wax"

Referring to his solidity as a man in terms of wealth.

LADY CAPULET
What say you?
 Can you love the gentleman?
This night you shall behold him at our feast,
Read over the volume of young Paris' face,
And find delight writ there with beauty's pen,
Examine every married lineament,
And see how one another lends content
And what obscured in this fair volume lies
Find written in the margent of his eyes.
This precious book of love,
This unbound lover,
To beautify him, only lacks a cover:
The fish lives in the sea, and 'tis much pride
For fair without the fair within to hide:
That book in many's eyes
Doth share the glory,
That in gold clasps locks in the golden story,
So shall you share all that he doth possess,
By having him, making yourself no less.
Nurse
No less! Nay, bigger - women grow by men!
LADY CAPULET
Speak briefly, can you like of Paris' love?
JULIET
I'll look to like, if looking liking move:
But no more deep, will I endart mine eye;
Than your consent
Gives strength to make it fly.

[*Enter* PETER]

PETER
Madam, the guests are come,
Supper served up, you called,
My young lady asked for,
The Nurse cursed in the pantry,
And everything in extremity.
I must hence to wait,
I beseech you, follow straight.
LADY CAPULET
We follow thee. Juliet, the County stays.
Nurse
Go, girl, seek happy nights to happy days.

[*Exeunt*]

Lady Capulet makes use of 2 repetitive rhetorical questions,

"What say you?
 Can you love the gentleman?"

One can suggest that she is hesitant about Juliet's feelings for Paris, and she doubts whether Juliet will marry Paris willingly.

She urges Juliet to look at the beauty in Paris' face,

"Read over the volume of young Paris' face, And
 find delight writ there with beauty's pen"

Perhaps her hesitancy leads her to present Juliet with a very persuasive imagery of a book full of love where Juliet can find love with Paris. They can be bound together by marriage just like the binding of a book because Paris needs a wife and he 'lacks a cover.'

"This precious book of love,
 This unbound lover,
 To beautify him, only lacks a cover"

She says that Juliet will be happy at how handsome Paris is because beauty's pen has sculpted Paris' face very finely and beautifully.

We will have to take note of the Nurse's wavering opinions of the men in Juliet's life, especially after she meets Romeo.

Shakespeare uses the character of the nurse to appear at strategic points in the play in order to cut the tension in a very serious play.

She is portrayed as cheerful and bawdy and here her speech reeks of sexual overtones, suggesting that Juliet must find a man who will make her happy in bed.

"Go girl seek happy nights to happy days"

A Street

[*Enter* ROMEO, MERCUTIO, BENVOLIO, *with six Maskers, Torch–bearers, and others*]

ROMEO
What!
Shall this speech be spoke for our excuse?
Or shall we on without apology?
BENVOLIO
The date is out of such prolixity:
We'll have no Cupid hoodwinked with a scarf,
Bearing a Tartar's painted bow of lath,
Scaring the ladies like a crow–keeper,
Nor no without–book prologue, faintly spoke
After the prompter, for our entrance:
But let them measure us by what they will,
We'll measure them a measure and be gone.
ROMEO
Give me a torch: I am not for this ambling,
Being but heavy, I will bear the light.
MERCUTIO
Nay, gentle Romeo, we must have you dance.
ROMEO
Not I, believe me: you have dancing shoes
With nimble soles: I have a soul of lead
So stakes me to the ground I cannot move.
MERCUTIO
You are a lover; borrow Cupid's wings,
And soar with them above a common bound.
ROMEO
I am too sore empierced with his shaft
To soar with his light feathers, and so bound,
I cannot bound a pitch above dull woe:
Under love's heavy burden do I sink.
MERCUTIO
And, to sink in it, should you burden love,
Too great oppression for a tender thing.
ROMEO
Is love a tender thing?
It is too rough, too rude, too boisterous,
And it pricks like thorn.

[Enter ROMEO, MERCUTIO and BENVOLIO]

GUESTS arriving at CAPULET's HOUSE

We once again meet the lovesick Romeo and he describes his heavy heart with a pun and associates it to dancing,

"With nimble soles: I have a soul of lead"

Lead is heavy and Romeo compares his heart to lead because of the pain caused by Rosaline's unrequited love.

"Under love's heavy burden do I sink"

Once again Romeo repeats the fact that love is a heavy burden that he must bear.

He goes on to accuse love of being,

"too rough, too rude, too boisterous"

Here Romeo vents his frustration about love being too rocky, difficult and painful.

Romeo also uses a simile saying that love is painful and it,

"pricks like a thorn"

MERCUTIO
If love be rough with you, be rough with love,
Prick love for pricking,
And you beat love down.
Give me a case to put my visage in:
A visor for a visor! What care I
What curious eye doth cote deformities?
Here are the beetle brows shall blush for me.

[*They put on their visors - (masks)*]
BENVOLIO
Come, knock and enter; and no sooner in,
But every man betake him to his legs.
ROMEO
A torch for me: let wantons light of heart
Tickle the senseless rushes with their heels,
For I am proverbed with a grandsire phrase,
I'll be a candleholder and look on.
The game was never so fair, and I am done.
MERCUTIO
Tut, dun's the mouse,
The constable's own word:
If thou art Dun, we'll draw thee
From the mire of this sir–reverence love,
Wherein thou stickst up to the ears.
Come, we burn daylight, ho!
ROMEO
Nay, that's not so.
MERCUTIO
I mean, sir, in delay
We waste our lights in vain, like lamps by day.
Take our good meaning, for our judgment sits
Five times in that, ere once in our five wits.
ROMEO
And we mean well in going to this masque,
But 'tis no wit to go.
MERCUTIO
Why, may one ask?
ROMEO
I dreamt a dream tonight.
MERCUTIO
And so did I.
ROMEO
Well, what was yours?
MERCUTIO
That dreamers often lie.
ROMEO
In bed asleep,
While they do dream things true.

Shakespeare creates a discussion on love.
Mercutio's view is

"If love be rough with you, be rough with love"

**MERCUTIO, ROMEO, BENVOLIO
discussing the meaning of love**

But Romeo's view is different, more caring,

"let wantons light of heart
Tickle the senseless rushes"

**ROMEO, MURCUTIO and BENVOLIO waiting to
enter CAPULET's HOUSE**

Mercutio dismisses Romeo's dream as unworthy of
truth by saying

"That dreamers often lie"

But Romeo is insistent by saying

"In bed asleep,
While they do dream things true"

MERCUTIO
O, then,
I see Queen Mab hath been with you.

BENVOLIO
Queen Mab! What's she!

MERCUTIO
She is the fairies' midwife, and she comes
In shape no bigger than an agate–stone
On the forefinger of an alderman,
Drawn with a team of little atomi
Over men's noses as they lie asleep,
Her wagon spokes made of long spiders' legs
The cover of the wings of grasshoppers,
Her traces of the smallest spider's web,
Her collars of the moonshine's watery beams,
Her whip of cricket's bone, the lash of film,
Her wagoner a small grey–coated gnat,
Not half so big as a round little worm
Pricked from the lazy finger of a maid,
Her chariot is an empty hazelnut
Made by the joiner squirrel or old grub,
Time out o' mind the fairies' coachmakers.
And in this state
She gallops night by night
Through lovers' brains,
And then they dream of love,
O'er courtiers' knees,
That dream on court'sies straight,
Over lawyers' fingers,
Who straight dream on fees,
Over ladies' lips,
Who straight on kisses dream,
Which oft the angry Mab with blisters plagues
Because their breaths
With sweetmeats tainted are:
Sometime she gallops o'er a courtier's nose,
And then dreams he of smelling out a suit,
And sometime comes
She with a tithe–pig's tail
Tickling a parson's nose as a' lies asleep,
Then dreams he of another benefice.
Sometime she driveth over a soldier's neck,
And then dreams he of cutting foreign throats
Of breaches, ambuscadoes, Spanish blades,
Of healths five fathom deep; and then anon
Drums in his ear,

Shakespeare introduces wit and mocking humour through Mercutio's retelling of the story of Queen MAB. Mercutio remarks to Romeo,

"I see Queen Mab hath been with you"

Then in response to Benvolio, Mercutio tells his comrades who Queen Mab is,

She is the fairies' midwife"

MERCUTIO telling the story of QUEEN MAB to BENVOLIO and ROMEO

Mercutio description of Queen Mab is full of fanciful nonsense designed to belittle Romeo's dream that what he dreamt was nature's truth revealed in sleep.

Queen Mab is the fairy Queen and a mythological creature.

She is responsible for creating fantasies to people when they are asleep.

"And in this state
She gallops night by night
Through lovers' brains,
And then they dream of love"

Mercutio says that lovers are forced to dream things about love that is untrue because of Queen Mab's influence on lovers whilst they are asleep as is in Romeo's case.

She also plays tricks on lawyers who dream of fees and parsons who dream of more money and soldiers who are victorious in battle.

MERCUTIO (*continues*)
At which he starts and wakes
And being thus frighted
Swears a prayer or two
And sleeps again.
This is that very Mab
That plats the manes of horses in the night,
And bakes the elf-locks in foul sluttish hairs,
Which, once untangled,
Much misfortune bodes.
This is the hag,
When maids lie on their backs,
That presses them
And learns them first to bear,
Making them women of good carriage:
This is she —
ROMEO
Peace, peace, Mercutio, peace!
Thou talk'st of nothing.
MERCUTIO
True, I talk of dreams,
Which are the children of an idle brain,
Begot of nothing but vain fantasy,
Which is as thin of substance as the air
And more inconstant than the wind,
Who woos even now,
The frozen bosom of the north,
And, being angered, puffs away from thence,
Turning his face to the dew–dropping south.
BENVOLIO
This wind, you talk of,
Blows us from ourselves
Supper is done, and we shall come too late.
ROMEO
I fear, too early: for my mind misgives
Some consequence yet hanging in the stars
Shall bitterly begin his fearful date
With this night's revels and expire the term
Of a despised life closed in my breast
By some vile forfeit of untimely death.
But He, that hath the steerage of my course,
Direct my sail! On, lusty gentlemen.
BENVOLIO
Strike, drum.

[*Exeunt*]

Romeo, eventually, intervenes having heard enough saying,

"Peace, peace, Mercutio, peace!
Thou talk'st of nothing."

BENVOLIO

Benvolio brings the discussion to an end by reminding all that

"Supper is done, and we shall come too late"

Fate is an important motif that runs throughout the play and here Romeo talks about the stars,

"some consequence yet hanging in the stars"

And he foreshadows his death,

"By some vile forfeit of untimely death"

Shakespeare uses the theme of fate because the Elizabethans believed that the stars determined your fate.

Shakespeare uses foreshadowing when Romeo 'predicts' his death.

This we should note is the start of his journey towards his death. This ball that he is going to attend and meet Juliet which will steer him towards his death.

A Hall in Capulet's House

[*Musicians waiting*]

[*Enter the* MASQUERS
who march round the Hall, and stand aside]

[*Enter Serving men with napkins*]

PETER
Where's Potpan,
That he helps not to take away?
He shift a trencher?
He scrape a trencher!
First Servant
When good manners
Shall lie all in one- or two-men's hands
And they unwashed too,
'tis a foul thing.
PETER
Away with the joint–stools,
Remove the court–cupboard,
Look to the plate.
Good thou, save me a piece of marchpane,
And, as thou lovest me,
Let the porter let in Susan Grindstone
And Nell - Antony, and Potpan!
Second Servant
Ay, boy, ready.
PETER
You are looked for and called for,
Asked for and sought for,
In the great chamber.
Second Servant
We cannot be here and there too.
Cheerly, boys,
Be brisk awhile,
And the longer liver take all.

[*Exit* PETER *and the* Serving men]

[*Enter* CAPULET, *his* WIFE, JULIET,
NURSE, TYBALT, Capulet's COUSIN,
and others of the house, meeting ROMEO,
BENVOLIO, MERCUTIO, *and all other*
GUESTS, *joining the* MASQUERS]

[Enter CAPULETS and TYBALT]

Lord Capulet plays the perfect host, he welcomes everyone and urges them to dance. He is very jovial, and he summons the musicians to play.

We have to very carefully observe and analyse Capulet's changing behaviour in various parts of the play. However controversial his behaviour seems at times, he can weigh it out by being sensible at times when the need arises, as we will witness at this party.

Masks for the guests

Festivities in the Hall

CAPULET
Welcome, gentlemen!
Ladies that have their toes
Unplagued with corns
Will have a bout with you.
Ah ha, my mistresses!
Which of you all will now deny to dance?
She that makes dainty,
She, I'll swear, hath corns,
Am I come near ye now?
Welcome, gentlemen! I have seen the day
That I have worn a visor and could tell
A whispering tale in a fair lady's ear,
Such as would please:
'tis gone, 'tis gone, 'tis gone:
You are welcome, gentlemen!
Come, musicians, play.

[*Music plays, and they dance*]

A hall, a hall! Give room!
And foot it, girls!
More light, you knaves,
And turn the tables up,
And quench the fire,
The room is grown too hot.
Ah, sirrah, this unlooked for sport comes well.
Nay, sit, nay, sit, good cousin Capulet,
For you and I are past our dancing days:
How long is't now since last yourself and I
Were in a masque?
Capulet's COUSIN
By'r Lady, thirty years
CAPULET
What, man!
'Tis not so much, 'tis not so much:
'Tis since the nuptials of Lucentio,
Come Pentecost as quickly as it will,
Some five and twenty years
And then we masqued
Capulet's COUSIN
'Tis more, 'tis more, his son is elder, sir,
His son is thirty.
CAPULET
Will you tell me that?
His son was but a ward two years ago.

CAPULET welcoming the guest

MUSICIANS play

BENVOLIO, ROMEO, MERCUTIO look-on

Romeo has noticed Juliet and he is immediately awestruck. He uses light imagery to describe Juliet's beauty.

ROMEO
[*To a* Servingman]
What lady is that,
Which doth enrich the hand
Of yonder knight?
Servant
I know not, sir.
ROMEO
O, she doth teach the torches to burn bright!
It seems she hangs upon the cheek of night
Like a rich jewel in an Ethiope's ear;
Beauty too rich for use, for earth too dear!
So shows a snowy dove trooping with crows,
As yonder lady o'er her fellows shows.
The measure done,
I'll watch her place of stand,
And, touching hers,
Make blessed my rude hand.
Did my heart love till now? forswear it, sight!
For I never saw true beauty till this night

O she doth teach the torches to burn bright!

He says that she shows the torches how to illuminate. He goes further and uses a metaphor to describe her amazing beauty;

"she hangs upon the cheek of night"

And she is conspicuous in the dark;

"Like a rich jewel in an Ethiope's ear"

The simile associates her beauty to a stunning, beautiful jewel hanging from an Ethiopian's ear. Her beauty, he says is too good for this world,

"Beauty too rich for use, for earth too dear!"

Romeo echoes Benvolio's words,

"So shows a snowy dove trooping with crows

The use of the colour imagery, 'snowy' can be associated with Juliet's purity and innocence. The dove is the symbol of peace which we hope will reign between these two warring families because Romeo and Juliet represented peace and love.

'Doves' can be juxtaposed to 'crows' and the crows can represent not only evil and death but also the intense hate that existed between these two families and their children had to pay the ultimate price - death.

Now Romeo sees Juliet as the beautiful 'dove' among all the ugly 'crows' at the ball just as Benvolio had predicted. He says that when the dance is over, he will touch her smooth hand with his rough one.

One will say that Romeo is rather fickle because just a very short while ago, he was moping and distraught about his unrequited love for Rosaline but now he changed his tone and exclaims,

"Did my heart love till now?"

He also insisted that nobody was as beautiful as Rosaline yet he now says,

"For I never saw true beauty till This night"

ROMEO admiring JULIET

JULIET admiring ROMEO

TYBALT
This, by his voice, should be a Montague.
Fetch me my rapier, boy.

[*Exit Page*]

What dares the slave
Come hither,
Covered with an antic face,
To fleer and scorn at our solemnity?
Now, by the stock and honour of my kin,
To strike him dead, I hold it not a sin.
CAPULET
Why, how now, kinsman!
Wherefore storm you so?
TYBALT
Uncle, this is a Montague, our foe,
A villain that is hither come in spite,
To scorn at our solemnity this night.
CAPULET
Young Romeo is it?
TYBALT
'Tis he, that villain Romeo.
CAPULET
Content thee, gentle coz, let him alone,
He bears him like a portly gentleman,
And, to say truth, Verona brags of him
To be a virtuous and well–governed youth:
I would not for the wealth of all the town
Here in my house do him disparagement:
Therefore, be patient, take no note of him:
It is my will, the which if thou respect,
Show a fair presence
And put off these frowns,
And ill–beseeming semblance for a feast.
TYBALT
It fits, when such a villain is a guest:
I'll not endure him.
CAPULET
He shall be endured:
What, goodman boy!
I say, he shall: go to;
Am I the master here, or you? Go to.
You'll not endure him!
God shall mend my soul!
You'll make a mutiny among my guests!
You will set cock–a–hoop!
You'll be the man!

when he saw Juliet at the ball.

Now Tybalt is enraged when he suspects that a Montague had infiltrated their ball.

He immediately summons for his sword.

"Fetch me my rapier"

Once again Shakespeare foreshadows Tybalt's hot, passionate temper and his lack of reasoning which will be his downfall later in the play.

Here Capulet displays a sense of decency when he deliberately reprimands Tybalt for his unreasonable behaviour towards Romeo.

He describes Romeo in a very favourable light despite him being the 'enemy'

"To be a virtuous and well - governed youth"

TYBALT restrained by LORD CAPULET

Lord Capulet is very forceful when he warns
Tybalt of his irrational behaviour and insists that,

"It is my will, the which if thou respect,
Show a fair presence
And put off these frowns"

But Tybalt is adamant and insists that

"I'll not endure him"

Capulet was very firm with Tybalt,

"Am I the master here or you?"

TEXT Act 1 scene 5

TYBALT
Why, uncle, 'tis a shame.
CAPULET
Go to, go to,
You are a saucy boy: is't so, indeed?
This trick may chance to scathe you,
I know what:
You must contrary me! Marry, 'tis time.
Well said, my hearts!
You are a princox; go:
Be quiet, or—More light, more light!
For shame! I'll make you quiet.
What, cheerly, my hearts!
TYBALT
Patience perforce with wilful choler meeting
Makes my flesh tremble
In their different greeting.
I will withdraw but this intrusion shall
Now seeming sweet convert to bitter gall.

[*Exit* TYBALT]

ROMEO
[*taking* JULIET's *hand*]
If I profane with my unworthiest hand
This holy shrine, the gentle fine is this:
My lips, two blushing pilgrims, ready stand
To smooth that rough touch with a tender kiss.
JULIET
Good pilgrim,
You do wrong your hand too much,
Which mannerly devotion shows in this,
For saints have hands
That pilgrims' hands do touch,
And palm to palm is holy palmers' kiss.
ROMEO
Have not saints' lips, and holy palmers too?
JULIET
Ay, pilgrim, lips that they must use in prayer.
ROMEO
O, then, dear saint, let lips do what hands do,
They pray, grant thou, lest faith turn to despair.
JULIET
Saints do not move,
Though grant for prayers' sake.

EXPLANATION

But Tybalt ironically says that this intrusion shall,

"convert to bitterest gall"

Meaning that he will take revenge.

TYBALT told to go by LORD CAPULET

Romeo takes Juliet's hand, and he uses biblical imagery by saying that it's a 'holy shrine.'

He goes on to say that his lips are,

"two blushing pilgrims"

That can solve any problem with a kiss.

JULIET and ROMEO about to kiss

Notice how Juliet uses biblical imagery, 'pilgrims' hence associating their love to God and purity.

ROMEO
Then move not,
While my prayer's effect I take.
[ROMEO *kisses her*]
Thus from my lips, by yours, my sin is purged.
JULIET
Then have my lips the sin that they have took.
ROMEO
Sin from thy lips?
O trespass sweetly urged!
Give me my sin again.
[*They kiss again*]
JULIET
You kiss by the book.
Nurse
Madam, your mother craves a word with you.

[JULIET *goes to her mother*]

ROMEO
What is her mother?
Nurse
Marry, bachelor,
Her mother is the lady of the house,
And a good lady, and a wise and virtuous
I nursed her daughter, that you talked withal,
I tell you, he that can lay hold of her
Shall have the chinks.
ROMEO
Is she a Capulet?
O dear account!
My life is my foe's debt.
BENVOLIO
Away, begone,
The sport is at the best.
ROMEO
Ay, so I fear,
The more is my unrest.
CAPULET
Nay, gentlemen, prepare not to be gone,
We have a trifling foolish banquet towards.
[*the* Masquers *excuse themselves*]
Is it even so?
Why, then, I thank you all
I thank you, honest gentlemen, good night.
More torches here,
Come on! Then let's to bed.

[Servants *bring torches to escort guests out*]

Pilgrims worship statues and holy shrines and by them touching hands, it represents a holy kiss.

Their first conversation is based on holiness, but leads to passion

"While my prayer's effect I take"

And they kiss.

NURSE interrupts to tell JULIET her mother craves a word

Romeo is somewhat distraught to learn that Juliet is a Capulet,

"My life is my foe's debt"

ROMEO, MERCUTIO, BENVOLIO leaving the feast

CAPULET
Ah, Sirrah, by my fay, it waxes late:
I'll to my rest.

[*Exeunt all but* JULIET *and* Nurse]

JULIET
Come hither, nurse.
What is yond gentleman?
Nurse
The son and heir of old Tiberio.
JULIET
What's he that now is going out of door?
Nurse
Marry, that, I think, be young Petrucio.
JULIET
What's he that follows there,
That would not dance?
Nurse
I know not.
JULIET
Go ask his name: if he be married,
My grave is like to be my wedding bed.

[Nurses *goes across the room and returns*]

Nurse
His name is Romeo, and a Montague,
The only son of your great enemy.
JULIET
My only love sprung from my only hate!
Too early seen unknown and known too late!
Prodigious birth of love it is to me,
That I must love a loathed enemy.
Nurse
What's this? What's this?
JULIET
A rhyme I learned even now
Of one I danced withal.

[*One calls within 'Juliet!'*]

Nurse
Anon, anon!
Come, let's away; the strangers all are gone.

[*Exeunt*]

NURSE telling JULIET that ROMEO is a MONTAGUE the son of her greatest foe

He believes that his life belongs to his enemy. Juliet asks the nurse to enquire who Romeo is and she foreshadows her fate by saying,

"if he be married,
My grave is like to be my wedding bed"

Ironically her grave became her wedding bed.

She goes on to say that,

"Prodigious birth of love it is to me,
That I must love a loathed enemy"

When analyzing Juliet's character, we note that she does not fit the stereotypical actions of a fourteen-year-old of that era.

Her boldness and instant tendency to lie somewhat shocks the reader. Here she lies to the nurse telling her that it's a rhyme she has learnt but in reality, she is referring to her love for her enemy Romeo.

Children of the Elizabethan era were expected to be docile and follow their parents' orders.

[1st quatrain]

Now old desire doth in his deathbed lie,
And young affection gapes to be his heir,
That fair for which Love groaned for and would die,
With tender Juliet matched, is now not fair.

[2nd quatrain]

Now Romeo is beloved, and loves again,
Alike bewitched by the charm of looks:
But to his foe supposed he must complain,
And she steal love's sweet bait from fearful hooks:

[3rd quatrain]

Being held a foe, he may not have access
To breathe such vows as lovers use to swear,
And she as much in love, her means much less
To meet her new beloved anywhere:

[rhyming couplet]

But passion lends them power, time means, to **meet**
Tempering extremities with extreme **sweet**.

[Exit]

The prologue sung by the chorus in the Elizabethan Era foreshadows the story of the play in a nutshell and using dramatic irony, the audience is aware of certain events unravelling before the actors do.

Using an AB-AB rhyme scheme, in the 1st quatrain, the prologue spells out that Romeo's feelings of love for Rosaline is dying,

'Now old desire doth in his deathbed lie'

Note the foreshadowing of the noun 'deathbed' now uttered by the Chorus, signalling an eerie foreboding of death.

In the 2nd quatrain, Shakespeare uses a fishing imagery to express Juliet's love.

And she steal love's sweet bait from fearful hooks

Juliet's love is bait for Romeo's hook whom she was supposed to fear.

In the 3rd quatrain, they find it difficult to meet each other because of their circumstances.

In the rhyming couplet, their love conquers all because it gives them power to meet.

'But passion lends them power, time means, to **meet**'

A Lane by the Wall of Capulet's Orchard

[*Enter* ROMEO *alone in the lane*]

ROMEO

Can I go forward when my heart is here?
Turn back, dull earth, and find thy centre out.

[*He climbs the wall, and leaps down within it*]

[*Enter* BENVOLIO *and* MERCUTIO *in the lane*
ROMEO listens behind the wall]

BENVOLIO
Romeo! My cousin Romeo!
MERCUTIO
He is wise,
And, on my lie, hath stolen him home to bed.
BENVOLIO
He ran this way, and leaped this orchard wall:
Call, good Mercutio.
MERCUTIO
Nay, I'll conjure too.
Romeo! Humours!
Madman! Passion! Lover!
Appear thou in the likeness of a sigh:
Speak but one rhyme, and I am satisfied,
Cry but 'Ay me!',
Pronounce but 'love' and 'dove',
Speak to my gossip Venus one fair word,
One nickname for her purblind son and heir,
Young Abram Cupid, he that shot so trim,
When King Cophetua loved the beggar maid!
He heareth not, he stirreth not, he moveth not
The ape is dead, and I must conjure him.
I conjure thee by Rosaline's bright eyes,
By her high forehead and her scarlet lip,
By her fine foot, straight leg,
And quivering thigh
And the demesnes that there adjacent lie,
That in thy likeness thou appear to us!
BENVOLIO
And if he hears thee, thou wilt anger him.

[ENTER ROMEO]

Benvolio and Mercutio look for Romeo but in vain. He seems to have alluded them and they say that he has been blinded by love and they go home.

Romeo is distraught, he said that he cannot go away while his heart is here. He must go back and follow his heart, his love.

"Turn back dull earth and find thy centre out"

He goes to Juliet's garden in the hope of seeing her.

ROMEO at the orchard wall

Once again Mercutio makes fun of the love-sick Romeo.

"Romeo! Humours! Madman!
Passions! Lover!"

Benvolio warns Mercutio that Romeo will get angry if he hears him.

"And if he hears thee, thou wilt anger him"

MERCUTIO
This cannot anger him:
'Twould anger him
To raise a spirit in his mistress' circle
Of some strange nature, letting it there stand
Till she had laid it and conjured it down,
That were some spite:
My invocation is fair and honest,
And in his mistress' name
I conjure only but to raise up him.
BENVOLIO
Come!
He hath hid himself among these trees,
To be consorted with the humorous night:
Blind is his love and best befits the dark.
MERCUTIO
If love be blind, love cannot hit the mark.
Now will he sit under a medlar tree,
And wish his mistress were that kind of fruit
As maids call medlars,
When they laugh alone.
O Romeo, that she were,
O, that she were an open-arse,
And thou a poperin pear!
Romeo, good night:
I'll to my truckle–bed,
This field–bed is too cold for me to sleep:
Come, shall we go?
BENVOLIO
Go, then; for 'tis in vain
To seek him here that means not to be found.

[*Exeunt* BENVOLIO *and* MERCUTIO]

BENVOLIO and MERCUTIO search for ROMEO by the orchard wall

Shakespeare draws a clear distinction between the characters of Mercutio and Benvolio.

Benvolio appears to always be sensible, and he gives good advice. His speeches are short and polite as well whereas Mercutio's speeches are always bawdy, rude and careless.

In portraying Mercutio in this light one can infer that Shakespeare is preparing the audience for Mercutio's impending doom.

It is, after all his impulsive actions and impolite speeches that contributes ultimately to his sad death.

Benvolio says of Romeo,

"Blind is his love and best befits the dark"

We can sense a warning tone in Benvolio's voice. He is fearful that Romeo is acting out of love without thinking because he just met Juliet and he is already lovesick. Hence, he is afraid that this impulsive behaviour will lead to Romeo's destruction.

Mercutio echoes Benvolio's sentiments

"If love be blind, love cannot hit the mark"

Capulet's Orchard

[*Enter* ROMEO]

ROMEO
He jests at scars that never felt a wound.

[JULIET *appears above at a window*]

JULIET at a window with ROMEO below

But, soft!
What light through yonder window breaks?
It is the east, and Juliet is the sun.
Arise, fair sun, and kill the envious moon,
Who is already sick and pale with grief,
That thou her maid art far more fair than she:
Be not her maid since she is envious.
Her vestal livery is but sick and green,
And none but fools do wear it; cast it off.
It is my lady, O, it is my love!
O, that she knew she were!
She speaks yet she says nothing:
What of that?
Her eye discourses,
I will answer it.

[Enter ROMEO]

He says that love is a wound and the scars that it makes should not be laughed at,

"He jests at scars that never felt a wound"

[JULIET Appears above are a window]

Romeo is so overwhelmed at seeing her. He uses light imagery to describe her beauty,

"But, soft!"
"What light through yonder window breaks?"

He says that she is the east, where the sun rises from and that she represents the sun,

"It is the east and Juliet is the sun"

He goes on to use the heavenly bodies to describe her amazing beauty. He challenges the moon saying that it is jealous of Juliet's beauty and that the sun should kill it.

"Arise, fair sun and kill the envious moon"

The moon (Diana the goddess of the moon and patron of the Virgins) is,

"sick and pale with grief"

Because Juliet is far more beautiful than her. Shakespeare uses colour imagery 'green' which is associated with jealousy and envy.

Romeo is overwhelmed when he sees Juliet on her balcony,

"It is my lady, O, it is my love!
O, that she knew she were!"

Romeo's use of the repeated exclamation marks can suggest that he is in awe of Juliet's presence and that he is really excited to see her.

ROMEO (*continues*)
I am too bold, 'tis not to me she speaks:
Two of the fairest stars in all the heaven,
Having some business, do entreat her eyes
To twinkle in their spheres till they return.

Romeo says that the moon is jealous because it is still a virgin and had never felt love. Her virginal uniform 'vestal livery' is but sick and green. Romeo urges Juliet to cast off her virginity because only fools 'Wear it' and that it causes Diana goddess of the moon to be jealous of her beauty.

The repetition of the 'O' uttered by Romeo suggests that he is smitten by Juliet's beauty. She is uttering something which he says he is bold enough to answer, although she says nothing to him, but her eyes are speaking. Once again, he uses the heavenly bodies to describe her beauty,

"Two of the fairest stars in all the heavens"

Her eyes, he says are like two stars twinkling in the heavens and that two stars who were busy on business entrusted her with the job of twinkling for them.

"Having some business, do entreat her eyes
 To twinkle in their spheres till they return"

ROMEO in the garden near the window

ROMEO (*continues*)
What if her eyes were there, they in her head?
The brightness of her cheek
Would shame those stars,
As daylight doth a lamp,
Her eyes in heaven
Would thro' the airy region stream so bright
That birds would sing
And think it were not night.
See, how she leans her cheek upon her hand!
O, that I were a glove upon that hand,
That I might touch that cheek!
JULIET
Ay me!
ROMEO
She speaks:
O, speak again, bright angel!
For thou art
As glorious to this night, being over my head
As is a winged messenger of heaven
Unto the white–upturned wondering eyes
Of mortals that fall back to gaze on him
When he bestrides the lazy–pacing clouds
And sails upon the bosom of the air.

[JULIET is unaware of ROMEO's presence]

JULIET
O Romeo, Romeo!
Wherefore art thou Romeo?
Deny thy father and refuse thy name
Or, if thou wilt not, be but sworn my love,
And I'll no longer be a Capulet.
ROMEO
[*Aside*]
Shall I hear more, or shall I speak at this?

And if her eyes were in the sky and the stars replace her eyes, the brightness of her glowing cheeks will outshine the glow of the stars in the same manner, that the brightness of the day

"The brightness of her cheek
 Would shame those stars,
 As daylight doth a lamp"

She leans her cheek upon her hand!

Her eyes in the night sky would shine so brightly that they would confuse the birds into thinking that it was day, and they will begin to sing.

"That birds would sing
 And think it were not night"

Romeo wishes that he was the glove upon Juliet's hand so that he can touch her cheek. Romeo uses very endearing terms when addressing Juliet. He associates her to an angel, highlighting her purity and innocence.

"O, speak again, bright angel!"

He says that she shines like an angel from heaven, who make men gaze wondrously at the angel in the clouds.

Juliet is just as smitten by love, whispering to herself, and asking Romeo to deny his father and refuse his name

"O Romeo, Romeo!
 Wherefore art thou Romeo?
 Deny thy father and refuse thy name"

JULIET
'Tis but thy name that is my enemy,
Thou art thyself, though not a Montague.
What's Montague?
It is nor hand, nor foot, nor arm, nor face,
Nor any other part belonging to a man.
O be some other name!
What's in a name?
That which we call a rose
By any other name would smell as sweet,
So, Romeo would, were he not Romeo called
Retain that dear perfection
Which he owes without that title.
Romeo, doff thy name,
And for that name which is no part of thee
Take all myself
ROMEO
I take thee at thy word:
Call me but love, and I'll be new baptized,
Henceforth I never will be Romeo.
JULIET
What man art thou
That thus bescreened in night
So stumblest on my counsel?
ROMEO
By a name
I know not how to tell thee who I am:
My name, dear saint, is hateful to myself,
Because it is an enemy to thee,
Had I it written I would tear the word.
JULIET
My ears have not yet drunk a hundred words
Of that tongue's utterance,
Yet I know the sound:
Art thou not Romeo and a Montague?
ROMEO
Neither, fair saint, if either thee dislike.
JULIET
How camest thou hither,
Tell me, and wherefore?
The orchard walls are high and hard to climb,
And the place death,
Considering who thou art,
If any of my kinsmen find thee here.

Just the way the men gaze admiringly at the angels in the sky, Romeo gazes up in awe at Juliet who is on the balcony, and he is down in the garden.

Juliet is unaware that Romeo is listening, and she asks him to renounce his name and love her. She asks,

"What's in a name?
That which we call a rose
By any other name would smell as sweet"

Meaning that Romeo would still be that amazing person even if he wasn't a Montague, because that name does not reflect him.

Romeo agrees to give up his name for Juliet and he tells her that he hates his name because,

"It is an enemy to thee"

ROMEO says "It is an enemy to thee"

Juliet asks Romeo how he came into the orchard, and she is puzzled because she says that,

"The orchard walls are high and hard to climb"

She also warns him that it is certainly a place of death for an enemy like him.

ROMEO
With love's light wings
Did I o'er–perch these walls,
For stony limits cannot hold love out,
And what love can do
That dares love attempt,
Therefore, thy kinsmen are no stop to me.

JULIET
If they do see thee, they will murder thee.

ROMEO
Alack, there lies more peril in thine eye
Than twenty of their swords:
Look thou but sweet,
And I am proof against their enmity.

JULIET
I would not for the world they saw thee here.

ROMEO
I have
night's cloak to hide me from their sight
And but thou love me, let them find me here:
My life were better ended by their hate,
Than death prorogued, wanting of thy love.

JULIET
By whose direction
Foundst thou out this place?

ROMEO
By love, who first did prompt me to inquire,
He lent me counsel and I lent him eyes.
I am no pilot,
Yet, wert thou as far as that vast shore Washed with
the farthest sea,
I would adventure for such merchandise.

---

or she will no longer be a Capulet.

He uses a metaphor in reply to her fears,

"With love's light wings

 Did I O'er perch these walls"

He flew over the wall with wings of love and that no wall irrespective of its height can keep him out;

"For stony limits cannot hold love out"

Even her relatives, with the threat of death cannot stop him,

"Therefore, thy kinsmen are no stop to me"

Shakespeare goes further in using a metaphor to describe Romeo's boldness,

"night's cloak to hide me from their sight"

Suggesting that the dark will hide his presence.

He tells Juliet that if she doesn't love him, then he would be glad to die instead of his life being prolonged and him yearning for her love.

"My life were better ended by their hate"

Once again, we have to note the fore shadowing of death so early in the play which prepares the audience for the deaths to come. Juliet questions Romeo about how he came to know where her bedroom was and he tells her that,

"By love, that first did prompt me to inquire"

He assures her that if she was, across the furthest sea, he would risk it all to find her - such is the extent of his love. Shakespeare uses a metaphor

"Yet, wert thou as far as that vast shore
 Washed with the farthest sea"

JULIET
Thou knowst the mask of night is on my face,
Else would a maiden blush bepaint my cheek
For that which thou hast
Heard me speak to–night
Fain would I dwell on form, fain, fain deny
What I have spoke, but farewell compliment!
Dost thou love me? I know thou wilt say 'Ay,'
And I will take thy word: yet if thou swearest
Thou mayst prove false, at lovers' perjuries
Then say, Jove laughs. O gentle Romeo,
If thou dost love, pronounce it faithfully:
Or if thou think'st I am too quickly won,
I'll frown and be perverse an say thee nay,
So thou wilt woo; but else, not for the world.
In truth, fair Montague, I am too fond,
And therefore
thou mayst think my behaviour light:
But trust me, gentleman,
I'll prove more true than those
That have more cunning to be strange.
I should have been more strange,
I must confess,
But that thou overheardst, ere I was ware,
My true love's passion:
Therefore, pardon me,
And not impute this yielding to light love,
Which the dark night hath so discovered.
ROMEO
Lady, by yonder blessed moon I vow
That tips with silver all these fruit tree tops —

Juliet admonishes Romeo

"the mask of night is on my face"

Referring to the dark night, which is hiding her blushes,

"blush bepaint my cheek"

And she urges him to also declare his love for her,

"If thou dost love, pronounce it faithfully"

Here it is obvious that Juliet does not obey the rules of contemporary Elizabethan ethics where ladies had no voice and were expected to be coy and subdued and wait for the man to woo them but here Juliet is rather forthright in expressing her love for Romeo. And she doesn't stop there. Throughout the play we see a rather strong-willed Juliet and she always act against the norms of Elizabethan society and sadly her actions end in disaster.

"But trust me, gentlemen,
 I'll prove more true than those
That have more cunning to be strange"

Juliet expresses her profoundly deep love and desire for Romeo,

"My true's love passion"

Once again Romeo attaches spirituality to their love and confesses that he loves her,

"by yonder blessed moon I vow"

Enhancing the purity of their love.
Juliet expresses her dissatisfaction when Romeo swore his love by the moon.

JULIET
O, swear not by the moon,
The inconstant moon,
That monthly changes in her circled orb,
Lest that thy love prove likewise variable.
ROMEO
What shall I swear by?
JULIET
Do not swear at all,
Or, if thou wilt, swear by thy gracious self,
Which is the god of my idolatry,
And I'll believe thee.
ROMEO
If my heart's dear love —
JULIET
Well, do not swear; although I joy in thee,
I have no joy of this contract to-night:
It is too rash, too unadvised, too sudden,
Too like the lightning, which doth cease to be
Ere one can say 'It lightens'.
Sweet, good night!
This bud of love,
By summer's ripening breath,
May prove a beauteous flower
When next we meet.
Good night, good night!
As sweet repose and rest
Come to thy heart as that within my breast!
ROMEO
O, wilt thou leave me so unsatisfied?
JULIET
What satisfaction canst thou have to-night?
ROMEO
The exchange of
Thy love's faithful vow for mine
JULIET
I gave thee mine before thou didst request it:
And yet I would it were to give again.

She believes that the moon is inconsistent and that it is constantly changing with the changing seasons, and she didn't want Romeo's love to be inconsistent like the changing moon,

"Lest that thy love proves likewise variable"

She prefers him to swear by himself, who she says, she idolises like a God.

"Which is the god of my Idolatry"

Once again note the use of biblical imagery attached to their love suggesting that it is pure and heavenly.

JULIET: "It is too rash, too unadvisedly"

Juliet describes her love as being,

"It is too rash, too unadvised, too sudden,
Too like the lightning, which doth cease to be"

This love we will later see, ends in disaster because Juliet is aware of her impulsiveness, yet she takes sweeping steps to consummate this love with her 'enemy' Romeo.

Juliet uses a flower imagery to describe her growing love for Romeo,

"This bud of love,
By summer's ripening breadth,
May prove a beauteous flower
When next we meet"

ROMEO
Wouldst thou withdraw it?
For what purpose, love?

JULIET
But to be frank and give it thee again.
And yet I wish but for the thing I have:
My bounty is as boundless as the sea,
My love as deep; the more I give to thee,
The more I have, for both are infinite.

[Nurse *calls within*]

I hear some noise within,
Dear love, adieu!
Anon, good Nurse!
Sweet Montague be true.
Stay but a little, I will come again.

[JULIET *goes in*]

ROMEO
O blessed, blessed night!
I am afeard being in night,
All this is but a dream,
Too flattering sweet to be substantial.

[JULIET *returns*]

JULIET
Three words, dear Romeo,
And good night indeed.
If that thy bent of love be honourable,
Thy purpose marriage,
Send me word to–morrow,
By one that I'll procure to come to thee,
Where and what time
Thou wilt perform the rite,
And all my fortunes at thy foot I'll lay
And follow thee my lord throughout the world.
Nurse
[*Within*]
Madam!
JULIET
I come, anon.—
But if thou meanest not well,
I do beseech thee —

Juliet uses a flower imagery saying that her their love is like a bud and that it will burst into a flower the next time they meet. She says that their love is infinite, and she leaves.

NURSE calls for JULIET

Romeo is excited and he thinks that it is all a dream,

"All this is but a dream,
Too flattering sweet to be substantial"

Juliet reappears and asks Romeo to marry her. Romeo decides to go and see the Friar to tell him about his good fortune and ask for his help.

ROMEO remarks "All this is but a dream"

Nurse
[*Within*]
Madam!
JULIET
By and by, I come: —
To cease thy suit, and leave me to my grief:
Tomorrow will I send.
ROMEO
So thrive my soul —
JULIET
A thousand times good night!

[JULIET *goes in*]

ROMEO
A thousand times the worse, to want thy light!
Love goes toward love,
As schoolboys from their books,
But love from love,
Toward school with heavy looks.

[*Retiring*]
[JULIET *returns*]
JULIET
Hist! Romeo, hist!
O, for a falconer's voice,
To lure this tassel–gentle back again!
Bondage is hoarse,
And may not speak aloud,
Else would I tear the cave where Echo lies,
And make her airy tongue
More hoarse than mine,
With repetition of 'My Romeo'.
ROMEO
It is my soul that calls upon my name:
How silver–sweet
Sound lovers' tongues by night,
Like softest music to attending ears!
JULIET
Romeo!
ROMEO
My niess!
JULIET
At what o'clock to–morrow
Shall I send to thee?
ROMEO
At the hour of nine.
JULIET
I will not fail: 'tis twenty years till then.
I have forgot why I did call thee back.

Shakespeare makes use of bird analogue to express their newfound bliss and devotion: ROMEO is the falconer, and JULIET the Falcon.

JULIET remarks,

"O, for a falconer's voice,
To lure this tassel gentle back again!"

Juliet is afraid to speak loudly because she is confined to her father's house and she is afraid of calling Romeo's name too loudly.

"Bondage is hoarse,
And may not speak aloud,
Else would I tear the cave where echo lies"

Echo was a mythological creature and she loved Narcissus who didn't love her. Grief-stricken, she lived in a cave and deteriorated until all that was left was her voice.

Shakespeare uses a simile to describe how melodious and sweet lovers sound when they speak to each other.

Romeo says,

"How silver-sweet
Sound lovers' tongues by night,
Like softest music to attending ears!"

JULIET says "I will not fail"

ROMEO
Let me stand here till thou remember it.
JULIET
I shall forget, to have thee still stand there,
Remembering how I love thy company.
ROMEO
And I'll still stay, to have thee still forget,
Forgetting any other home but this.
JULIET
'Tis almost morning; I would have thee gone:
And yet no further than a wanton's bird,
Who lets it hop a little from her hand,
Like a poor prisoner in his twisted gyves,
And with a silk thread plucks it back again,
So loving–jealous of his liberty.
ROMEO
I would I were thy bird.
JULIET
Sweet, so would I:
Yet I should kill thee with much cherishing.
Good night, good night!
Parting is such sweet sorrow,
That I shall say good night till it be morrow.

[*Exit above*]

ROMEO
Sleep dwell upon thine eyes,
Peace in thy breast!
Would I were sleep and peace
So sweet to rest!
Hence will I to my ghostly father's cell,
His help to crave, and my dear hap to tell.

[*Exit* ROMEO *to Friar Laurence's cell*]

Romeo and Juliet just cannot say goodbye to each other.

Juliet uses the imagery of a bird saying that Rome is like a bird in a spoilt child's hand.

The child loves the bird and ties it up and holds it prisoner. She lets it hop for a little while and plucks it back again.

Juliet does the same to Romeo, she doesn't want him to leave. She says,

"Good night, good night!
Parting is such sweet sorrow,
That I shall say good night till it be morrow"

JULIET and ROMEO say Goodnight

Shakespeare personifies sleep and peace, and Romeo wishes that he could be at peace and rest with Juliet.

"Would I were sleep and peace,
So sweet to rest!"

Romeo is preparing to go to Friar Lawrence's cell to tell him about his woes and ask him for help.

"Hence will I to my ghostly father's cell,
His help to crave, and my dear hap to tell"

Friar Laurence's Cell

FRIAR LAURENCE's cell inside Monastery

[*Enter* FRIAR LAURENCE, *with a basket*]

FRIAR LAURENCE
The grey–eyed morn smiles
On the frowning night,
Checkering the eastern clouds
With streaks of light,
And flecked darkness like a drunkard reel
From forth day's path
And Titan's fiery wheels:
Now, ere the sun advance his burning eye,
The day to cheer and night's dank dew to dry,
I must upfill this osier cage of ours
With baleful weeds
And precious–juiced flowers.
The earth that's nature's mother is her tomb,
What is her burying grave that is her womb
And, from her womb, children of divers kind
We sucking on her natural bosom find,
Many for many virtues excellent,
None but for some and yet all different.
O, mickle is the powerful grace that lies
In herbs, plants, stones,
And their true qualities:
For nought so vile that on the earth doth live
But to the earth some special good doth give,
Nor aught so good
But strained from that fair use

[Enter FRIAR LAURENCE carrying a basket]

Shakespeare sets the scene for forth-coming events by getting Friar Laurence to recite a soliloquy on nature and its interaction with night and day, which can be juxtaposed with the star crossed-lovers eventual sorrow and joy

"The grey-eyed morn smiles
On the frowning night"

Friar Laurence is in the garden, and he uses many rhyme schemes in his speech as though he is enlightening for us the unique rhythm that exists between nature and man.

'Night-light'

'tomb-womb'

He also uses personifications to make nature come alive by giving inanimate objects animate qualities,

"morn smiles
On the frowning night"

And

"flecked darkness like a drunkard reels
From forty day's path"

He gives us an in-depth description of the power of nature and how earth's womb creates so many amazing plants that provide excellent virtues.

"But to the earth some special good doth give"

He says that Earth is Mother Nature and also nature's grave.

Monastery garden

FRIAR LAURENCE (*continues*)
Revolts from true birth, stumbling on abuse:
Virtue itself turns vice, being misapplied,
And vice sometimes by action dignified.
Within the infant rind of this weak flower
Poison hath residence and medicine power:
For this, being smelt,
With that part cheers each part,
Being tasted, stays all senses with the heart.
Two such opposed kings encamp them still
In man as well as herbs, grace and rude will,
And where the worser is predominant,
Full soon the canker death eats up that plant.

FRIAR LAURENCE studying herbs

[*Enter* ROMEO]

ROMEO
Good morrow, father.

He also talks about vice turning to virtue if it is used properly.

One can connote that his utterances about vice can be a foreshadowing for the Capulet's and Montague's hate and sadly the sacrifice of their children's life had to put an end to this strife.

Ironically, it was these very herbs itself that was instrumental in bringing about the deaths of Romeo and Juliet and turning vice to virtue in the end.

Another way of interpreting and analysing Friar Laurence's quote,

"Virtue itself turns vice, being misapplied, And vice sometime by action dignified"

This can be applied to Friar Laurence himself because it can be argued that his actions were inappropriate - being a man of God. Here he tries to justify his actions and firmly believing that if he manages to marry Romeo and Juliet then their parent's strife would end. Unfortunately, his well-laid plans did not materialise and ended in disaster although the families did unite at the end.

Friar Laurence said that everything both man and nature has opposing forces - good and evil,

"In man as well as herbs, grace and rude will"

He goes on to give us a visual imagery of a plant that is infected by canker, a destructive disease that destroys plants, in the same way
cancer destroys the body. When evil is rampant, death takes control of the body. These explanations cannot be seen in isolation, but it is imperative that it is seen in comparison to the text.

Being a man of God, we can assume that this is a grave warning for Man to mend his ways or suffer the consequences.

[Enter ROMEO]

FRIAR LAURENCE
Benedicite!
What early tongue so sweet saluteth me?
Young son, it argues a distempered head
So soon to bid good morrow to thy bed:
Care keeps his watch in every old man's eye,
And where care lodges, sleep will never lie,
But where unbruised youth
With unstuffed brain doth couch his limbs,
There golden sleep doth reign:
Therefore thy earliness doth me assure
Thou art up–roused by some distemperature,
Or if not so, then here I hit it right,
Our Romeo hath not been in bed tonight.

ROMEO
That last is true; the sweeter rest was mine.

FRIAR LAURENCE
God pardon sin! Wast thou with Rosaline?

ROMEO
With Rosaline, my ghostly father? No!
I have forgot that name, and that name's woe

FRIAR LAURENCE
That's my good son!
But where hast thou been, then?

ROMEO
I'll tell thee, ere thou ask it me again.
I have been feasting with mine enemy,
Where on a sudden one hath wounded me,
That's by me wounded: both our remedies
Within thy help and holy physic lies:
I bear no hatred, blessed man, for, lo,
My intercession likewise steads my foe.

FRIAR LAURENCE
Be plain, good son, and homely in thy drift,
Riddling confession finds but riddling shrift.

ROMEO
Then plainly know my heart's dear love is set
On the fair daughter of rich Capulet:
As mine on hers, so hers is set on mine,
And all combined,
Save what thou must combine
By holy marriage:
When and where and how we met,
We wooed and made exchange of vow
I'll tell thee as we pass,
But this I pray,
That thou consent to marry us today.

Friar Lawrence is a wise and perceptive man because he immediately sensed that Romeo is troubled.

"Young son, it argues a distempered head"

Romeo tells Friar Lawrence that he has been wounded with love. Note the repetition of the verb 'wounded' ironically this love has really wounded him and caused him much pain.

ROMEO asking FRIAR LAURENCE - "that thou consent to marry us today"

Note also that Romeo's impatience proves to be his great downfall later in the play. We can conclude that Romeo's heart rules his head,

"know my heart's dear love is set"

There is a sense of impatience in Romeo's voice because he doesn't tell Friar Lawrence how and where he met Juliet but insists that he marry them immediately,

"That thou consent to marry us today"

FRIAR LAURENCE
Holy Saint Francis, what a change is here!
Is Rosaline, whom thou didst love so dear,
So soon forsaken?
Young men's love then lies
Not truly in their hearts, but in their eyes.
Jesu Maria, what a deal of brine hath washed
Thy sallow cheeks for Rosaline!
How much salt water thrown away in waste
To season love, that of it doth not taste!
The sun not yet thy sighs from heaven clears,
Thy old groans ring yet in my ancient ears,
Lo, here upon thy cheek the stain doth sit
Of an old tear that is not washed off yet:
If ever thou wast thyself and these woes
thine,
Thou and these woes were all for Rosaline:
And art thou changed?
Pronounce this sentence then,
Women may fall,
When there's no strength in men.
ROMEO
Thou chid'st me oft for loving Rosaline.
FRIAR LAURENCE
For doting, not for loving, pupil mine.
ROMEO
And bad'st me bury love.
FRIAR LAURENCE
Not in a grave,
To lay one in, another out to have.
ROMEO
I pray thee, chide not,
She whom I love now
Doth grace for grace and love for love allow,
The other did not so.
FRIAR LAURENCE
O, she knew well
Thy love did read by rote and could not spell.
But come, young waverer, come, go with me,
In one respect I'll thy assistant be,
For this alliance may so happy prove,
To turn your households' rancour to pure love
ROMEO
O let us hence; I stand on sudden haste.
FRIAR LAURENCE
Wisely and slow; they stumble that run fast.

[*Exeunt*]

Even the Friar is shocked at Romeo's sudden change in circumstances,

"Holy Saint Francis, what a change is here!"

The exclamation mark can denote the friar's shock at the change in Romeo because he forgot Rosaline so quickly,

"Thou and these woes were all for Rosaline"

Friar Lawrence foreshadows Romeo's fate when he mentions the grave,

"Not in a grave,
To lay one in, another out to have"

Meaning that Romeo is getting rid of Rosaline to replace her with Juliet.

Note that the friar calls Romeo a wave'er and earlier Juliet said that she didn't want his love to waver like the moon. This can suggest that Romeo's behaviour is inconsistent.

The friar has good intentions and agrees to help Romeo so that the hatred between their families will abate.

"To turn your households' rancour to pure love"

As I mentioned before Romeo is too hasty,

"I stand on sudden haste"

The friar noticed his impatience and warns him,

"Wisely and slow; they stumble that run fast"

Making it clear that impatience can breed disaster.

A public place in Verona

[*Enter* BENVOLIO *and* MERCUTIO]

MERCUTIO
Where the devil should this Romeo be?
Came he not home to–night?
BENVOLIO
Not to his father's, I spoke with his man.
MERCUTIO
Why, that same pale hard–hearted wench,
That Rosaline torments him so,
That he will sure run mad.
BENVOLIO
Tybalt, the kinsman of old Capulet,
Hath sent a letter to his father's house.
MERCUTIO
A challenge, on my life.
BENVOLIO
Romeo will answer it.
MERCUTIO
Any man that can write may answer a letter.
BENVOLIO
Nay, he will answer the letter's master,
How he dares, being dared.
MERCUTIO
Alas poor Romeo! He is already dead,
Stabbed with a white wench's black eye,
Shot through the ear with a love song,
The very pin of his heart cleft
With the blind bow–boy's butt–shaft:
And is he a man to encounter Tybalt?
BENVOLIO
Why, what is Tybalt?
MERCUTIO
More than Prince of Cats, I can tell you.
He is the courageous captain of compliments
He fights as you sing prick–song,
Keeps time, distance, and proportion,
Rests me his minim rest, one, two,
And the third in your bosom:
The very butcher of a silk button,
A duellist, a duellist,
A gentleman of the very first house,
Of the first and second cause:
Ah, the immortal passado!
The punto reverso! The hai!

[Enter BENVOLIO and MERCUTIO]

Benvolio and Mercutio are looking for Romeo and Benvolio reveals that Tybalt has sent a letter in which he wants to challenge Romeo to a duel.

"Tybalt, the kinsman of old Capulet,
 Hath sent a letter to his father's house"

BENVOLIO with letter from TYBALT

Shakespeare presents Mercutio as a very irrational and boisterous character, giving us an inkling of his impending doom.

Here his speech is filled with violent imagery. He says that Romeo is already dead,

"Stabbed with a white wench's black eye,
 Shot through the air with a love song"

Ironically, he is just about to be stabbed and he dies by Tybalt's sword.

Furthermore, Mercutio outlines for us in detail Tybalt's expertise and skill in fencing, yet he became the victim of that skill.

"A duellist, a duellist"

BENVOLIO
The what?
MERCUTIO
The pox of such antic,
Lisping, affecting fantasticoes,
These new tuners of accents!'
By Jesu, a very good blade!
A very tall man! A very good whore!'
Why, is not this a lamentable thing, grandsire,
That we should be thus afflicted with
These Strange flies,
These fashion–mongers,
These perdona–mi's,
Who stand so much on the new form,
That they cannot at ease on the old bench?
O, their bones, their bones!

[*Enter* ROMEO]

BENVOLIO
Here comes Romeo, here comes Romeo!
MERCUTIO
Without his roe, like a dried herring.
O, flesh, flesh, how art thou fishified!
Now is he for the numbers
That Petrarch flowed in:
Laura, to his lady, was but a kitchen–wench-
Marry, she had a better love to be–rhyme her!
Dido a dowdy; Cleopatra a gipsy,
Helen and Hero hildings and harlots,
Thisbe a grey eye or so,
But not to the purpose.
Signior Romeo, bonjour!
There's a French salutation -
To your French slop.
You gave us the counterfeit fairly last night.
ROMEO
Good morrow to you both.
What counterfeit did I give you?
MERCUTIO
The slip, sir, the slip,
Can you not conceive?
ROMEO
Pardon, good Mercutio,
My business was great;
And in such a case as mine
A man may strain courtesy.

Mercutio continues his denunciation of foreigners by calling them 'strange flies',

"That we should be thus afflicted with
These strange flies,
These fashion-mongers,
These persona-mi's"

BENVOLIO listens to MERCUTIO views on TYBALT and his skills in sword play

[Enter ROMEO]

Mercutio starts his tirade on love and the role of women in trapping men,

"Helen and Hero hildings and harlots"

Mercutio asks Romeo why he gave them the slip last night and Romeo says that his,

"business was great"

Mercutio talks about losing his battle of wits with Romeo but ironically, despite all his big talk he later loses his battle of duels with Tybalt, and he is killed by Tybalt's sword.

MERCUTIO
That's as much as to say,
Such a case as yours constrains
A man to bow in the hams.

ROMEO
Meaning, to curtsy?

MERCUTIO
Thou hast most kindly hit it.

ROMEO
A most courteous exposition.

MERCUTIO
Nay, I am the very pink of courtesy.

ROMEO
Pink for flower?

MERCUTIO
Right.

ROMEO
Why, then is my pump well flowered.

MERCUTIO
Sure wit!
Follow me this jest now
Till thou hast worn out thy pump,
That when the single sole of it is worn,
The jest may remain
After the wearing sole singular.

ROMEO
O single–soled jest,
Solely singular for the singleness!

MERCUTIO
Come between us, good Benvolio;
My wits faint.

ROMEO
Switch and spurs, switch and spurs,
Or I'll cry a match.

MERCUTIO
Nay, if thy wits run the wild–goose chase,
I have done, for thou hast
More of the wild–goose in one of thy wits
Than I am sure, I have in my whole five.
Was I with you there for the goose?

ROMEO
Thou wast never with me for anything
When thou wast not there for the goose.

MERCUTIO
I will bite thee by the ear for that jest.

ROMEO
Nay, good goose, bite not.

MERCUTIO
Thy wit is a very bitter sweeting,
It is a most sharp sauce.

Mercutio teases Romeo on love, fate and courtship, comparing it to a pump - a light dancing shoe and a flower.

BENVOLIO, MERCUTIO and ROMEO exchanging wit and innuendos on love

Mercutio is tired of this battle of wits with Romeo, so he asks Benvolio to help him.

"Come between us, good Benvolio,
 My wits faint"

This foreshadows the duel that Mercutio is involved in later in the play with Tybalt. This duel costed him his life, and he curses the families.

Mercutio points-out to Romeo that he is more than a wild-goose chaser (a serial chaser of woman) than himself,

"for thou hast
 More of the wild-goose in one of thy wits
 Than I"

ROMEO
And is it not well served into a sweet goose?
MERCUTIO
O here's a wit of cheverel,
That stretches from an inch
Narrow to an ell broad!
ROMEO
I stretch it out for that word 'broad;'
Which added to the goose,
Proves thee far and wide a broad goose.
MERCUTIO
Why, is not this better now
Than groaning for love?
Now art thou sociable,
Now art thou Romeo,
Now art thou what thou art,
By art as well as by nature:
For this drivelling love is like a great natural,
That runs lolling up and down
To hide his bauble in a hole.
BENVOLIO
Stop there, stop there.
MERCUTIO
Thou desirest me to stop
In my tale against the hair?
BENVOLIO
Thou wouldst else have made thy tale large.
MERCUTIO
O, thou art deceived,
I would have made it short:
For I was come to the whole depth of my tale,
And meant, indeed,
To occupy the argument no longer.
ROMEO
Here's goodly gear!

[*Enter* Nurse *and* PETER]

MERCUTIO
A sail, a sail!
BENVOLIO
Two, two,
A shirt and a smock.
Nurse
Peter!
PETER
Anon!
Nurse
My fan, Peter.

MERCUTIO jests with ROMEO on love

Mercutio is once again attacking Romeo for being love-sick. He points out to Romeo that jesting around is better,

"Than groaning for love?"

And that it is better to be sociable than be consumed by love.

Benvolio stops Mercutio's rantings in case it leads to trouble,

"Stop there, stop there"

Mercutio is adamant that Romeo's wit and argument are invalid,

"O, thou art deceived"

[Enter NURSE and PETER]

Mercutio's blatant rudeness shocks the audience.

MERCUTIO
Good Peter, to hide her face,
For her fan's the fairer face.
Nurse
God ye good morrow, gentlemen.
MERCUTIO
God ye good den, fair gentlewoman.
Nurse
Is it good den?
MERCUTIO
'Tis no less, I tell you,
For the bawdy hand of the dial
Is now upon the prick of noon.
Nurse
Out upon you!
What a man are you?
ROMEO
One, gentlewoman,
That God hath made for himself to mar.
Nurse
By my troth, it is well said,
'For himself to mar,' quoth a'?
Gentlemen, can any of you tell me
Where I may find the young Romeo?
ROMEO
I can tell you,
But young Romeo will be older
When you have found him
Than he was when you sought him.
I am the youngest of that name,
For fault of a worse.
Nurse
You say well.
MERCUTIO
Yea, is the worst well?
Very well took, I' faith!
Wisely, wisely!
Nurse
If you be He, sir,
I desire some confidence with you.
BENVOLIO
She will endite him to some supper.
MERCUTIO
A bawd, a bawd, a bawd! So ho!
ROMEO
What hast thou found?

ROMEO, MERCUTIO, BENVOLIO meeting NURSE and PETER her servant

He verbally attacks Nurse and says that she needs to hide her face,

"For her fan's the fairer face"

Suggesting that her fan is more beautiful than she is.

Mercutio is also very crude in his jokes and he uses a lot of puns in his speeches,

"For the bawdy hand of the dial
Is now upon the prick of noon"

His behaviour infuriates the Nurse, and she yells,

"Out upon you!
What a man are you?".

Ironically, he says that God made him to ruin himself. How true because he does ruin himself by his bizarre behaviour.

"That God hath made, himself to mar"

MERCUTIO
No hare, sir,
Unless a hare, sir, in a Lenten pie
That is something stale,
And hoar ere it be spent.
[He *walks by* Nurse *and sings*]
   An old hare hoar,
   And an old hare hoar,
   Is very good meat in Lent
   But a hare that is hoar
   Is too much for a score
   When it hoars ere it be spent.
[He *speaks*]
Romeo, will you come to your father's?
We'll to dinner, thither.
ROMEO
I will follow you.
MERCUTIO
Farewell, ancient lady; farewell,
[*Singing*]
   'lady, lady, lady.'

[*Exeunt* MERCUTIO *and* BENVOLIO]

Nurse
Marry, farewell!
I pray you, sir,
What saucy merchant was this
That was so full of his ropery?
ROMEO
A gentleman, Nurse,
That loves to hear himself talk,
And will speak more in a minute
Than he will stand to in a month.
Nurse
[*speaks to* ROMEO]
And if he speaks anything against me,
I'll take him down,
If he were lustier than he is,
And twenty such Jacks,
And if I cannot, I'll find those that shall.
Scurvy knave!
I am none of his flirt–gills,
I am none of his skains–mates.
[*now speaks to* PETER]
And thou must stand by too,
And suffer every knave
To use me at his pleasure!

Mercutio sings a lewd poem to discredit Nurse and the portent of her message.

In response, Nurse comments,

"What saucy merchant was this
That was so full of his ropery?"

PETER looking-on as NURSE and ROMEO

Romeo tries to defuse the Nurse's indignation by excusing Mercutio's indiscretion as,

"A gentleman,
That loves to hear himself talk"

Nurse continues to berate Romeo and then her servant Peter for not admonishing Mercutio about his scandalous attack on her dignity. She threatens to attack Mercutio because she is furious

"And if he speaks anything against me
I'll take him down"

PETER
I saw no man use you at his pleasure:
If I had,
My weapon should quickly have been out,
I warrant you,
I dare draw as soon as another man,
If I see occasion in a good quarrel,
And the law on my side.
Nurse
Now, afore God, I am so vexed,
That every part about me quivers.
Scurvy knave! Pray you, sir, a word:
And as I told you,
My young lady bade me inquire you out,
What she bade me say,
I will keep to myself:
But first let me tell ye,
If ye should lead her into a fool's paradise,
As they say,
It were a very gross kind of behaviour,
As they say:
For the gentlewoman is young,
And, therefore,
If you should deal double with her,
Truly it were an ill thing to be offered
To any gentlewoman,
And very weak dealing.
ROMEO
Nurse,
Commend me to thy lady and mistress.
I protest unto thee —
Nurse
Good heart, and, I' faith,
I will tell her as much:
Lord, Lord, she will be a joyful woman.
ROMEO
What wilt thou tell her, Nurse?
Thou dost not mark me!
Nurse
I will tell her, sir,
That you do protest,
Which, as I take it,
Is a gentlemanlike offer.

Peter pacifies Nurse by proclaiming his manly duty of defending her should the need arise,

"My weapon should quickly have been out"

followed by

"If I see occasion in a good quarrel"

Nurse questions Romeo's motives as to his true intent towards Juliet, and issues a moral judgement

"If you should deal double with her,
 Truly it were an ill thing to be offered
 To any gentlewoman,
 And very weak dealing"

Romeo reassures her that he will be true to Juliet. We note once again the Nurse's love and loyalty for Juliet's well-being.

"Nurse,
 Commend me to thy lady and mistress.
 I protest unto thee"

The nurse is very polite to Romeo. She sees him in a favourable light.

We also witness the Nurse's excitement for Juliet because she repeats the words, 'Lord.' And one can denote a sense of excitement in her tone,

"I will tell her as much:
 Lord, Lord, she will be a joyful woman"

ROMEO
Bid her devise
Some means to come to shrift this afternoon,
And there she shall at Friar Laurence' cell
Be shrived and married.
Here is for thy pains.
Nurse
No truly sir; not a penny.
ROMEO
Go to; I say you shall.
Nurse
This afternoon, sir?
Well, she shall be there.
ROMEO
And, good nurse, behind the abbey wall:
Within this hour my man shall be with thee
And bring thee cords made like a tackled stair
Which to the high top–gallant of my joy
Must be my convoy in the secret night.
Farewell: be trusty, and I'll quit thy pains:
Farewell: commend me to thy mistress.
Nurse
Now God in heaven bless thee!
Hark you, sir.
ROMEO
What say'st thou, my dear Nurse?
Nurse
Is your man secret?
Did you never hearsay
'Two may keep counsel, putting one away'?
ROMEO
I warrant thee, my man's as true as steel.
Nurse
Well, sir; my mistress is the sweetest lady —
Lord, Lord! When 'twas a little prating thing:
O, there is a nobleman in town, one Paris,
That would fain lay knife aboard,
But she, good soul, had as lief see a toad,
A very toad, as see him.
I anger her sometimes
And tell her that Paris
Is the properer man,
But I'll warrant you,
When I say so,
She looks as pale as
Any clout in the versal world.
Doth not Rosemary and Romeo
Begin both with a letter?

Romeo tells the nurse to tell Juliet to come to Friar Lawrence's cell to be married.

"And there she shall at Friar Laurence' cell
Be shrived and married"

NURSE listening to ROMEO's instructions for him and JULIET to wed

The nurse tells Romeo of Paris' intention to marry Juliet.

Shakespeare uses the phrase

"lay knife abroad"

as an analogy by Nurse to show Paris' intent to establish or pursue his claim.

**NURSE tells ROMEO
about PARIS' desire to wed JULIET**

ROMEO
Ay, Nurse; what of that?
Both with an R.
Nurse
Ah. Mocker!
That's the dog's name;
R is for the — No,
I know it begins with some other letter: —
And she hath the prettiest sententious of it,
Of you and Rosemary,
That it would do you good to hear it.
ROMEO
Commend me to thy lady.
Nurse
Ay, a thousand times.

[*Exit* Romeo]

Peter!
PETER
Anon!
Nurse
Peter, take my fan, and go before and apace.

[*Exeunt*]

Shakespeare uses the letter R to link the first letter of Romeo's name to the growl of a dog.

"Ay, Nurse; what of that?
 Both with an R"

The Nurse muses on this connection

"Ah. Mocker!
 That's the dog's name"

Capulet's Orchard

[*Enter* JULIET]

JULIET

The clock struck nine
When I did send the Nurse,
In half an hour she promised to return.
Perchance she cannot meet him:
That's not so. O, she is lame!
Love's heralds should be thoughts,
Which ten times faster
Glide than the sun's beams,
Driving back shadows over louring hills:
Therefore,
Do nimble–pinioned doves draw love,
And therefore,
Hath the wind–swift Cupid wings.
Now is the sun upon the high most hill
Of this day's journey, and from nine till twelve
Is three long hours, yet she is not come.
Had she affections and warm youthful blood,
She would be as swift in motion as a ball,
My words would bandy her to my sweet love,
And his to me:
But old folks, many feign as they were dead,
Unwieldy, slow, heavy and pale as lead.
O God, she comes!

[*Enter* Nurse *and* PETER]

O honey nurse, what news?
Hast thou met with him?
Send thy man away.
Nurse
Peter, stay at the gate.

[*Exit* PETER]

JULIET
Now, good sweet nurse -
O Lord, why look'st thou sad?
Though news be sad,
Yet tell them merrily; if good,
Thou shamest the music of sweet news
By playing it to me with so sour a face.

[Enter JULIET]

Juliet is just as impatient as Romeo when she waits for news from the nurse. We can see Juliet's impatience in her voice when she accuses the nurse of not being,

"as swift in motion as a ball"

And that,

"old folks, many feign as they were dead"

When the Nurse arrives, Juliet is excited, but the Nurse decides to play a few tricks which agitates Juliet.

Nurse
I am aweary, give me leave awhile:
Fie, how my bones ache!
What a jaunt have I had!
JULIET
I would thou hadst my bones, and I thy news:
Nay, come, I pray thee, speak,
Good, good Nurse, speak.
Nurse
Jesu, what haste!
Can you not stay awhile?
Do you not see that I am out of breath?
JULIET
How art thou out of breath,
When thou hast breath
To say to me that thou art out of breath?
The excuse that thou dost make in this delay
Is longer than the tale thou dost excuse.
Is thy news good, or bad? Answer to that,
Say either and I'll stay the circumstance:
Let me be satisfied, is't good or bad?
Nurse
Well, you have made a simple choice,
You know not how to choose a man:
Romeo! No, not he.
Though his face be better than any man's,
Yet his leg excels all men's
And for a hand, and a foot, and a body,
Though they be not to be talked on,
Yet they are past compare:
He is not the flower of courtesy,
But I'll warrant him, as gentle as a lamb.
Go thy ways, wench; serve God.
What, have you dined at home?
JULIET
No, no: but all this did I know before.
What says he of our marriage? What of that?
Nurse
Lord, how my head aches!
What a head have I!
It beats as it would fall in twenty pieces.
My back o' t' other side,
O, my back, my back!
Beshrew your heart for sending me about, To catch my death
With jaunting up and down!

The nurse is creating a lot of suspense here by deliberately delaying the news thereby exasperating Juliet. Just like the Friar, the nurse is observant enough to detect Juliet's impatience which can lead to her destruction,

"Jesus, what haste!"

Shakespeare presents the nurse as a comic character whose light banter and bawdiness cuts the tension and the seriousness of the play. Instead of giving desperate Juliet the news from Romeo, she embarks on a prolonged description of his physical appearance and his character. She then goes on to ask a very irate Juliet if she had lunch, and then she complains about her headache and her aching back.

We find the nurse to be hilarious with the ability to create nerve-wracking suspense.

The nurse's hilarity makes her endearing to the audience because her amusing antics leaves them in stitches.

Shakespeare very deliberately created this light-hearted ambiance to weigh up the horror that is about to unfold. Hence allowing the audience some reprieve.

JULIET
I' faith, I am sorry that thou art not well.
Sweet, sweet, sweet Nurse,
Tell me, what says my love?
Nurse
Your love says, like an honest gentleman,
And a courteous, and a kind,
And a handsome, and I warrant, a virtuous, -
Where is your mother?
JULIET
Where is my mother! Why, she is within,
Where should she be?
How oddly thou repliest!
'Your love says, like an honest gentleman,
Where is your mother?'
Nurse
O God's lady dear!
Are you so hot? Marry, come up, I trow!
Is this the poultice for my aching bones?
Henceforward do your messages yourself.
JULIET
Here's such a coil! Come, what says Romeo?
Nurse
Have you got leave to go to shrift to–day?
JULIET
I have.
Nurse
Then hie you hence to Friar Laurence' cell,
There stays a husband to make you a wife,
Now comes,
The wanton blood up in your cheeks,
They'll be in scarlet straight at any news.
Hie you to church; I must another way,
To fetch a ladder, by the which your love
Must climb a bird's nest soon when it is dark:
I am the drudge and toil in your delight,
But you shall bear the burden soon at night.
Go; I'll to dinner: hie you to the cell.
JULIET
Hie to high fortune! Honest Nurse, farewell.

[*Exeunt*]

JULIET receiving the news of marriage from NURSE

One would think that by now she would give Juliet the news that she is craving for but oh no, she embarks on a further tirade when she delivers the news.

"Your love says like an honest gentleman,
 And a courteous, and a kind,
 And a handsome, and I warrant, a virtuous –
 Where is your mother?"

The Nurse then reverts to Juliet's mother's whereabouts and as you can imagine by now that Juliet is incensed by the Nurse's frivolous behaviour.

Alas! She finally delivers Romeo's message to Juliet, hence ending in a bawdy tone,

"I am the drudge and toil in your delight,
 But you shall bear the burden soon at night"

Friar Laurence's Cell

[*Enter* FRIAR LAURENCE *and* ROMEO]

[Enter FRIAR LAWRENCE and ROMEO]

The friar marries Romeo and Juliet, and he uses a personification to bless the marriage.

FRIAR LAURENCE
So smile the heavens upon this holy act,
That after hours with sorrow chide us not!

"So smile the heavens upon this holy act"

Ironically, the Friar says that he hopes no misfortune befalls them after this.

ROMEO
Amen, amen! But come what sorrow can,
It cannot countervail the exchange of joy
That one short minute gives me in her sight:
Do thou but close our hands with holy words,
Then love–devouring death do what he dare
It is enough I may but call her mine.

Romeo says that no amount of sorrow can eclipse the joy that he is feeling.

He urges the friar to get them married quickly,

"Do thou but close our hands with holy words"

FRIAR LAURENCE
These violent delights have violent ends
And in their triumph die, like fire and powder,
Which as they kiss consume:
The sweetest honey is loathsome
In his own deliciousness
And in the taste confounds the appetite:
Therefore, love moderately; long love doth so,
Too swift arrives as tardy as too slow.
Here comes the lady.

Then Romeo challenges death by saying that love destroying death can do whatever it wants as long as he can call Juliet his very own.

The friar makes a very poignant remark here which foreshadows Romeo and Juliet's deaths which are very violent,

"These violent delights have Violent ends"

[*Enter* JULIET, *somewhat fast*]

[Enter JULIET]

Ironically the Friar says that she,

O, so light a foot
Will never wear out the everlasting flint!
A lover may bestride the gossamer
That idles in the wanton summer air,
And yet not fall; so light is vanity.

"Will never wear out the everlasting flint!"

Well, she never did, did she?
A right merry mess it ended in.

JULIET
Good even to my ghostly confessor.

The road to their love was really rocky, and difficult to endure, culminating in their deaths.

FRIAR LAURENCE
Romeo shall thank thee, daughter, for us both.
JULIET
As much to him, else is his thanks too much.

[ROMEO *and* JULIET *embrace*]

ROMEO

Ah, Juliet, if the measure of thy joy
Be heaped like mine
And that thy skill be more
To blazon it, then sweeten with thy breath
This neighbour air,
And let rich music's tongue
Unfold the imagined happiness that both
Receive in either by this dear encounter.

JULIET

Conceit, more rich in matter than in words,
Brags of his substance, not of ornament:
They are but beggars
That can count their worth,
But my true love is grown to such excess
I cannot sum up sum of half my wealth.

FRIAR LAURENCE

Come, come with me,
And we will make short work,
For, by your leaves, you shall not stay alone
Till holy church incorporate two in one.

[*Exeunt*]

NURSE and FRIAR looking-on as ROMEO and JULIET greet with joy each other

Romeo and Juliet greet each other with words justifying their union. Romeo says,

"Ah, Juliet, if the measure of thy joy
 Be heaped like mine"

Juliet responds,

"But my true love is grown to such excess
 I cannot sum up sum of half my wealth"

JULIET and ROMEO kneel in front of FRIAR LAURENCE ready to be married

To cement their union, and hoping to reconcile the two houses by their marriage, Friar Laurence tells the star-crossed lovers,

"Come, come with me,
 And we will make short work,
 For, by your leaves, you shall not stay alone
 Till holy church incorporate two in one"

A Public Place

[*Enter* MERCUTIO, BENVOLIO, *Page, others*]

BENVOLIO
I pray thee, good Mercutio, let's retire:
The day is hot, the Capulets, abroad,
And, if we meet, we shall not scape a brawl,
For now, these hot days,
Is the mad blood stirring.
MERCUTIO
Thou art like one of those fellows
That when he enters the confines of a tavern
Claps me his sword upon the table
And says, 'God send me no need of thee!'
And by the operation of the second cup,
Draws it on the drawer,
When indeed there is no need.
BENVOLIO
Am I like such a fellow?
MERCUTIO
Come, come, thou art as hot a Jack
In thy mood as any in Italy,
And as soon moved to be moody,
And as soon moody to be moved.
BENVOLIO
And what to?
MERCUTIO
Nay, an there were two such,
We should have none shortly,
For one would kill the other.
Thou! Why, thou wilt quarrel with a man
That hath a hair more, or a hair less,
In his beard, than thou hast:
Thou wilt quarrel with a man for cracking nuts
Having no other reason
But because thou hast hazel eyes:
What eye but such an eye
Would spy out such a quarrel?
Thy head is as full of quarrels
As an egg is full of meat,
And yet thy head hath been beaten
As addle as an egg for quarrelling:
Thou hast quarrelled with a man
For coughing in the street,
Because he hath wakened thy dog
That hath lain asleep in the sun.

[Enter MERCUTIO and BENVOLIO]

Benvolio is seen as a very benevolent character, and we can see that it is somewhat reflected in his name.

He desperately urges Mercutio to retire, and he is afraid that they would encounter a brawl with the Capulet's if they stayed on the streets.

Mercutio is furious with Benvolio, and he embarks on a tirade of abuse, shaming Benvolio about his bad temper and detailing all the times he picked petty fights with people. He says that Benvolio will quarrel with a man for having less hair, and with another for cracking nuts, yet we don't see any evidence of Benvolio behaving badly. He is always the rational, calm one, giving advice to Mercutio who is always getting into trouble.

"Thy head is as full of quarrels"

MERCUTIO
Didst thou not fall out with a tailor
For wearing his new doublet before Easter?
With another,
For tying his new shoes with old riband?
And yet thou wilt tutor me from quarrelling!
BENVOLIO
An I were so apt to quarrel as thou art,
Any man should buy the fee–simple of my life
For an hour and a quarter.
MERCUTIO
The fee–simple? O simple!
BENVOLIO
By my head, here come the Capulets.
MERCUTIO
By my heel, I care not.

[*Enter* TYBALT *and others*]

TYBALT
Follow me close, for I will speak to them.
Gentlemen, goodden: a word with one of you
MERCUTIO
And but one word with one of us?
Couple it with something,
Make it a word and a blow.
TYBALT
You shall find me apt enough to that, sir,
An you will give me occasion.
MERCUTIO
Could you not take
Some occasion without giving?
TYBALT
Mercutio, thou consortest with Romeo, —
MERCUTIO
Consort!
What, dost thou make us minstrels?
An thou make minstrels of us,
Look to hear nothing but discords:
Here's my fiddlestick;
Here's that shall make you dance.
'Zounds, 'consort'!
BENVOLIO
We talk here in the public haunt of men:
Either withdraw unto some private place,
Or reason coldly of your grievances,
Or else depart; here all eyes gaze on us.

Mercutio ends his outbursts by saying,

"yet thou wilt tutor me from quarrelling!"

Now once again Shakespeare portrays Mercutio's fiery temper thus preparing us for his fate. It's a case of: 'You live by the sword, and you die by the sword'.

Mercutio seems to always be inviting trouble with his irrational behaviour.

The audience becomes troubled and anxious for him.

[Enter TYBALT and others]

Tybalt wants a word with one of them, but as usual Mercutio starts to 'Fuel a fire' by exclaiming,

"Make it a word and a blow"

Mercutio is proving to be confrontational in his behaviour which does not augur well for him.

TYBALT, BENVOLIO, MERCUTIO who says "Make it a word and a blow"

He is stirring up trouble because he points his sword and tells Tybalt that it will challenge him,

"Here's my fiddlestick.
Here's that shall make you dance"

MERCUTIO
Men's eyes were made to look,
And let them gaze,
I will not budge for no man's pleasure, I.

[*Enter* ROMEO]

TYBALT
Well, peace be with you, sir:
Here comes my man.
MERCUTIO
But I'll be hanged, sir, if he wear your livery:
Marry, go before to field,
He'll be your follower,
Your worship in that sense may call him 'man'
TYBALT
Romeo, the hate I bear thee can afford
No better term than this, — thou art a villain.
ROMEO
Tybalt, the reason that I have to love thee
Doth much excuse the appertaining rage
To such a greeting: Villain am I none,
Therefore farewell: I see thou knowest me not
TYBALT
Boy, this shall not excuse the injuries
That thou hast done me,
Therefore turn and draw.
ROMEO
I do protest, I never injured thee,
But love thee better than thou canst devise,
Till thou shalt know the reason of my love:
And so, good Capulet, — which name I tender
As dearly as my own, — be satisfied.
MERCUTIO
O calm, dishonourable, vile submission!
'Alla stoccata' carries it away.

[MERCUTIO d*raws his rapier*]

Tybalt, you rat–catcher, will you walk?
TYBALT
What wouldst thou have with me?

Benvolio senses some sense of discord and urges them to go somewhere private to settle their grievances. But Mercutio is adamant and insists that he will never move,

"I will not budge for no man's pleasure, I"

[Enter ROMEO]

Tybalt on seeing Romeo hurls abuse at him calling him, 'a villain' but Romeo dismisses his insults by saying,

"Tybalt the reason that I have to love thee
 Doth much excuse the appertaining rage"

Romeo is referring to his love for Juliet and hence his willingness to forgive the insults and he bids Tybalt farewell.

But Tybalt challenges Romeo to a duel,

"Therefore turn and draw"

Romeo once again expresses his love for Tybalt,

"But love thee better than thou canst devise,
Till thou shalt know the reason of my love"

Mercutio draws his sword,

"Tybalt, you rat-catcher, will you walk?"

MERCUTIO tells TYBALT:
"Tybalt, you rat-catcher, will you walk?"

MERCUTIO
Good King of Cats,
Nothing but one of your nine lives,
That I mean to make bold withal,
And as you shall use me hereafter,
Dry-beat the rest of the eight.
Will you pluck your sword
Out of his pilcher by the ears?
Make haste, lest mine be about your ears
Were it be out.
TYBALT
I am for you.

[TYBALT *draws his rapier (sword)*]

ROMEO
Gentle Mercutio put thy rapier up.
MERCUTIO
Come, sir, your passado.

[MERCUTIO *and* TYBALT *fight*]

ROMEO
Draw, Benvolio,
Beat down their weapons.
Gentlemen, for shame, forbear this outrage!
Tybalt, Mercutio, the Prince expressly hath
Forbid this bandying in Verona streets:
Hold, Tybalt! Good Mercutio!

[*Under* ROMEO's arm,
TYBALT *stabs* MERCUTIO.
TYBALT *then hurries away with his followers*]

MERCUTIO
I am hurt.
A plague o' both your houses! I am sped
Is he gone, and hath nothing?
BENVOLIO
What, art thou hurt?
MERCUTIO
Ay, ay, a scratch, a scratch,
Marry, 'tis enough.
Where is my page?
Go, villain, fetch a surgeon.

[*Exit* Page]

Mercutio provokes Tybalt, and Tybalt draws his sword, and they fight.

Romeo begs them to,

"Beat down their weapons"

Romeo tries to break up the fight but Tybalt stabs Mercutio under Romeo's arm.

MERCUTIO attacking TYBALT with ROMEO trying to intervene to stop it

Romeo's intervention impedes Mercutio's ability to fight, so later Romeo feels he is responsible for Mercutio death.

TYBALT kills MERCUTIO

[TYBALT *flees with his followers*]

Mercutio curses both the families for his fate,

"A plague o' both your houses! I am sped"

But he denies being seriously hurt claiming,

Ay, ay, a scratch, a scratch"

But then realises he death is near.

ROMEO
Courage, man; the hurt cannot be much.
MERCUTIO
No, 'tis not so deep as a well,
Nor so wide as a church–door,
But 'tis enough,'twill serve:
Ask for me tomorrow,
And you shall find me a grave man.
I am peppered, I warrant, for this world.
A plague o' both your houses!
Zounds, a dog, a rat, a mouse, a cat,
To scratch a man to death!
A braggart, a rogue, a villain,
That fights by the book of arithmetic!
Why the devil came you between us?
I was hurt under your arm.
ROMEO
I thought all for the best.
MERCUTIO
Help me into some house, Benvolio,
Or I shall faint.
A plague o' both your houses!
They have made worms' meat of me:
I have it, and soundly too! Your houses!

[*Exeunt* MERCUTIO *and* BENVOLIO]

ROMEO
This gentleman, the Prince's near ally,
My very friend, hath got his mortal hurt
In my behalf, my reputation stained
With Tybalt's slander - Tybalt, that an hour
Hath been my kinsman! O sweet Juliet,
Thy beauty hath made me effeminate
And in my temper softened valour's steel!

[*Re–enter* BENVOLIO]

BENVOLIO
O Romeo, Romeo, brave Mercutio is dead!
That gallant spirit hath aspired the clouds,
Which too untimely here did scorn the earth.
ROMEO
This day's black fate
On more days doth depend,
This but begins the woe others must end.
BENVOLIO
Here comes the furious Tybalt back again.

Mercutio rants and raves to his death, claiming that,

"They have made worms' meat of me"

Meaning that now he is going to die, and he will become meals for the worms.

Romeo is very distraught, and he thinks that his love for Juliet had weakened him like a woman. He believes that he is now soft and his bravery which used to be hard as steel is gone.

"And in my temper softened Valour's steel!"

[Re-Enter BENVOLIO]

He announces Mercutio's death, and we are made aware of the motif of 'fate' because Romeo mentions fate and we will see fate's interventions in Romeo and Juliet's lives throughout the play.

The atmosphere is very tense, and Romeo speaks in a very bitter tone. He uses dark imagery, 'black fate' and warns that today's event will breed more grief and sadness in the future.

"This but begins the woe others must end"

BENVOLIO tells ROMEO that MERCUTIO is dead

ROMEO
Alive, in triumph! And Mercutio slain!
Away to heaven, respective lenity,
And fire–eyed fury be my conduct now!

[*Re–enter* TYBALT]

Now, Tybalt, take the 'villain' back again,
That late thou gavest me; for Mercutio's soul
Is but a little way above our heads
Staying for thine to keep him company:
Either thou, or I, or both, must go with him.
TYBALT
Thou, wretched boy,
That didst consort him here,
Shalt with him hence.
ROMEO
This shall determine that.

[*They fight*; TYBALT *falls and dies*]

BENVOLIO
Romeo, away, be gone!
The citizens are up, and Tybalt slain.
Stand not amazed:
The prince will doom thee death,
If thou art taken, hence, be gone, away!
ROMEO
O, I am Fortune's fool!
BENVOLIO
Why dost thou stay?

[*Exit* ROMEO]

[*Enter Citizens*]

First Citizen
Which way ran he that killed Mercutio?
Tybalt, that murderer, which way ran he?
BENVOLIO
There lies that Tybalt.
First Citizen
Up, sir, go with me,
I charge thee in the Prince's name, obey.

[*Enter* PRINCE, *attended*, MONTAGUE, CAPULET, *their Wives, and others*]

Enter TYBALT]

Romeo is furious with Tybalt, and he tells him that,

"Either thou or I, or both, must go with him"

Romeo and Tybalt fight and Tybalt falls. Benvolio urges Romeo to flee or suffer the consequence of death.

TYBALT fights ROMEO

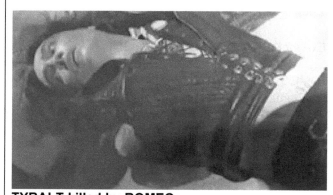

TYBALT killed by ROMEO

BENVOLIO tells ROMEO: "be gone!"

PRINCE
Where are the vile beginners of this fray?
BENVOLIO
O noble Prince, I can discover all
The unlucky manage of this fatal brawl:
There lies the man, slain by young Romeo,
That slew thy kinsman, brave Mercutio.
LADY CAPULET
Tybalt, my cousin! O my brother's child!
O prince! O cousin! O husband!
O, the blood is spilt of my dear kinsman!
Prince, as thou art true,
For blood of ours, shed blood of Montague.
O cousin, cousin!
PRINCE
Benvolio, who began this bloody fray?
BENVOLIO
Tybalt, here slain,
Whom Romeo's hand did slay,
Romeo that spoke him fair, bade him bethink
How nice the quarrel was,
And urged withal
Your high displeasure:
All this uttered with gentle breath, calm look,
Knees humbly bowed, could not take truce
With the unruly spleen of Tybalt deaf to peace
But that he tilts with piercing steel
At bold Mercutio's breast,
Who all as hot, turns deadly point to point,
And, with a martial scorn,
With one hand beats cold death aside,
And with the other sends it back to Tybalt,
Whose dexterity retorts it.
Romeo, he cries aloud,
'Hold, friends! Friends, part!'
And, swifter than his tongue, his agile arm
Beats down their fatal points,
And 'Twixt them rushes,
Underneath whose arm,
An envious thrust From Tybalt
Hit the life of stout Mercutio,
And then Tybalt fled,
But by and by comes back to Romeo,
Who had but newly entertained revenge,
And to it they go like lightning,
For, ere I could draw to part them,
Was stout Tybalt slain.
And, as he fell, did Romeo turn and fly.
This is the truth or let Benvolio die.

[Enter PRINCE, MONTAGUES & CAPULETS]

MERCUTIO and TYBALT dead

PRINCE presiding on ROMEO's fate

CAPULETS awaiting judgement

MONTAGUES awaiting judgement

LADY CAPULET
He is a kinsman to the Montague,
Affection makes him false,
He speaks not true:
Some twenty of them fought
In this black strife,
And all those twenty could but kill one life.
I beg for justice,
Which thou, Prince, must give:
Romeo slew Tybalt!
Romeo must not live!
PRINCE
Romeo slew him,
He slew Mercutio,
Who now,
The price of his dear blood doth owe?
MONTAGUE
Not Romeo, Prince,
He was Mercutio's friend,
His fault concludes,
But what the law should end -
The life of Tybalt.
PRINCE
And for that offence
Immediately we do exile him hence:
I have an interest in your hate's proceeding,
My blood for your rude brawls
Doth lie a–bleeding,
But I'll amerce you with so strong a fine
That you shall all repent the loss of mine:
I will be deaf to pleading and excuses,
Nor tears nor prayers
Shall purchase out abuses:
Therefore, use none:
Let Romeo hence in haste,
Else, when he's found, that hour is his last.
Bear hence this body and attend our will:
Mercy but murders, pardoning those that kill.

[*Exeunt*]

The prince is furious at these tragic, vile turn of events. Benvolio explains exactly what happened.

Naturally, Lady Capulet is extremely distraught over Tybalt's death, and she urges the prince to take revenge on the house of Montague's. She insists that Romeo,

"Romeo slew Tybalt!
 Romeo must not live!"

Shakespeare once again highlights for us the bitter feud and intense hate that existed between these two families.

When we look at Lady Capulet's reasoning, we are astounded at how her hate can overrule justice.

She immediately calls for revenge citing that Romeo killed Tybalt so Romeo must be punished.

She ignored the fact that Tybalt killed Mercutio from the house of Montague's.

Shakespeare clearly highlights for us the stubborn nature of these two feuding families even in death.

It's obvious that a heavy price needs to be paid to stop this ongoing hate.

The prince made a decree that Romeo should be banned from Verona,

"But I'll amerce you with so strong a fine
 That you shall all repent the loss of mine"

The prince is furious because Mercutio was a kinsman of his. He vows that he will take no excuses. We can juxtapose the prince's reaction to Romeo and Juliet's death in the end.

He is regretful of his decision that he made here which he thinks was rather too lenient.

Capulet's House

[*Enter* JULIET]

JULIET
Gallop apace, you fiery–footed steeds,
Towards Phoebus' lodging!
Such a wagoner as
Phaethon would whip you to the west,
And bring in cloudy night immediately.
Spread thy close curtain,
Love–performing night,
That runaway's eyes may wink
And Romeo leap to these arms,
Untalked of and unseen.
Lovers can see to do their amorous rites
By their own beauties,
Or, if love be blind,
It best agrees with night.
Come, civil night,
Thou sober–suited matron, all in black,
And learn me how to lose a winning match,
Played for a pair of stainless maidenhoods:
Hood my unmanned blood,
Bating in my cheeks,
With thy black mantle,
Till strange love, grown bold,
Think true love acted simple modesty.
Come, night; come, Romeo,
Come, thou day in night,
For thou wilt lie upon the wings of night
Whiter than new snow on a raven's back.
Come, gentle night,
Come, loving, black–browed night,

Enter JULIET]

Once again Juliet's impatience is quite evident when she is waiting for Romeo to come to her.

She associates herself to Phoebus - the Greek God of Light and she summons the horses to bring Romeo to her.

"Gallop apace, you fiery–footed steeds,
Towards Phoebus' lodging!"

She wishes for the night to come so that she can make love to Romeo.

"And bring cloudy night immediately"

She goes on to describe Romeo with a simile and contrasting colour imagery.

"Whiter than new snow on a raven's back"

There is a juxtaposition here between

'black' raven and 'white' swan

This can suggest good versus evil.

Despite the intense hate that exists between their families, these two can unite in pure love and create a deep physical bond. Good will ultimately triumph over evil.

Furthermore, in this soliloquy Juliet repeats the colour imagery, 'black' -

'black mantle' and 'black-browed night'

The raven it was thought symbolized death In Elizabethan times.

One can connote that there is a foreboding, eerie darkness about their meeting.

JULIET (*continues*)
Give me my Romeo,
And when he shall die,
Take him and cut him out in little stars,
And he will make the face of heaven so fine
That all the world will be in love with night
And pay no worship to the garish sun.
O, I have bought the mansion of a love,
But not possessed it,
And, though I am sold,
Not yet enjoyed:
So tedious is this day
As is the night before some festival
To an impatient child that hath new robes
And may not wear them.
O, here comes my Nurse,
And she brings news,
And every tongue that speaks
But Romeo's name
Speaks heavenly eloquence.

[*Enter* Nurse, *with cords*]

Now, Nurse, what news?
What hast thou there?
The cords that Romeo bid thee fetch?
Nurse
Ay, ay, the cords.

[Nurse *throws the cords down*]

JULIET
Ay me! What news?
Why dost thou wring thy hands?
Nurse
Ah, well–a–day!
He's dead, he's dead, he's dead!
We are undone, lady, we are undone!
Alack the day!
He's gone, he's killed, he's dead!
JULIET
Can heaven be so envious?

She goes on to say that when she dies, Romeo must be cut into little stars. This utterance can foreshadow their deaths,

"And when he shall die,
 Take him and cut him out in little stars"

The use of the biblical imagery,

"And he will make the face of heaven so fine"

Once again, she associates their love to being pure and godly. The use of the metaphor,

"O, I have bought the mansion of a love"

Suggesting Juliet's powerful, great and unending love for Romeo.
She says that she feels like a child who has new clothes but can't wear them. She loves Romeo but she can't enjoy his company and she is thoroughly impatient to meet him.

[Enter NURSE with cords]

Shakespeare's use of the repeated question marks can suggest Juliet's impatience once again,

"Ay me! What news?
 Why dost thou wring thy hands?"

Well we trust the Nurse to use dramatic irony when she relays the news to Juliet about Romeo's banishment;

"He's dead, he's dead, he's dead!"

"He's gone, he's killed, he's dead!"

Shakespeare's continued use of the repetitive exclamation marks and constant reference to death highlights for us the calamitous manner in which the nurse delivered the sad news to Juliet.

Once again, the Nurse is toying with Juliet's emotions. She is deliberately delaying the deliverance of the sad news, keeping Juliet in painful suspense.

Nurse
Romeo can,
Though heaven cannot:
O Romeo, Romeo!
Whoever would have thought it?
Romeo!
JULIET
What devil art
Thou that dost torment me thus?
This torture should be roared in dismal hell.
Hath Romeo slain himself?
Say thou but 'Ay'!
And that bare vowel 'I' shall poison more
Than the death–darting eye of cockatrice:
I am not I, if there be such an I
Or those eyes shut,
That make thee answer 'I'.
If he be slain, say 'I'; or if not, no:
Brief sounds determine of my weal or woe.
Nurse
I saw the wound,
I saw it with mine eyes, -
God save the mark! -
Here on his manly breast:
A piteous corse,
A bloody piteous corse;
Pale, pale as ashes,
All bedaubed in blood,
All in gore–blood,
I swounded at the sight.
JULIET
O, break, my heart!
Poor bankrupt - break at once!
To prison, eyes, never look on liberty!
Vile earth, to earth resign,
End motion here,
And thou and Romeo
Press one heavy bier!

The Nurse's antics are really irking Juliet and she is furious,

"What devil art
Thou that dost torment me thus?"

This torture is like hell, but the nurse ignores Juliet and once again she embarks on a vivid description of the wound that she saw,

"I saw the wound,
 I saw it with mine eyes"

Shockingly Juliet is actually echoing God's words here when he made man. The use of the words

"Pale, pale as ashes"

echoes God's words 'Ashes to Ashes, Dust to Dust' in the Old Testament.

When God created Man, he took the dust of the earth and breathe into it. He said that man was created from dust and when he dies, he will return to the earth. And now Juliet wants to go back to the earth. It's as though she is having some kind of premonition about her impending death.

Juliet is extremely distraught,

"O, break my heart!
 Poor bankrupt, break at once!"

She exclaims that her eyes will be imprisoned and that it will never be free to look on anything again.

"To prison, eyes, never look on liberty!"

Once again Juliet is foreshadowing their deaths. She promises to give her body back to the earth,

"Vile earth, to earth resign"

She also wants hers and Romeo's body to lie in the same coffin.

Nurse
O Tybalt, Tybalt, the best friend I had!
O courteous Tybalt! Honest gentleman!
That ever I should live to see thee dead!
JULIET
What storm is this that blows so contrary?
Is Romeo slaughtered?
And is Tybalt dead?
My dear–loved cousin,
And my dearer lord?
Then, dreadful trumpet,
Sound the general doom!
For who is living,
If those two are gone?
Nurse
Tybalt is gone, and Romeo banished,
Romeo that killed him, he is banished.
JULIET
O God!
Did Romeo's hand shed Tybalt's blood?
Nurse
It did, it did; alas the day, it did!
JULIET
O serpent heart hid with a flowering face!
Did ever dragon keep so fair a cave?
Beautiful tyrant! Fiend angelical!
Dove–feathered raven!
Wolvish–ravening lamb!
Despised substance of divinest show!
Just opposite to what thou justly seamst,
A damned saint, an honourable villain!
O nature, what hadst thou to do in hell,
When thou didst bower the spirit of a fiend
In moral paradise of such sweet flesh?
Was ever book containing such vile matter
So fairly bound?
O that deceit should dwell
In such a gorgeous palace!
Nurse
There's no trust,
No faith, no honesty in men; all perjured,
All forsworn, all naught, all dissemblers.
Ah, where's my man?
Give me some aqua vitae:
These griefs, these woes,
These sorrows make me old.
Shame come to Romeo!

Now Nurse is still ranting and raving about Tybalt's death, still very meticulously withholding the main message from Juliet. In so doing, Nurse is creating a very tense atmosphere and the suspense is palpable.

Juliet is overwrought with grief, and she bombards the nurse with a number of continuous questions,

"Is Romeo slaughtered?
And is Tybalt dead?"

"For who is living,
If those two are gone?"

This line of questioning, however, can suggest Juliet's mounting dilemma and dread.

She concludes that if these two people are dead, then life is not worth living.

Finally, the Nurse delivers the news. Juliet is shocked to learn that Romeo shed Tybalt's blood.

"Did Romeo's hand shed Tybalt's blood?"

We can draw a parallel here between Romeo's speech at the beginning when he uses many paradoxes to describe his love for Rosaline, "O loving hate" (Act 1 scene 1).

Here Juliet is also using many paradoxes to describe Romeo,

"O serpent heart, hid with a flowering face!"

She is basically saying that he is a devil in disguise. A snake with a beautiful face to mislead people.

"Beautiful tyrant! Fiend angelical!"

We see clear paradoxes here when Juliet calls Romeo a tyrant as being beautiful and an angel as being devilish.
The Nurse changes her tune, and she curses Romeo,

"Shame come to Romeo!"

JULIET
Blistered be thy tongue for such a wish!
He was not born to shame:
Upon his brow shame is ashamed to sit,
For 'tis a throne
Where honour may be crowned
Sole monarch of the universal earth.
O, what a beast was I to chide at him!
Nurse
Will you speak well of him
That killed your cousin?
JULIET
Shall I speak ill of him that is my husband? Ah, poor
my lord,
What tongue shall smooth thy name,
When I, thy three–hours wife,
Have mangled it?
But, wherefore,
Villain, didst thou kill my cousin?
That villain cousin
Would have killed my husband:
Back, foolish tears,
Back to your native spring,
Your tributary drops belong to woe,
Which you, mistaking, offer up to joy.
My husband lives,
That Tybalt would have slain,
And Tybalt's dead,
That would have slain my husband:
All this is comfort; wherefore weep I then?
Some word there was,
Worser than Tybalt's death,
That murdered me, I would forget it fain,
But, O, it presses to my memory,
Like damned guilty deeds to sinners' minds:
'Tybalt is dead, and Romeo—banished',
That 'banished,' that one word 'banished',
Hath slain ten thousand Tybalts
Tybalt's death was woe enough,
If it had ended there:
Or, if sour woe delights in fellowship
And needly will be ranked with other griefs,
Why followed not,
When she said, 'Tybalt's dead,'
Thy father, or thy mother, nay, or both,
Which modern lamentations
Might have moved?
But with a rearward following Tybalt's death,
'Romeo is banished!'

But Juliet defends Romeo and reprimands the Nurse,

"Blistered be thy tongue for such a wish!"

JULIET reprimands NURSE:
Blistered be thy tongue for such a wish!

Juliet is angry with the Nurse and she wishes that the nurse's mouth be plagued with sores. Juliet is loyal and she defends Romeo,

"Shall I speak ill of him that is my husband?"

Juliet displays a deep sense of maturity here for a girl of just fourteen years old.

She weighs out the pros and cons of Romeo's actions and concludes that if he didn't kill Tybalt then Tybalt would have surely killed him.

The repetition of the verb 'banished' can reveal Juliet's pain. This short, snappy sentence,

"Romeo is banished!"

Causes Juliet unimaginable pain and distress.

That verb 'banished' echoed death.

JULIET
To speak that word,
Is father, mother, Tybalt, Romeo, Juliet,
All slain, all dead.
'Romeo is banished!'
There is no end, no limit, measure, bound,
In that word's death,
No words can that woe sound.
Where is my father, and my mother, Nurse?
Nurse
Weeping and wailing over Tybalt's corse:
Will you go to them?
I will bring you thither.
JULIET
Wash they his wounds with tears:
Mine shall be spent,
When theirs are dry,
For Romeo's banishment.
Take up those cords:
Poor ropes, you are beguiled,
Both you and I,
For Romeo is exiled:
He made you for a highway to my bed,
But I, a maid, die maiden–widowed.
Come, cords, come, Nurse:
I'll to my wedding bed,
And death, not Romeo,
Take my maidenhead!
Nurse
Hie to your chamber:
I'll find Romeo
To comfort you:
I wot well where he is.
Hark ye! Your Romeo will be here at night:
I'll to him; he is hid at Laurence's cell.
JULIET
O find him!
Give this ring to my true knight,
And bid him come to take his last farewell.

[*Exeunt*]

JULIET: "Shall I speak ill of him"- Romeo

The rope ladder was a means of getting Romeo to then visit her chambers and consummates their marriage but now she is very sad that she is going to die a virgin, maidenhead, and she ironically blurts out,

"death, not Romeo,
 Take my maidenhead"

It's very often that the Nurse's antics annoy the audience but her love and loyalty to Juliet is rather endearing to us. She tells Juliet that she will find Romeo to comfort her.

"Hark ye! Your Romeo will be here at night:
I'll to him; he is hid at Laurence's cell."

Juliet is desperate and she gives Nurse a ring to give to Romeo and instructs the Nurse to tell him to come to say his last goodbye

NURSE tells JULIET she will bring ROMEO

Ironically, this is indeed the last time that Juliet sees Romeo.
"And bid him come to say his last farewell"

Friar Laurence's Cell

[*Enter* FRIAR LAURENCE]

FRIAR LAURENCE
Romeo, come forth,
Come forth, thou fearful man:
Affliction is enamoured of thy parts,
And thou art wedded to calamity.

[*Enter* ROMEO]

ROMEO
Father, what news?
What is the Prince's doom?
What sorrow craves acquaintance at my hand
That I yet know not?
FRIAR LAURENCE
Too familiar
Is my dear son with such sour company!
I bring thee tidings of the Prince's doom.
ROMEO
What less than Doomsday
Is the Prince's doom?
FRIAR LAURENCE
A gentler judgment vanished from his lips,
Not body's death, but body's banishment.
ROMEO
Ha, banishment?
Be merciful, say 'death',
For exile hath more terror in his look,
Much more than death:
Do not say 'banishment'.
FRIAR LAURENCE
Hence from Verona art thou banished:
Be patient, for the world is broad and wide.
ROMEO
There is no world without Verona walls,
But purgatory, torture, hell itself.
Hence 'banished' is 'banished from the world',
And world's exile is death: then banished,
Is death mis–termed:
Calling death banishment,
Thou cuttest my head off with a golden axe,
And smilest upon the stroke that murders me.

[Enter FRIAR LAURENCE]

Friar Laurence is very perceptive, and he calls out to Romeo telling him that he invites trouble and that he is married to disaster,

"Affliction is enamoured of thy parts,
And thou art wedded to calamity"

[Enter ROMEO]

The repetition of the adjective 'doom'

In Friar Laurence's and Romeo's speech is important because right from the outset the relationship between Romeo and Juliet was doomed.

Once again fate played a cruel trick which ended in Romeo's banishment and his separation from Juliet.

"What less than Doomsday
Is the Prince's doom?"

We can draw a parallel here between Juliet's reaction to the words, 'banishment' or 'banished', and Romeo's. Both of them likened it to 'death'. He says that exile is more terrible than death itself. He says that if he has to leave Verona and be away from Juliet then that would be,

"But purgatory, torture and hell Itself"

The friar is annoyed at Romeo's response to his being banished.

FRIAR LAURENCE
O deadly sin! O rude unthankfulness!
Thy fault our law calls death,
But the kind Prince, taking thy part,
Hath rushed aside the law,
And turned that black word
'Death' to 'Banishment':
This is dear mercy, and thou seest it not.
ROMEO
'Tis torture, and not mercy: heaven is here,
Where Juliet lives, and every cat and dog
And little mouse, every unworthy thing,
Live here in heaven and may look on her,
But Romeo may not: more validity,
More honourable state, more courtship lives
In carrion–flies than Romeo: they my seize
On the white wonder of dear Juliet's hand
And steal immortal blessing from her lips,
Who even in pure and vestal modesty,
Still blush, as thinking their own kisses sin,
This may flies do when I from this must fly
And say'st thou yet that exile is not death?
But Romeo may not; he is banished:
Flies may do this, but I from this must fly:
They are free men, but I am banished.
And say'st thou yet that exile is not death?
Hadst thou no poison mixed,
No sharp – ground knife,
No sudden mean of death,
Though never so mean,
But 'banished' to kill me? — Banished'!
O Friar, the damned use that word in hell,
Howlings attend it:
How hast thou the heart,
Being a divine, a ghostly confessor,
A sin–absolver, and my friend professed,
To mangle me with that word 'banished'?
FRIAR LAURENCE
Thou fond mad man,
Hear me but speak a word.
ROMEO
O, thou wilt speak again of banishment.
FRIAR LAURENCE
I'll give thee armour to keep off that word:
Adversity's sweet milk, philosophy,
To comfort thee, though thou art banished.

"Thy fault our law calls death"

He tells Romeo that the prince was kind enough to banish him because he was supposed to be put to death for murder. Romeo's short, snappy sentence,

"heaven is here"

Indicates his great love for Juliet and his grief at leaving her.

He bemoaned the fact that all the animals can see Juliet, flies can touch her hand and kiss her lips', but he has to be banished.

"Flies may do this, but I from this must fly"

ROMEO tells FRIAR LAURENCE:
"Flies may do this, but I from this must fly"

ROMEO
Yet 'banished'? Hang up philosophy!
Unless philosophy can make a Juliet,
Displant a town, reverse a Prince's doom,
It helps not, it prevails not; talk no more.
FRIAR LAURENCE
O, then I see that madmen have no ears.
ROMEO
How should they,
When that wise men have no eyes?
FRIAR LAURENCE
Let me dispute with thee of thy estate.
ROMEO
Thou canst not speak of
That thou dost not feel:
Wert thou as young as I, Juliet thy love,
An hour but married, Tybalt murdered,
Doting like me and like me banished,
Then mightst thou speak,
Then mightst thou tear thy hair,
And fall upon the ground, as I do now,
Taking the measure of an unmade grave.
[*Knocking within*]
FRIAR LAURENCE
Arise; one knocks; good Romeo, hide thyself.
ROMEO
Not I; unless the breath of heartsick groans,
Mist—like, infold me from the search of eyes.
[*Knocking*]
FRIAR LAURENCE
Hark, how they knock! Who's there?
Romeo, arise,
Thou wilt be taken. Stay awhile! Stand up,
[*Loud knocking*]
Run to my study.
By and by! God's will,
What simpleness is this!
I come, I come!
[*Louder knocking*]
Who knocks so hard?
Whence come you?
What's your will?
Nurse
Let me come in,
And you shall know my errand,
I come from Lady Juliet.
FRIAR LAURENCE
Welcome, then.

Friar Laurence tries to solve his problem,

"Let me dispute with thee of thy estate"

But Romeo is agitated, and he yells at the friar accusing him of not understanding his situation. That the friar is not as young as he is and not in love the way he loves Juliet and that he is not the one being banished and waiting for death as he is.

"Taking the measure of an unmade grave"

Friar Laurence hears a knocking and tries to get Romeo to hide but Romeo is so stubborn that he refused.

FRIAR LAURENCE tells ROMEO:
"Hark, how they knock! Who's there?"

The Nurse come in with news from Juliet.

[*Enter* Nurse]

Nurse
O holy friar, O, tell me, holy friar,
Where is my lady's lord? Where's Romeo?
FRIAR LAURENCE
There on the ground,
With his own tears made drunk.
Nurse
O, he is even in my mistress' case,
Just in her case!
O woeful sympathy!
Piteous predicament!
Even so lies she,
Blubbering and weeping,
Weeping and blubbering.
Stand up, stand up!
Stand, and you be a man:
For Juliet's sake, for her sake, rise and stand,
Why should you fall into so deep an O?
ROMEO
Nurse!
Nurse
Ah sir! ah sir! Well, death's the end of all.
ROMEO
Spakest thou of Juliet?
How is it with her?
Doth she not think me an old murderer,
Now I have stained the childhood of our joy
With blood removed but little from her own?
Where is she? And how doth she?
And what says
My concealed lady to our cancelled love?
Nurse
She says nothing, sir, but weeps and weeps,
And now falls on her bed; and then starts up,
And Tybalt calls; and then on Romeo cries,
And then down falls again.
ROMEO
As if that name,
Shot from the deadly level of a gun,
Did murder her as that name's cursed hand
Murdered her kinsman.
O, tell me, friar, tell me,
In what vile part of this anatomy
Doth my name lodge?
Tell me, that I may sack the hateful mansion.

[ROMEO *offers to stab himself,*
but NURSE *snatches the dagger away*]

[Enter NURSE]

Friar Laurence tells the nurse that Romeo is getting drunk on his own tears. She tells Friar Laurence that he is aching just like Juliet.

"Piteous predicament!
Even so lies she"

Once again, the nurse gets all dramatic by using onomatopoeias and repetition to express Juliet's feelings.

"Blubbering and weeping,
Weeping and blubbering"

We can actually hear and feel Juliet's distress by the nurse's description.

We can now compare Juliet's speech with the nurse when she wanted news about Romeo. Juliet asked many questions and now Romeo is doing the same, he's asking many questions about Juliet showing his grief.

"Spakest thou of Juliet?
How is it with her?
Doth she think me an old murderer?"

There are lots of similarities in Romeo's and Juliet's behaviour.

He is in anguish about his name, and he says that it's as though his name was like a bullet from his gun that did murder Juliet.

Romeo becomes very dramatic and enquires of the friar,

"In what vile part of this anatomy
Doth my name lodge?"

He draws out his dagger to cut it out.

FRIAR LAURENCE

Hold thy desperate hand:
Art thou a man? Thy form cries out thou art:
Thy tears are womanish; thy wild acts denote
The unreasonable fury of a beast:
Unseemly woman in a seeming man!
Or ill—beseeming beast in seeming both!
Thou hast amazed me: by my holy order,
I thought thy disposition better tempered.
Hast thou slain Tybalt? Wilt thou slay thyself?
And stay thy lady too that lives in thee,
By doing damned hate upon thyself?
Why rail'st thou on thy birth,
The heaven, and earth?
Since birth, and heaven, and earth,
All three do meet in thee at once,
Which thou at once wouldst lose.
Fie, fie, thou shamest
Thy shape, thy love, thy wit,
Which, like a usurer, abound'st in all,
And usest none in that true use indeed
Which should bedeck
Thy shape, thy love, thy wit:
Thy noble shape is but a form of wax,
Digressing from the valour of a man,
Thy dear love sworn but hollow perjury,
Killing that love which
Thou hast vowed to cherish,
Thy wit, that ornament to shape and love,
Misshapen in the conduct of them both,
Like powder in a skilless soldier's flask,
Is set afire by thine own ignorance,
And thou dismembered
With thine own defence.
What, rouse thee, man!
Thy Juliet is alive,
For whose dear sake
Thou wast but lately dead; There art
thou happy:
Tybalt would kill thee,
But thou slewest Tybalt,
There are thou happy too:
The law that threatened death
Becomes thy friend and turns it to exile,
There art thou happy:
A pack of blessings lights up upon thy back,
Happiness courts thee in her best array,
But, like a misbehaved and sullen wench,
Thou pouts upon thy fortune and thy love:
Take heed, take heed, for such die miserable.

Friar Laurence is at his wits end about Romeo's irrational and strange behaviour. He accuses Romeo of acting like a woman.

"Thy tears are womanish; thy wild acts denote

He assures Romeo that he is lucky to be alive and that he should be brave like a man and not to digress,

"from the valour of a man"

Happiness in the best form is waiting for you,

"Happiness courts thee in her best array"

Friar Laurence reprimands Romeo for acting like a spoilt child who is frowning upon his good fortune and his love,

"But, like a misbehaved and sullen wench,
Thou pouts upon thou fortune and thy love"

The repetition of,

"Take heed, take heed, for such die miserable"

Can denote Friar Laurence's desperation to save Romeo and he warns him that his erratic behaviour can lead to a miserable death.

Ironically, in the end, Romeo did die a miserable death.

He tells Romeo to go to Juliet and then onto Mantua where he will reside.

Friar Laurence has big plans for Romeo's future. He hopes that he will be pardoned by the prince.

FRIAR LAURENCE (*continues*)
Go, get thee to thy love, as was decreed,
Ascend her chamber, hence and comfort her:
But look thou stay not till the watch be set,
For then thou canst not pass to Mantua,
Where thou shalt live, till we can find a time
To blaze your marriage,
Reconcile your friends,
Beg pardon of the Prince,
And call thee back with
Twenty Hundred Thousand times more joy
Than thou wentst forth in lamentation.
Go before, Nurse: commend me to thy lady,
And bid her hasten all the house to bed,
Which heavy sorrow makes them apt unto:
Romeo is coming.
Nurse
O Lord, I could have stayed here all the night
To hear good counsel: O, what learning is!
My lord, I'll tell my lady you will come.
ROMEO
Do so and bid my sweet prepare to chide.
Nurse
Here, sir, a ring she bid me give you, sir:
Hie you, make haste, for it grows very late.

[*Exit* Nurse]

ROMEO
How well my comfort is revived by this!
FRIAR LAURENCE
Go hence, good night,
And here stands all your state:
Either be gone before the watch be set,
Or by the break of day disguised from hence:
Sojourn in Mantua; I'll find out your man,
And he shall signify from time to time
Every good hap to you that chances here:
Give me thy hand; 'tis late:
Farewell; good night.
ROMEO
But that a joy past joy calls out on me,
It were a grief, so brief to part with thee:
Farewell.

[*Exeunt*]

Friar Laurence consents to Romeo and Juliet's marriage, hoping that this union will end the feud between their families.

The Nurse gives Romeo the ring

"Here, sir, a ring she bid me give you"

and leaves to give Juliet the good news.

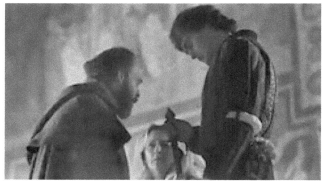

**FRIAR LAURENCE, NURSE,
ROMEO who says:**
"How well my comfort is revived by this!"

Friar Laurence bids Romeo good night and Romeo is upbeat and excited and says,

"But that a joy past joy calls out to me"

Romeo is excited to meet Juliet as he embarks on his journey to Mantua.

ROMEO arriving at Mantua

A Room in Capulet's House	
[*Enter* CAPULET, LADY CAPULET, PARIS]	[Enter CAPULETS and PARIS]
CAPULET Things have fallen out, sir, so unluckily, We have had no time to move our daughter: Look you, she loved her kinsman Tybalt dearly - And so did I Well, we were born to die. 'Tis very late, she'll not come down tonight: I promise you, but for your company, I would have been abed an hour ago.	Capulet apologies to Paris because, "We have had no time to move our daughter" In Elizabethan times marriage seemed to have been a contract between the males without the consent of the females. Being a patriarchal society, the woman had no say in the matter, and they were forced to marry whoever their fathers chose for them.
PARIS These times of woe afford no time to woo. Madam, good night: Commend me to your daughter.	This practice is clearly evident in the case of Juliet's. Paris is very gallant and understands that in times of grief there is no time to be courting,
LADY CAPULET I will, and know her mind early tomorrow Tonight she is mewed up to her heaviness.	"These times of woe afford no time to woo"
CAPULET Sir Paris, I will make a desperate tender Of my child's love: I think she will be ruled In all respects by me; Nay, more, I doubt it not. Wife, go you to her ere you go to bed, Acquaint her ear of my son Paris' love, And bid her, mark you me Wednesday next - But, soft! what day is this?	Capulet proves to be overbearing when he says that he will make every effort to convince Juliet to marry Paris and he adds "I think she will be ruled" In all respects by me" Clearly indicating that his decision will overrule her consent.
PARIS Monday, my lord,	

CAPULET
Monday! Ha, ha!
Well, Wednesday is too soon,
On Thursday let it be:
O' Thursday, tell her,
She shall be married to this noble earl.
Will you be ready?
Do you like this haste?
We'll keep no great ado, — a friend or two,
For, hark you, Tybalt being slain so late,
It may be thought we held him carelessly,
Being our kinsman, if we revel much:
Therefore, we'll have
Some half a dozen friends,
And there an end.
But what say you to Thursday?
PARIS
My lord,
I would that Thursday were tomorrow.
CAPULET
[*to his wife*]
Well get you gone:
O' Thursday be it, then.
Go you to Juliet ere you go to bed,
Prepare her, wife, against this wedding day
Farewell, my lord - Light to my chamber, ho!
Afore me! 'tis is so very very late,
That we may call it early by and by -
Good night.

[*Exeunt*]

Capulet didn't even tell Juliet of this match at this point, but he had already set a wedding date. They decided to have a small ceremony out of respect for Tybalt's memory,

"Tybalt being slain so late,
 It may be thought we held him carelessly"

Lord Capulet don't want people to think that he has no respect for Tybalt's death because he is planning Juliet's wedding so quickly.

Out of respect for Tybalt he decides to have a small function with a few friends.

PARIS says to Lord and Lady CAPULET
"My Lord,
 I would that Thursday were tomorrow"

Paris is excited and he says that,
"My Lord,
 I would that Thursday was tomorrow"

Lord Capulet is in high spirits and is eager for Juliet to prepare for her wedding day.

"Prepare her, wife, against this wedding day"

Capulet's Orchard

[*Enter* ROMEO *and* JULIET *on the balcony*]

JULIET
Wilt thou be gone? It is not yet near day:
It was the nightingale, and not the lark,
That pierced the fearful hollow of thine ear,
Nightly she sings on yon pomegranate tree:
Believe me, love, it was the nightingale.
ROMEO
It was the lark, the herald of the morn, -
No nightingale:
Look, love, what envious streaks
Do lace the severing clouds in yonder east:
Night's candles are burnt out, and Jocund day
Stands tiptoe on the misty mountain tops.
I must be gone and live or stay and die. **JULIET**
Yond light is not daylight, I know it, I:
It is some meteor that the sun exhales,
To be to thee this night a torch bearer,
And light thee on thy way to Mantua:
Therefore stay yet,
Thou needst not to be gone.
ROMEO
Let me be taken, let me be put to death,
I am content, so thou wilt have it so.
I'll say yon grey is not the morning's eye,
'Tis but the pale reflex of Cynthia's brow,
Nor that is not the lark, whose notes do beat
The vaulty heaven so high above our heads:
I have more care to stay than will to go:
Come, death, and welcome! Juliet wills it so.
How is't, my soul?
Let's talk; it is not day.
JULIET
It is, it is! Hie hence, be gone, away!
It is the lark that sings so out of tune,
Straining harsh discords
And unpleasing sharps.
Some say the lark makes sweet division,
This doth not so, for she divideth us:
Some say the lark
And loathed toad change eyes,
O, now I would they had changed voices too!
Since arm from arm that voice doth us affray,
Hunting thee hence with hunt's—up to the day,
O, now be gone; more light and light it grows.

[Enter ROMEO and JULIET]

Juliet doesn't want Romeo to go because it's not yet daybreak.

Shakespeare uses an imagery of birds suggesting flight or captivity, considering Romeo's plight at this point in time. He's like a captive bird that needs to fly away.

Romeo uses a personification to describe the day,

"Jocand day
 Stands tiptoe on the misty mountain tops"

Romeo tells Juliet that he can pretend that it is not daylight and get captured and be put to death. But he says that he doesn't mind dying if she wants it that way.

"Come, death and welcome! Juliet wills it so"

When she hears this, Juliet changes her tone, now it becomes one of utter panic and she urges Romeo to hasten away and save his life,

"Be gone, away!"

The exclamation mark can denote her panic and desperation.

JULIET and ROMEO together

ROMEO
More light and light,
More dark and dark our woes!

[*Enter* Nurse, *to the chamber*]

Nurse
Madam!
JULIET
Nurse?
Nurse
Your lady mother is coming to your chamber:
The day is broke: be wary, look about.

[*Exit* Nurse]

JULIET
Then, window, let day in, and let life out.
ROMEO
Farewell, farewell! One kiss, and I'll descend.
[*they kiss, and he descends the balcony*]

JULIET
Art thou gone so?
Love, lord, ay, husband, friend!
I must hear from thee every day in the hour,
For in a minute there are many days:
O, by this count I shall be much in years
Ere I again behold my Romeo!
ROMEO
[*from below*]
Farewell!
I will omit no opportunity
That may convey my greetings, love, to thee.
JULIET
O, thinkest thou we shall ever meet again?
ROMEO
I doubt it not; and all these woes shall serve
For sweet discourses in our time to come.
JULIET
O God, I have an ill–divining soul!
Methinks I see thee, now thou art so low,
As one dead in the bottom of a tomb:
Either my eyesight fails, or thou lookest pale.
ROMEO
And trust me, love, in my eye so do you:
Dry sorrow drinks our blood. Adieu, adieu!

[*Exit* ROMEO]

Romeo says that the more light they get, the deeper their sorrow becomes.

"More light and light,
 More dark and dark our woes!"

[Enter NURSE]

JULIET and ROMEO warned by NURSE of her mother's imminent arrival

Juliet says goodbye to Romeo and asks,

"thinkest thou we shall ever meet again?"

She foreshadows the fact that they will never meet again- only in their graves. But Romeo is positive, and he assures her that all these troubles will only become legends for later in life.

Juliet has some sort of an eerie premonition and predicts exactly what is going to happen.

"Methinks I see thee, now thou art so low,
 As one dead in the bottom of a tomb"

ROMEO says Adieu, adieu! to JULIET

[Exit ROMEO]

JULIET
O Fortune, Fortune!
All men call thee fickle:
If thou art fickle, what dost thou with him.
That is renowned for faith?
Be fickle, Fortune,
For then, I hope, thou wilt not keep him long,
But send him back

LADY CAPULET
[*Within*]
Ho, daughter! are you up?

JULIET
Who is't that calls? Is it my lady mother?
Is she not down so late, or up so early?
What unaccustomed cause
Procures her hither?

[*Enter* LADY CAPULET]

LADY CAPULET
Why, how now, Juliet!

JULIET
Madam, I am not well.

LADY CAPULET
Evermore weeping for your cousin's death?
What, wilt thou wash him
From his grave with tears?
An if thou couldst,
Thou couldst not make him live,
Therefore, have done:
Some grief shows much of love,
But much of grief shows
Still some want of wit.

JULIET
Yet let me weep for such a feeling loss.

LADY CAPULET
So shall you feel the loss, but not the friend
Which you weep for.

JULIET
Feeling so the loss,
Cannot choose but ever weep the friend.

LADY CAPULET
Well, girl,
Thou weep'st not so much for his death,
As that the villain lives which slaughtered him

JULIET
What villain madam?

LADY CAPULET
That same villain, Romeo.

[Enter LADY CAPULET]

Right at the outset we can see a certain detachment in the relationship between Juliet and her mother.

When her mother comes to her room Juliet asks,

"What unaccustomed cause
 Procures her hither?"

Juliet finds it strange that her mother is coming to her room which indicates that there is a distance between mother and daughter.

Furthermore, Juliet addresses her mother in very formal terms,

'Lady' 'madam' 'Ladyship'

Once again, we see a certain detachment and lack of emotional contact between mother and daughter.

Lady Capulet also misinterpreted Juliet's grief, thinking that she is still mourning Tybalt's death.

Lady Capulet wasn't able to understand the source of her daughter' grief and she attributes Juliet's sadness to stupidity.

"But much of grief shows
 Still some want of wit"

Lady Capulet tells Juliet that she cries more for the fact that Romeo, who killed Tybalt, is still alive and not punished.

"Thou weep'st not so much for his death,
 As that the villain lives which slaughtered him"

JULIET
Villain and he be many miles asunder. —
God Pardon him! I do, with all my heart,
And yet no man like he doth grieve my heart.

LADY CAPULET
That is because the traitor murderer lives.

JULIET
Ay madam from the reach of these my hands:
Would none but I
Might venge my cousin's death!

LADY CAPULET
We will have vengeance for it, fear thou not:
Then weep no more.
I'll send to one in Mantua,
Where that same banished runagate doth live
Shall give him such an unaccustomed dram,
That he shall soon keep Tybalt company:
And then, I hope, thou wilt be satisfied.

JULIET
Indeed, I never shall be satisfied
With Romeo, till I behold him — dead —
Is my poor heart for a kinsman vexed
Madam, if you could find out but a man
To bear a poison, I would temper it,
That Romeo should, upon receipt thereof,
Soon sleep in quiet. O, how my heart abhors
To hear him named and cannot come to him.
To wreak the love I bore my cousin Tybalt
Upon his body that slaughtered him!

LADY CAPULET
Find thou the means, and I'll find such a man.
But now I'll tell thee joyful tidings, girl.

JULIET
And joy comes well in such a needy time:
What are they, I beseech your ladyship?

LADY CAPULET
Well, well, thou hast a careful father, child,
One who, to put thee from thy heaviness,
Hath sorted out a sudden day of joy,
That thou expect'st not nor I looked not for.

JULIET
Madam, in happy time. What day is that?

LADY CAPULET
Marry, my child, early next Thursday morn,
The gallant, young and noble gentleman,
The County Paris, at Saint Peter's Church,
Shall happily make thee there a joyful bride.

Lady Capulet is speaking with a very bitter, caustic tone about Romeo insisting that they,

"will have vengeance"

We have to take note of lady Capulet's intense, unabated hate despite the life of Tybalt being sacrificed for their hate.

"Shall give him such an unaccustomed dram,
That he shall soon keep Tybalt company"

Juliet is portrayed as being manipulative, she makes her mother believe that she is mourning Tybalt's death and she is pretending to hate Romeo. This behaviour is totally out of character for a docile, fourteen-year-old from the Elizabethan era.

"Madam, if you could find out but a man
To bear the poison, I would temper it"

Juliet seems to flout all the norms set out for females in Elizabethan times.

LADY CAPULET tells JULIET to marry PARIS, but JULIET reject the proposal - in secret, she is already married to ROMEO

JULIET

Now, by Saint Peter's Church and Peter too,
He shall not make me there a joyful bride.
I wonder at this haste, that I must wed
Ere he that should be husband comes to woo
I pray you, tell my lord and father, madam,
I will not marry yet; and, when I do, I swear,
It shall be Romeo, whom you know I hate,
Rather than Paris. These are news indeed!

LADY CAPULET

Here comes your father; tell him so yourself And
see how he will take it at your hands.

[*Enter* CAPULET *and* Nurse]

CAPULET

When the sun sets, the air doth drizzle dew,
But for the sunset of my brother's son
It rains downright.
How now, a conduit, girl? What, still in tears?
Evermore showering? In one little body
Thou counterfeit a bark, a sea, a wind,
For still thy eyes, which I may call the sea,
Do ebb and flow with tears,
The bark thy body is, sailing in this salt flood,
The winds, thy sighs, who raging with thy tear
And they with them, without a sudden calm,
Will overset thy tempest–tossed body.
How now, wife!
Have you delivered to her our decree?

LADY CAPULET

Ay, sir;
But she will none, she gives you thanks.
I would the fool were married to her grave!

CAPULET

Soft!
Take me with you, take me with you, wife
How, will she none?
Doth she not give us thanks?
Is she not proud?
Doth she not count her blest,
Unworthy as she is,
That we have wrought
So worthy a gentleman
To be her bridegroom?

JULIET

Not proud, you have,
But thankful, that you have:
Proud can I never be of what I hate,
But thankful even for hate, that is meant love

When her mother tells her that she must marry Paris she replies,

"He shall not make me there a joyful bride"

Lady Capulet is unsympathetic to her daughter's plight,

"I pray you, tell my lord and father, madam"

Once again, we see lady Capulet's cold, emotionless response to Juliet's pleas,

"Here comes your father; tell him so yourself"

[Enter CAPULET and NURSE]

When Capulet enters, he sees Juliet crying and he associates her tears to a downpour of rain. He uses an imagery of a ship to describe Juliet's grief. He compares her body to the ship and her eyes, to the sea, that are raging with tears. Her tears ebb and flow like the waves and her sighs are the winds and that her body is tempest tossed with grief.

Lady Capulet tells Capulet that Juliet refuses to marry Paris. She foreshadows Juliet's fate when she remarks,

"I would the fool were married to the grave!"

Ironically, Juliet ended up being 'married' to the grave.

Capulet's speech consists of many questions which denotes his mounting anger towards Juliet.

"How, will she none?
 Doth she not give us thanks?
 Is she not proud?
 Doth she not count her blest,
 Unworthy as she is,
 That we have wrought
 So worthy a gentleman
 To be her bridegroom?"

CAPULET
How now, how now, chop–logic!
What is this? 'Proud,' and 'I thank you,'
And 'I thank you not;'
And yet 'not proud,' mistress minion, you,
Thank me no thanking's,
Nor, proud me no prouds!
But:
Fettle your fine joints against Thursday next,
To go with Paris to Saint Peter's Church,
Or I will drag thee on a hurdle thither.
Out, you green–sickness carrion!
Out, you baggage! You tallow–face!
LADY CAPULET
Fie, fie! what, are you mad?
JULIET
[*kneeling before her father, pleading*]
Good father, I beseech you on my knees,
Hear me with patience but to speak a word.
CAPULET
Hang thee, young baggage!
Disobedient wretch!
I tell thee what:
Get thee to church o' Thursday,
Or never after look me in the face:
Speak not, reply not, do not answer me;
My fingers itch.
Wife, we scarce thought us blest
That God had lent us but this only child;
But now I see this one is one too much,
And that we have a curse in having her:
Out on her, hilding!

JULIET receiving her father anger for rejecting PARIS as a suitor

Capulet is overbearing and he displays a tyrannical behaviour towards Juliet, and he orders her to;

"Fettle your fine joints against Thursday next
 To go with Paris to Saint Peter's Church"

His dominant attitude is unnerving, and his superiority must be respected, such were the traits of the patriarchal society of Elizabethan times.

Shakespeare shows Capulet's mounting fury in the onomatopoeia,

"Or I will drag thee on a hurdle thither"

Once again exerting his power and influence over Juliet. Capulet is enraged, he is ranting and raving about Juliet's disobedience. He hurls abuse at her,

"Out you green-sickness carrion!"

Oops, this is very harsh, calling her pale face and the rotting flesh of animals.

"Out you baggage! You tallow-face!"

He is furious at her disobedience,

"Hang thee, young baggage!
 Disobedient wretch!"

Note the use of the repeated exclamation mark suggesting his inability to control his fury.

Capulet is firm and arrogant and yells,

"Speak not, reply not, do not answer me"

The use of these short, snappy imperative verbs and negatives suggests that Capulet's rage is boiling over and there's an increase in the pace and urgency in his voice.

"My fingers itch.
 Wife, we scarce thought us blest
 That God had lent us but this only child."

Nurse

God in heaven bless her!

You are to blame, my lord, to rate her so.

CAPULET

And why, my Lady Wisdom?

Hold your tongue, Good prudence,

Smatter with your gossips, go!

Nurse

I speak no treason.

CAPULET

O, God ye god–den.

Nurse

May not one speak?

CAPULET

Peace, you mumbling fool!

Utter your gravity o'er a gossip's bowl,

For here we need it not.

LADY CAPULET

You are too hot.

CAPULET

God's bread! It makes me mad:

Day, night, hour, tide, time, work, play,

Alone, in company, still my care hath been

To have her matched: and having now

Provided a gentleman of noble parentage,

Of fair demesnes, youthful, and nobly trained,

Stuffed, as they say, with honourable parts,

Proportioned as one's thought

Would wish a man,

And then to have a wretched puling fool,

A whining mammet, in her fortune's tender,

To answer: 'I'll not wed; I cannot love,

I am too young, I pray you, pardon me'.

But, as you will not wed, I'll pardon you:

Graze where you will,

You shall not house with me:

Look to it, think on it, I do not use to jest.

Thursday is near; lay hand on heart, advise:

An you be mine, I'll give you to my friend;

An you be not, hang, beg, starve,

Die in the streets,

For, by my soul, I'll never acknowledge thee,

Nor what is mine shall never do thee good:

Trust to it, bethink you; I'll not be forsworn.

[*Exit* CAPULET]

Capulet is so overwrought with fury, that he is now almost resorting to physical violence. Look at the verb 'lent'. Ironical, isn't it? God did lend Juliet to them, and he claimed her back.

We are going to later compare Capulet's behaviour here, and his attitude towards her death at the end.

We should also look at the endearing attitude of the Nurse and juxtapose it to that of lady Capulet,

"You are to blame, my Lord, to rate her so"

The Nurse defended Juliet by standing up to Lord Capulet for his unreasonable behaviour. Despite her lower status in the household, she was bold enough to voice her opinion.

Yet lady Capulet did not protect or defend Juliet.

The nurse was prepared to be the victim of Lord Capulet's wrath,

"Peace, you mumbling fool!"

Capulet carries on his abusive tirade with Juliet and the audience gets emotionally involved and they empathise with Juliet's agony,

"An you be mine, I'll give you to my friend;
An you be not, hang, beg, starve,
Die in the streets"

[Exit CAPULET]

JULIET

Is there no pity sitting in the clouds
That sees into the bottom of my grief?
O sweet my mother, cast me not away!
Delay this marriage for a month, a week,
Or, if you do not, make the bridal bed
In that dim monument where Tybalt lies.

LADY CAPULET

Talk not to me, for I'll not speak a word:
Do as thou wilt, for I have done with thee.

[*Exit* LADY CAPULET]

JULIET

O God! -
O Nurse, how shall this be prevented?
My husband is on earth, my faith in heaven;
How shall that faith return again to earth,
Unless that husband send it me
From heaven by leaving earth?
Comfort me. Counsel me.

JULIET consoled by NURSE

Alack, alack,
That heaven should practise stratagems
Upon so soft a subject as myself!
What sayst thou?
Hast thou not a word of joy?
Some comfort, Nurse.

By now Juliet is overwhelmed with grief and she begs her mother not to ignore her pain,

"O sweet mother, cast me not away!"

Once again Juliet unwittingly foreshadows her impending doom,

"make the bridal bed
In that dim monument where Tybalt lies"

Of course, her bridal bed was in the tomb where Tybalt's body lay.

Lady Capulet is annoyed with Juliet, so she ignores her,

"Do as thou wilt, for I have done with thee"

[Exit LADY CAPULET]

Juliet is now exasperated, and she clings to the nurse for support,

"O Nurse, how shall this be prevented?"

Juliet says,

"My husband is on earth, my faith in heaven"

She is talking about her marriage contract
which is sanctioned by God.

She acknowledges that the only way for her promise to last, is for Romeo to die and go to heaven and then send back the promise to her,

"Unless that husband send it me
From heaven by leaving Earth?"

Juliet is at her wits end. Her dilemma is that she is already married to Romeo but is expected to marry Paris now. The use of the alliteration,

"Comfort me. Counsel me"

Suggests her desperation and hence her inability to complete her sentence.

Nurse
Faith, here it is.
Romeo is banished,
And all the world to nothing,
That he dares never
Come back to challenge you,
Or, if he do, it needs must be by stealth.
Then, since the case so stands as now it doth
I think it best you married with the County.
O, he's a lovely gentleman!
Romeo's a dishclout to him:
An eagle madam hath not so green, so quick,
So fair an eye as Paris hath.
Beshrew my very heart,
I think you are happy in this second match,
For it excels your first - or if it did not,
Your first is dead,
Or 'twere as good he were,
As living here and you no use of him.
JULIET
Speakest thou from thy heart?
Nurse
And from my soul too
Else beshrew them both.
JULIET
Amen!
Nurse
What?
JULIET
Well,
Thou hast comforted me marvellous much.
Go in and tell my lady:
I am gone, having displeased my father,
To Laurence's cell,
To make confession and to be absolved.

**JULIET listens to NURSE but rejects her advice
to marry PARIS**

Once again Juliet foreshadows Romeo's death. We can revert back to the PROLOGUE when they talk about:

'STAR-CROSSED LOVERS'

and the role the hand of fate played in these lover's lives:

'FROM FORTH THE FATAL LOINS OF THESE TWO FOES'

Now we are going to very carefully analyse Nurse's wavering character. Now her opinions are changed in her comparison between Romeo and Paris. She now labels Paris,

"a lovely gentleman"

Earlier she praised Romeo's looks and character but now she describes him,

"a dishclout to him"

It is very easy to label Nurse 'inconsistent' but we admire her not only for her sense of loyalty to Juliet but also her sense of reasoning power. She weighed up the pros and cons and concluded that in Juliet's terrible situation her best option is to marry Paris.

The Nurse then delivers these wise words,

"Your first is dead,
 Or 'twere as good as it were,
 As living here and you no use of him"

Juliet's reaction is one of shock at Nurse's sudden change of heart,

"Speakest thou from the heart?"

We are going to discuss Juliet's character which is making a young fourteen-year-old look rather sheepish- what with all the lies and deceit. Once again, she lies that she is going to Friar Lawrence's cell,

"To make confession and be absolved"

Nurse
Marry, I will; and this is wisely done.

[*Exit* NURSE]

JULIET

Ancient damnation! O most wicked fiend! Is it
more sin to wish me thus forsworn?
Or to dispraise my lord with that same tongue
Which she hath praised him with above
Compare so many thousand times?
Go, counsellor,
Thou and my bosom henceforth shall be twain
I'll to the friar, to know his remedy:
If all else fail, myself have power to die.

[*Exit* JULIET]

For annoying her father. Even the nurse believes her,

"this is wisely done"

Juliet is furious with the nurse for changing her opinion,

"Ancient damnation! O most wicked fiend!"

Note her use of repeated exclamation marks suggest her disgust and disappointment in the nurse's sudden change in her stances.

Juliet vows to seek assistance from Friar Lawrence and if that fails at least she will have the capacity to take her own life,

"If all else fail, myself have power to die"

Sadly, she does exactly what she had predicted. She committed suicide in the end.

[Exit JULIET]

Friar Laurence's Cell

[*Enter* FRIAR LAURENCE *and* PARIS]

FRIAR LAURENCE
On Thursday, sir? The time is very short.
PARIS
My father Capulet will have it so,
And I am nothing slow to slack his haste.
FRIAR LAURENCE
You say you do not know the lady's mind?
Uneven is the course, I like it not.
PARIS
Immoderately she weeps for Tybalt's death,
And therefore, have I little talked of love,
For Venus smiles not in a house of tears.
Now, sir, her father counts it dangerous
That she doth give her sorrow so much sway,
And in his wisdom hastes our marriage,
To stop the inundation of her tears,
Which, too much minded by herself alone,
May be put from her by society:
Now do you know the reason of this haste.
FRIAR LAURENCE
[*Aside*]
I would I knew not why it should be slowed.
Look, sir -
Here comes the lady towards my cell.

[*Enter* JULIET]

PARIS
Happily met, my lady and my wife!
JULIET
That may be, sir, when I may be a wife.
PARIS

That may be must be, love, on Thursday next.
JULIET
What must be shall be.
FRIAR LAURENCE
That's a certain text.
PARIS
Come you to make confession to this father?
JULIET
To answer that, I should confess to you.

[Enter FRIAR LAURENCE and PARIS]

Paris tells Friar Lawrence that the wedding will take place on Thursday. Friar Lawrence tells him that it's too soon and he doesn't like the idea that Juliet's heart is not in it.

"Uneven is the course. I like it not"

Paris says that she is mourning over Tybalt's death and that issues of the heart has no place.

"For Venus smiles not in a house of tears"

[Enter JULIET]

Paris expresses his desire to meet his wife. Juliet's curt reply was,

"That may be, sir, when I may be a wife"

Notice the use of the repetitive modal verb 'may' suggesting that their union may be a possibility but not a surety. It is also important to take note of the structure of the text in the exchange of the conversation between Juliet and Paris.

You can juxtapose it with her conversations with Romeo which are written in verses or stanzas suggesting a very deep, meaningful conversations filled with love. Yet Juliet's conversation with Paris are single-lined sentences suggesting that it is forced and meaningless, just like their love.

PARIS
Do not deny to him that you love me.
JULIET
I will confess to you that I love him.
PARIS
So will ye, I am sure, that you love me.
JULIET
If I do so, it will be of more price,
Being spoke behind your back,
Than to your face.
PARIS
Poor soul, thy face is much abused with tears
JULIET
The tears have got small victory by that,
For it was bad enough before their spite.
PARIS
Thou wrong'st it,
More than tears with that report.
JULIET
That is no slander, sir, which is a truth,
And what I spake, I spake it to my face.
PARIS
Thy face is mine, and thou hast slandered it.
JULIET
It may be so, for it is not mine own.
Are you at leisure, holy father, now
Or shall I come to you at evening mass? **FRIAR
LAURENCE**
My leisure serves me, pensive daughter, now.
My lord, we must entreat the time alone.
PARIS
God shield I should disturb devotion!
Juliet, on Thursday early will I rouse ye:
Till then, adieu; and keep this holy kiss.

[PARIS kisses JULIET]
[*Exit* PARIS]

JULIET
O shut the door!
And when thou hast done so,
Come weep with me,
Past hope, past cure, past help!
FRIAR LAURENCE
O Juliet, I already know thy grief,
It strains me past the compass of my wits:
I hear thou must,
And nothing may prorogue it,
On Thursday next be married to this County.

PARIS tells JULIET:
"Do not deny to him that you love me"

[Exit PARIS]

Juliet is beyond consoling because she has lost all hope and her situation is critical.

"Come weep with me,
 Past hope, past cure, past help"

JULIET says to the Friar:
**"Come weep with me,
 Past hope, past cure, past help!"**

JULIET

Tell me not, friar, that thou hear'st of this,
Unless thou tell me how I may prevent it:
If, in thy wisdom, thou canst give no help,
Do thou but call my resolution wise,
And with this knife I'll help it presently.
God joined my heart and Romeo's,
Thou our hands; And ere this hand,
By thee to Romeo sealed,
Shall be the label to another deed,
Or my true heart with treacherous revolt
Turn to another, this shall slay them both:
Therefore, out of thy long–experienced time,
Give me some present counsel, or behold,
'Twixt my extremes and me this bloody knife
Shall play the umpire, arbitrating that
Which the commission of thy years and art
Could to no issue of true honour bring.
Be not so long to speak; I long to die,
If what thou speak'st speak not of remedy.

FRIAR LAURENCE

Hold, daughter: I do spy a kind of hope,
Which craves as desperate an execution.
As that is desperate which we would prevent.
If rather than to marry County Paris,
Thou hast the strength of will to slay thyself,
Then is it likely thou wilt undertake a thing
Like death to chide away this shame,
That copest with death himself
To scape from it
And, if thou darest,
I'll give thee remedy.

JULIET

O, bid me leap, rather than marry Paris,
From off the battlements of yonder tower
Or walk in thievish ways; or bid me lurk
Where serpents are,
Chain me with roaring bears,
Or hide me nightly in a charnel house,
Over-covered quite with
Dead men's rattling bones,
With reeky shanks and yellow chapless skulls
Or bid me go into a new–made grave
And hide me with a dead man in his shroud,
Things that, to hear them told,
Have made me tremble,
And I will do it without fear or doubt,
To live an unstained wife to my sweet love.

Juliet displays a determination and willpower that exceeds her years. She acts in a rather dramatic manner and threatened suicide with a knife and insists that the friar solve her problems,

"Twixt my extremes and me this bloody knife
Shall play the umpire"

JULIET tells FRIAR LAURENCE:
"Twixt my extremes and me this bloody knife
Shall play the umpire"

This headstrong Juliet is given some hope of a solution to her problems.

"Hold daughter, I do spy a kind of hope"

Her speech here is very ironical and she foreshadows her death yet once again.

"And hide me with a dead man in his shroud"

In the end this is exactly what happened to Juliet. She was still alive, hiding in a tomb with the dead.

Juliet is overjoyed and says that she would go to any lengths to be,

"an unstained wife to my sweet love"

FRIAR LAURENCE
Hold, then; go home, be merry, give consent
To marry Paris: Wednesday is tomorrow:
Tomorrow night look that thou lie alone,
Let not thy nurse lie with thee in thy chamber:
Take thou this vial, being then in bed,
And this distilled liquor drink thou off,
When presently through all thy veins shall run
A cold and drowsy humour, for no pulse
Shall keep his native progress, but surcease:
No warmth, no breath, shall testify thou livest,
The roses in thy lips and cheeks shall fade
To paly ashes, thy eyes' windows fall,
Like death, when he shuts up the day of life,
Each part, deprived of supple government,
Shall, stiff and stark and cold, appear like death
And in this borrowed likeness of shrunk death
Thou shalt continue two and forty hours,
And then awake as from a pleasant sleep.
Now, when the bridegroom in the morning
Comes to rouse thee from thy bed,
There art thou dead:
Then, as the manner of our country is,
In thy best robes uncovered on the bier
Thou shalt be borne to that same ancient vault
Where all the kindred of the Capulets lie.
In the meantime, against thou shalt awake,
Shall Romeo by my letters know our drift,
And hither shall he come, and he and I
Will watch thy waking, and that very night
Shall Romeo bear thee hence to Mantua.
And this shall free thee
From this present shame,
If no inconstant toy, nor womanish fear,
Abate thy valour in the acting it.
JULIET
Give me, give me!
O, tell not me of fear!
FRIAR LAURENCE
Hold; get you gone,
Be strong and prosperous in this resolve:
I'll send a friar with speed to Mantua,
With my letters to thy lord.
JULIET
Love give me strength!
And strength shall help afford.
Farewell, dear father!

[*Exeunt*]

Friar Lawrence concocted his plans, and he gives Juliet instructions on how to carry it out.

FRIAR tells JULIET: "Take thou this vial"

He tells her to drink the potion and it will induce her into a deathlike state.

"No warmth, no breath shall testify thou livest"

JULIET tells FRIAR:
"Give me, give me!
O, tell not me of fear!"

FRIAR tells JULIET:
"I'll send a friar with speed to Mantua"

Hall in Capulet's House

[*Enter* LORD CAPULET, LADY CAPULET, NURSE, *and two* SERVINGMEN]

CAPULET
So many guests invite as here are writ.

[*Exit* First Servant]
Sirrah, go hire me twenty cunning cooks.
Second Servant
You shall have none ill, sir,
For I'll try if they can lick their fingers.
CAPULET
How canst thou try them so?
Second Servant
Marry, sir, 'tis an ill cook
That cannot lick his own fingers:
Therefore he that cannot lick
His fingers goes not with me.
CAPULET
Go, be gone.
[*Exit* Second Servant]
We shall be much unfurnished for this time.
What, is my daughter gone to Friar Laurence
Nurse
Ay, forsooth.
CAPULET
Well, he may chance to do some good on her
A peevish self–will'd harlotry it is.
Nurse
See where she comes
From shrift with merry look.

[*Enter* JULIET]

CAPULET
How now, my headstrong!
Where have you been gadding?
JULIET
Where I have learned me
To repent the sin of disobedient opposition
To you and your behests, and am enjoined
By holy Laurence to fall prostrate here,
And beg your pardon.
Pardon, I beseech you!
Henceforward I am ever ruled by you.

[Enter LORD & LADY CAPULET and NURSE]

SERVANT: "You shall have none I'll, sir"

Capulet is overjoyed and he gives instructions for the wedding feast, and he enquires whether Juliet has gone to Friar Lawrence to absolve her sins. He is very excited to learn that she has,

"Well, he may chance to do some good on her
A peevish self-willed harlotry it is"

[Enter JULIET]

Juliet is putting on a real performance of lies and deceit. She falls to her knees and begs for her father's forgiveness.

"Pardon, I beseech you!
Henceforward I am ever ruled by you"

JULIET tells her father:
"Pardon, I beseech you!
Henceforward I am ever ruled by you"

CAPULET
Send for the County; go tell him of this:
I'll have this knot knit up tomorrow morning.
JULIET
I met the youthful lord at Laurence' cell,
And gave him what becomed love I might,
Not stepping over the bounds of modesty.
CAPULET
Why, I am glad on it; this is well: stand up:
This is as it should be.
Let me see the County,
Ay, marry, go, I say, and fetch him hither.
Now, afore God! This reverend holy friar!
Our whole city is much bound to him.
JULIET
Nurse, will you go with me into my closet,
To help me sort such needful ornaments
As you think fit to furnish me tomorrow?
LADY CAPULET
No, not till Thursday; there is time enough.
CAPULET
Go, nurse, Go with her.
We'll to church tomorrow.

[*Exeunt* JULIET *and* Nurse]

LADY CAPULET
We shall be short in our provision:
'Tis now near night.
CAPULET
Tush, I will stir about,
And all things shall be well,
I warrant thee, wife:
Go thou to Juliet, help to deck up her,
I'll not to bed tonight; let me alone,
I'll play the housewife for this once.
What, ho! They are all forth.
Well, I will walk myself to County Paris,
To prepare him up against tomorrow.
My heart is wondrous light,
Since this same wayward girl is so reclaimed.

[*Exeunt*]

Capulet is fooled by both Juliet and the Friar. He is ecstatic at this new turn of events, and declares that,

"Now, afore God! This reverend holy friar!
Our whole city is much bound to him"

Now Juliet is pretending to need some clothes and jewellery, but lady Capulet turns down her request, but Capulet is so excited that he grants her wish.

"Go Nurse. Go with her.
We'll to church tomorrow"

CAPULET tells NURSE:
"Go nurse. Go with her.
We'll to church tomorrow"

Capulet goes to Paris to prepare him for the wedding.

He is too thrilled at the favourable way that things had turned out and he didn't even sleep - such was his excitement.

"My heart is wondrous light,
Since this same wayward girl is so reclaimed"

Juliet's Chamber

[*Enter* JULIET *and* Nurse]

JULIET
Ay, those attires are best:
But, gentle Nurse, I pray thee,
Leave me to myself to—night,
For I have need of many orisons
To move the heavens to smile upon my state,
Which, well thou know'st,
Is cross, and full of sin.

[*Enter* LADY CAPULET]

LADY CAPULET
What, are you busy, ho?
Need you my help?
JULIET
No, madam; we have culled such necessaries
As are behoveful for our state tomorrow:
So please you, let me now be left alone,
And let the Nurse this night sit up with you;
For, I am sure, you have your hands full all,
In this so sudden business.
LADY CAPULET
Good night:
Get thee to bed, and rest; for thou hast need.

[*Exeunt* LADY CAPULET *and* Nurse]

JULIET
Farewell!
God knows when we shall meet again.
I have a faint cold fear thrills through my veins
That almost freezes up the heat of life:
I'll call them back again to comfort me:
Nurse! What should she do here?
My dismal scene I needs must act alone.
Come, vial.
What if this mixture do not work at all?
Shall I be married then tomorrow morning?
No, no! This shall forbid it. Lie thou there.

[*Laying down her dagger*]

[Enter JULIET and NURSE]

Now Juliet has to lie again, and she even blasphemed-speaking lies in God's name.

"For I have need of many orisons
To move the heavens to smile upon my state"

[Enter LADY CAPULET]

Now we see a sudden change of tone and mannerisms in Lady Capulet as compared to her earlier responses to Juliet. Now she is more cordial and polite. She even offers Juliet assistance.

"What, are you busy, ho?
Need you my help?"

JULIET debates with herself in a soliloquy the merits of taking the drug given to her by FRIAR LAURENCE

JULIET (*continues*)
What if it be a poison, which the Friar
Subtly hath ministered to have me dead,
Lest in this marriage
He should be dishonoured,
Because he married me before to Romeo?
I fear it is: and yet, methinks, it should not,
For he hath still been tried a holy man.
How if, when I am laid into the tomb,
I wake before the time that Romeo
Come to redeem me?
There's a fearful point!
Shall I not, then, be stifled in the vault,
To whose foul mouth
No health-some air breathes in,
And there die strangled
Ere my Romeo comes?
Or, if I live, is it not very like,
The horrible conceit of death and night,
Together with the terror of the place, —
As in a vault, an ancient receptacle,
Where for these many hundred years
The bones of all my buried ancestors
Are packed where bloody Tybalt,
Yet but green in earth,
Lies festering in his shroud,
Where, as they say, at some hours
In the night spirits resort; —
Alack, alack, is it not like that I,
So early waking,
What with loathsome smells and shrieks
Like mandrakes' torn out of the earth,
That living mortals, hearing them, run mad —
O, if I wake, shall I not be distraught,
Environed with all these hideous fears?
And madly play with my forefather's joints?
And pluck mangled Tybalt from his shroud?
And in rage with some great kinsman's bone,
As with club, dash out my desperate brains?
O, look! methinks I see my cousin's ghost
Seeking out Romeo, that did spit his body
Upon a rapier's point:
Stay, Tybalt, stay!
Romeo, I come!
This do I drink to thee.

[JULIET *drinks and falls upon her bed, within the curtains*]

Juliet is scared to take the potion, so she imagines all kinds of morbid, deathly scenarios related to the tomb and presence among the dead.

"The horrible conceit of death and night,
Together with the terror of the place"

She drinks the potion and falls down on her bed.

JULIET drinks the drug, trusting in FRIAR LAURENCE' prediction that she would awake after two and forty hours

JULIET fast asleep in a dead-like state

Hall in Capulet's House

[*Enter* LADY CAPULET *and* Nurse]

LADY CAPULET
Hold, take these keys,
And fetch more spices, Nurse.
Nurse
They call for dates and quinces in the pastry.

[*Enter* CAPULET]

CAPULET
Come, stir, stir, stir!
The second cock hath crowed,
The curfew bell hath rung, 'tis three o'clock:
Look to the baked meats, good Angelica:
Spare not for the cost.
Nurse
Go, you cot–quean, go,
Get you to bed,
Faith, you'll be sick to–morrow
For this night's watching.
CAPULET
No, not a whit:
What!
I have watched ere now
All night for lesser cause,
And never been sick.
LADY CAPULET
Ay, you have been
A mouse–hunt in your time,
But I will watch you from such watching now.

[*Exeunt* LADY CAPULET *and* Nurse]

CAPULET
A jealous hood, a jealous hood!

[*Enter three or four Serving men, with spits, logs, and baskets*]

Now, fellow, What's there?
First Servant
Things for the cook, sir,
But I know not what.

[Enter LADY CAPULET and NURSE]

Lady Capulet is busy with wedding preparations.

[Enter LORD CAPULET]

"Come, stir, stir, stir!"

The repetition, exclamation mark and the short, snappy sentences,

"The second cock hath crowed"
"The curfew bell hath rung"

Are all indications of Capulet's excitement and the pace. Is no more sluggish but fast and exciting. Capulet tells the servants not to spare any expenses but to splash out.

"Spare not for the cost"

LADY CAPULET, NURSE, LORD CAPULET who says "Spare not the cost"

Make haste, make haste, sirrah.

[*Exit* First Servant]

Fetch drier logs:
Call Peter, he will show thee where they are
Second Servant
I have a head, sir, that will find out logs,
And never trouble Peter for the matter.

[*Exit* Second Servant]

CAPULET
Mass, and well said,
A merry whoreson, ha!
Thou shalt be logger–head.
Good faith, 'tis day:
The County will be here with music straight,
For so he said he would: I hear him near.
[*Music within*]
Nurse! Wife! What, ho!
What, Nurse, I say!

[*Re–enter* Nurse]

Go waken Juliet, go and trim her up,
I'll go and chat with Paris.
Hie, make haste, Make haste
The bridegroom he is come already:
Make haste, I say.

[*Exeunt*]

And he tells them

"Make haste, make haste, sirrah"

Capulet tells the nurse to wake Juliet,

"Make haste, make haste"

We can feel Capulet's excitement and the flurry of activity that he is creating.

He is increasing the pace and the urgency of the situation as though he wants to marry Juliet off quickly in case she changes her mind.

Shakespeare creates a lot of suspense here and he uses dramatic irony for the events that follow.

NURSE and LORD CAPULET who says:
"Go waken Juliet, go and trim her up"

Juliet's Chamber

[*Enter* Nurse]

Nurse
Mistress! What, mistress! Juliet!
Fast, I warrant her, she:
Why, lamb! Why, lady! Fie, you slug–a–bed!
Why, love, I say! Madam!
Sweetheart! Why, bride!
What, not a word?
You take your pennyworths now,
Sleep for a week; for the next night, I warrant,
The County Paris hath set up his rest,
That you shall rest but little.
God forgive me!
Marry, and amen,
How sound is she asleep!
I must needs wake her.
Madam, madam, madam!
Ay, let the County take you in your bed,
He'll fright you up, I' faith!
Will it not be?
[Nurse *draws back the curtains*]
What, dressed and in your clothes!
And down again!
I must needs wake you;,
Lady! Lady! Lady!
Alas, alas! Help, help! My lady's dead!
O, well–a–day, that ever I was born!
Some aqua vitae, ho!
My lord! My lady!

[*Enter* LADY CAPULET]

LADY CAPULET
What noise is here?
Nurse
O lamentable day!
LADY CAPULET
What is the matter?
Nurse
Look, look! O heavy day!
LADY CAPULET
O me, O me! My child, my only life!
Revive, look up, or I will die with thee!
Help, help! Call help.

[Enter NURSE into JULIET's Chamber]

The nurse tries to wake Juliet up, spicing it up as usual with some bawdiness,

"Ay, let the county take you in your bed"

Shakespeare uses dramatic irony here and the nurses futile attempt to wake Juliet up creates a lot of suspense and tension. It reaches an anti-climax when she discovers that Juliet is dead. Shakespeare uses a range of different punctuations to denote the nurses shock,

"Lady! Lady! Lady!
Alas! Alas! Help, help! My lady's dead!"

Shakespeare's use of repeated exclamation marks, repetition and hyphens shows the nurses horror at finding Juliet dead.

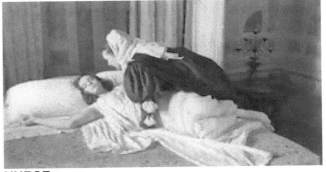

NURSE:
"Lady! Lady! Lady!
Alas, alas! Help, help! My lady's dead!"

The use of the hyphens can suggest that she is out of breath and that she is unable to control her distress.

[Enter LADY CAPULET]

Lady Capulet's demeanour has now changed, and she weeps profusely at seeing Juliet dead.

"O me, O me! My child, my only life!"

Her reaction seems a bit over exaggerated. This is a complete contrast to her earlier cold, detached self.

[*Enter* CAPULET]

CAPULET
For shame, bring Juliet forth; her lord is come
Nurse
She's dead, deceased, she's dead,
Alack the day!
LADY CAPULET
Alack the day,
She's dead, she's dead, she's dead!
CAPULET
Ha! Let me see her:
Out, alas! She's cold:
Her blood is settled, and her joints are stiff,
Life and these lips have long been separated:
Death lies on her like an untimely frost
Upon the sweetest flower of all the field.
Nurse
O lamentable day!
LADY CAPULET
O woeful time!
CAPULET
Death, that hath taken her
Hence to make me wail,
Ties up my tongue and will not let me speak.

[*Enter* FRIAR LAURENCE *and* PARIS, *with Musicians*]

FRIAR LAURENCE
Come, is the bride ready to go to church?
CAPULET
[*to* PARIS]
Ready to go, but never to return.
O son! The night before thy wedding day
Hath Death lain with thy wife.
There she lies,
Flower as she was, deflowered by him.
Death is my son–in–law, Death is my heir,
My daughter he hath wedded: I will die,
And leave him all; life, living, all is Death's.
PARIS
Have I thought long to see
This morning's face
And doth it give me such a sight as this?

[Enter CAPULET]

Shakespeare creates an air of woe. Capulet is beside himself at the loss of his only daughter,

"Death, that hath taken her
 Hence to make me wail"

[Enter FRIAR LAURENCE and PARIS with Musicians]

Enter Musicians with PARIS and FRIAR LAURENCE to greet CAPULET and wife

Now we have to juxtapose Capulet's behaviour. He is clearly very distraught to see Juliet lying dead, and he calls her a 'flower.'

He uses a very apt personification to describe her death. He hints that death has slept with Juliet and robbed her of her virginity on her wedding day.

"There she lies,
 Flower as she was, deflowered by him"

LADY CAPULET
Accursed, unhappy, wretched, hateful day!
Most miserable hour that ever time saw
In lasting labour of his pilgrimage!
But one, poor one, one poor and loving child,
But one thing to rejoice and solace in,
And cruel death hath catched it from my sight!
Nurse
O woe! O woeful, woeful, woeful day!
Most lamentable day, most woeful day,
That ever, ever, I did yet behold!
O day! O day! O day! O hateful day!
Never was seen so black a day as this:
O woeful day, O woeful day!
PARIS
Beguiled, divorced, wronged, spited, slain!
Most detestable death, by thee beguiled,
By cruel cruel thee quite overthrown!
O love! O life! Not life, but love in death!
CAPULET
Despised, distressed, hated, martyred, killed!
Uncomfortable time, why camest thou now
To murder, murder our solemnity?
O child! O child! My soul, and not my child!
Dead art thou! Alack! my child is dead,
And with my child my joys are buried.
FRIAR LAURENCE
Peace, ho, for shame!
Confusion's cure lives not in these confusions
Heaven and yourself had part in this fair maid
Now heaven hath all,
And all the better is it for the maid:
Your part in her could not keep from death,
But heaven keeps his part in eternal life.
The most you sought was her promotion,
'Twas your heaven he should be advanced
And weep ye now, seeing she is advanced
Above the clouds, as high as heaven itself?
O, in this love, you love your child so ill,
That you run mad, seeing that she is well:
She's not well married that lives married long,
But she's best married dies married young
Dry up your tears, and stick your rosemary
On this fair corse; and, as the custom is,
In all her best array bear her to church:
For though fond nature bids us an lament,
Yet nature's tears are reason's merriment.

Shakespeare uses the literary device of word-synonym repetition to reinforce the emotions generated by Juliet's death:

Lady Capulet:
Accursed, unhappy, wretched, hateful day!
Nurse:
O woe! O woeful, woeful, woeful day!
Paris:
Beguiled, divorced, wronged, spited, slain!
Lord Capulet:
Despaired, distressed, hated, martyred, killed!

NURSE, Lord CAPULET, Lady CAPULET and PARIS each express their sorrow

Everybody is weeping and wailing over Juliet's death, but Friar Laurence intervenes and consoles them and says that heaven has claimed her and that they should be happy for her.

"Yet nature's tears are reason's merriment"

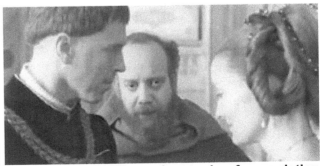

FRIAR LAURENCE speaks words of consolation to Lord and Lady CAPULET

CAPULET

All things that we ordained festival,
Turn from their office to black funeral,
Our instruments to melancholy bells,
Our wedding cheer to a sad burial feast,
Our solemn hymns to sullen dirges change,
Our bridal flowers serve for a buried corse,
And all things change them to the contrary.

FRIAR LAURENCE

Sir, go you in; and, madam, go with him,
And go, Sir Paris; everyone prepare
To follow this fair corse unto her grave:
The heavens do lour upon you for some ill.
Move them no more
By crossing their high will.

[*Exeunt* CAPULET, LADY CAPULET, PARIS, *and* FRIAR LAURENCE]

First Musician

Faith, we may put up our pipes, and be gone.

Nurse

Honest goodfellows, ah, put up, put up,
For, well you know, this is a pitiful case.

Second Musician

Ay, by my troth, the case may be amended.

[*Exit* NURSE] [*Enter* PETER]

PETER

Musicians, O, musicians,
'*Heart's Ease, Heart's Ease!*'
O, an you will have me live,
Play '*Heart's Ease*'

First Musician

Why '*Heart's Ease?*'

PETER

O, musicians, because my heart itself plays
'*My heart is full of woe*'.
O play me some merry dump, to comfort me.

First Musician

Not a dump we; 'tis no time to play now.

PETER

You will not, then?

First Musician

No.

PETER

I will then give it you soundly.

First Musician

What will you give us?

Capulet uses continuous repetition of the possessive pronoun 'our' and earlier in the play he said that Juliet belonged to him,

"An you be mine, I'll give you to my friend"
(Act 3 scene 5 line 190)

He treats her as his possession to do as he pleases with her life. Now he uses the pronoun our,

"Our instruments to melancholy bells,
Our wedding cheer to a sad burial feast,
Our solemn hymns to sullen dirges change,
Our bridal flowers serve for a buried corse"

This indicates that it was everybody's ceremony, yet we know that Juliet was not part of this whole marriage business, it would have been better if he had rather used the pronoun 'My.'

Friar Laurence asks them to go and see Juliet and he tries to make them feel guilty by targeting their conscience, warning them that God is punishing them for their past sins, implying that they forced Juliet into marriage and their intense hate for the Montague's.

He also tells them that they must not make the Heaven's angry by going against God's will,

"The heavens do lour upon you for some ill.
Move them no more
By crossing their high will"

PETER
No money, on my faith, but the gleek;
I will give you the minstrel.

First Musician
Then I will give you the serving creature.

PETER
Then will I lay
The serving creature's dagger on your pate.
I will carry no crotchets:
I'll 'RE' you, I'll 'FA' you; do you note me?

First Musician
An you 'RE' us and 'FA' us, you note us.

Second Musician
Pray you,
Put up your dagger and put out your wit.

PETER
Then have at you with my wit!
I will dry–beat you with an iron wit,
And put up my iron dagger.
Answer me like men:
  'When griping grief the heart doth wound'
  'And doleful dumps the mind oppress'
  'Then music with her silver sound'
Why *'silver sound'*?
Why *'music with her silver sound'*?
What say you, Simon Catling?

Musician
Marry, sir, because silver hath a sweet sound

PETER
Pretty! What say you, Hugh Rebeck?

Second Musician
I say *'silver sound'*,
Because musicians sound for silver.

PETER
Pretty too! What say you, James Soundpost?

Third Musician
Faith, I know not what to say.

PETER
O, I cry you mercy; you are the singer:
I will say for you.
It is *'music with her silver sound'*,
Because musician have no gold for sounding:
  'Then music with her silver sound'
  'With speedy help doth lend redress'

First Musician
What a pestilent knave is this same!

Second Musician
Hang him, Jack!
Come, we'll in here,
Tarry for the mourners and stay dinner.[*Exeunt*]

The Musicians who came with PARIS

The atmosphere is both tense and solemn. Everyone is very distraught about Juliet's death. Shakespeare tries to ease the tension by adding some light-hearted banter between Peter and the musicians.

This gives the audience a little breathing space after all the suspense and tension that they are experiencing.

Peter remarks,

"Then have at you with my wit!"

PETER challenges the MUSICIANS to a battle of wits:
"Then have at you with my wit!"

Mantua. A Street

[*Enter* ROMEO]

ROMEO
If I may trust the flattering truth of sleep,
My dreams presage some joyful news at hand
My bosom's lord sits lightly in his throne,
And all this day an unaccustomed spirit
Lifts me above the ground
With cheerful thoughts.
I dreamt my lady came and found me dead—
Strange dream that gives
A dead man leave to think!
And breathed such life with kisses in my lips,
That I revived and was an emperor.
Ah me! How sweet is love itself possessed,
When but love's shadows are so rich in joy!

[*Enter* BALTHASAR, *Romeo's man*]

News from Verona! — How now, Balthasar?
Dost thou not bring me letters from the friar?
How doth my lady? Is my father well?
How fares my Juliet? That I ask again,
For nothing can be ill if she be well.
BALTHASAR
Then she is well, and nothing can be ill:
Her body sleeps in Capel's monument,
And her immortal part with angels' lives.
I saw her laid low in her kindred's vault,
And presently took post to tell it you:
O pardon me for bringing these ill news,
Since you did leave it for my office, sir.
ROMEO
Is it even so? Then I defy you, stars!
Thou know'st my lodging:
Get me ink and paper,
And hire post–horses; I will hence to–night.
BALTHASAR
I do beseech you, sir, have patience:
Your looks are pale and wild,
And do import some misadventure.
ROMEO
Tush, thou art deceived:
Leave me and do the thing I bid thee do.
Hast thou no letters to me from the friar?

[Enter ROMEO]

This final scene opens with a very excited Romeo revealing his dream. Ironically, he foreshadows his final moments of his impending death.

"I dreamt my lady came and found me dead"

This was some kind of a weird premonition because that's exactly what happened. Juliet did find him dead in the tomb.

[Enter BALTHASAR]

Balthasar reveals that Juliet is dead and that her body lies in the Capulet's tomb,

"Her body sleeps in Capel's monument,
And her immortal part with angels' lives"

Romeo is angry that he has to be banished and he curses the stars,

"Then I defy you, stars!"

BALTHASAR tells ROMEO:
"Her body sleeps in Capel's monument,
And her immortal part with angels' lives"

BALTHASAR
No, my good lord.
ROMEO
No matter: get thee gone,
And hire those horses,
I'll be with thee straight.

[*Exit* BALTHASAR]

Well, Juliet, I will lie with thee to–night.
Let's see for means: O mischief, thou art swift
To enter in the thoughts of desperate men!
I do remember an apothecary, —
And hereabouts he dwells, —
Which late I noted
In tattered weeds, with overwhelming brows,
Culling of simples,
Meagre were his looks,
Sharp misery had worn him to the bones:
And in his needy shop a tortoise hung,
An alligator stuffed, and other skins
Of ill–shaped fishes; and about his shelves
A beggarly account of empty boxes,
Green earthen pots,
Bladders and musty seeds
Remnants of packthread
And old cakes of roses,
Were thinly scattered, to make up a show.
Noting this penury, to myself I said
'An if a man did need a poison now,
Whose sale is present death in Mantua,
Here lives a caitiff wretch would sell it him.'
O, this same thought did but forerun my need And
this same needy man must sell it me.
As I remember, this should be the house.
Being holiday, the beggar's shop is shut.
What, ho! Apothecary!

[*Enter* APOTHECARY]

Apothecary
Who calls so loud?

He plans to leave for Mantua that very night and vows,

"Well, Juliet, I will lie with thee tonight"

Shakespeare builds suspense by getting Romeo to recall a past encounter,

"To enter in the thoughts of desperate men!
　I do remember an apothecary"

Shakespeare then uses adjectives as a literary device to build curiosity and suspense in the storyline,

"Green earthen pots,
　Bladders and musty seeds
　Remnants of packthread
　And old cakes of roses"

And motive for Romeo's actions,

"to myself I said
'An if a man did need a poison now,
　Whose sale is present death in Mantua,
　Here lives a caitiff wretch would sell it him'"

ROMEO
Come hither, man. I see that thou art poor:
Hold, there is forty ducats:
Let me have a dram of poison,
Such soon–speeding gear
As will disperse itself through all the veins
That the life–weary taker may fall dead
And that the trunk
May be discharged of breath
As violently as hasty powder fired
Doth hurry from the fatal cannon's womb.

Apothecary
Such mortal drugs I have, but Mantua's law
Is death to any he that utters them.

ROMEO
Art thou so bare and full of wretchedness,
And fear'st to die? Famine is in thy cheeks,
Need and oppression starveth in thine eyes,
Contempt and beggary hang upon thy back,
The world is not thy friend nor the world's law
The world affords no law to make thee rich,
Then be not poor, but break it, and take this.

Apothecary
My poverty, but not my will, consents.

ROMEO
I pay thy poverty, and not thy will.

Apothecary
Put this in any liquid thing you will,
And drink it off; and if you had the strength
Of twenty men, it would dispatch you straight.

ROMEO
There is thy gold, -
Worse poison to men's souls,
Doing more murders in this loathsome world,
Than these poor compounds
That thou mayst not sell.
I sell thee poison; thou hast sold me none.
Farewell: buy food and get thyself in flesh.

[*Exit* Apothecary]

Come, cordial and not poison, go with me
To Juliet's grave, for there must I use thee.

[*Exeunt*]

APOTHECARY tells ROMEO:
"Such mortal drugs I have, but Mantua's law
 Is death to any he that utters them"

Romeo goes and buy some poison from the poor Apothecary. He takes the poison and head for Juliet's grave,

"Come, cordial and not poison, go with me
 To Juliet's grave, for there I must use thee"

POISON with the BAG of GOLD. ROMEO says:
"Come, cordial and not poison, go with me
 To Juliet's grave, for there must I use thee"

Friar Laurence's Cell

[*Enter* FRIAR JOHN]
FRIAR JOHN
Holy Franciscan friar! brother, ho!
[*Enter* FRIAR LAURENCE]
FRIAR LAURENCE
This same should be the voice of Friar John.
Welcome from Mantua: what says Romeo?
Or, if his mind be writ, give me his letter.
FRIAR JOHN
Going to find a bare–foot brother out
One of our order, to associate me,
Here in this city visiting the sick,
And finding him, the searchers of the town,
Suspecting that we both were in a house
Where the infectious pestilence did reign,
Sealed up the doors,
And would not let us forth,
So that my speed to Mantua there was stayed
FRIAR LAURENCE
Who bare my letter, then, to Romeo?
FRIAR JOHN
I could not send it, — here it is again, —
Nor get a messenger to bring it thee,
So fearful were they of infection.
FRIAR LAURENCE
Unhappy fortune! By my brotherhood,
The letter was not nice but full of charge
Of dear import, and the neglecting it
May do much danger.
Friar John, go hence, get me an iron crow,
And bring it straight unto my cell.
FRIAR JOHN
Brother, I'll go and bring it thee.
[*Exit* FRIAR JOHN]
FRIAR LAURENCE
Now must I to the monument alone,
Within three hours will fair Juliet wake:
She will beshrew me much that Romeo
Hath had no notice of these accidents,
But I will write again to Mantua,
And keep her at my cell till Romeo come,
Poor living corse,
Closed in a dead man's tomb!
[Exit]

[Enter FRIARS' JOHN and LAURENCE]

Once again, we witness the hand of fate playing its deadly game because the plague had prevented Friar John from delivering a
very important letter to Romeo.

Friar Laurence's plans went awry, and he is most disturbed,

"The letter was not nice but full of charge,
Of dear import, and the neglecting it
May do much danger"

FRIAR LAURENCE tells FRIAR JOHN:
"The letter was not nice but full of charge
Of dear import, and the neglecting it
May do much danger"

Friar Lawrence plans to go to the tomb and when Juliet awakes, he will take her to his cell until Romeo arrives,

"Poor living corse,
Closed in a dead man's tomb!"

A Churchyard
in it a Tomb belonging to the Capulets

[*Enter* PARIS, *and his Page bearing flowers and a torch*]

PARIS
Give me thy torch, boy.
Hence, and stand aloof.
Yet put it out, for I would not be seen.
Under yond yew–trees lay thee all along,
Holding thine ear close to the hollow ground,
So shall no foot upon the churchyard tread,
Being loose, unfirm, with digging up of graves
But thou shalt hear it:
Whistle then to me, as signal
That thou hear'st something approach.
Give me those flowers.
Do as I bid thee; go.
PAGE
[*Aside*]
I am almost afraid to stand alone
Here in the churchyard, yet I will adventure.

[PAGE *withdraws*]

PARIS
Sweet flower, with flowers
Thy bridal bed I strew, —
O woe! Thy canopy is dust and stones! —
Which with sweet water nightly I will dew
Or, wanting that, with tears distilled by moans:
The obsequies that I for thee will keep
Nightly shall be to strew thy grave and weep.

[PAGE *whistles*]

The boy gives warning
Something doth approach.
What cursed foot wanders this way tonight,
To cross my obsequies and true love's rite?
What with a torch! Muffle me, night, awhile.

[PAGE *retires*]

Inside the CAPULETS Tomb

[Enter PARIS and his PAGE]

PARIS outside the CAPULETS Tomb

Paris scatters flowers on Juliet's tomb. He is overwrought with grief and we can assume that Shakespeare's use of hyphens suggests this,

"Sweet flower, with flowers
 Thy bridal bed I strew"

He says that her tomb has become her 'bridal bed'. It was supposed to be their wedding night to consummate their marriage instead the tomb is now her bridal bed.

[*Enter* ROMEO *and* BALTHASAR, *who bears a torch, mattock (pick) and a crow of iron (crowbar)*]

ROMEO
Give me that mattock and the wrenching iron.
Hold, take this letter,
Early in the morning, see thou deliver it
To my lord and father.
Give me the light:
Upon thy life, I charge thee,
Whatever thou hear'st or seest, stand all aloof
And do not interrupt me in my course.
Why I descend into this bed of death,
Is partly to behold my lady's face,
But chiefly to take thence
From her dead finger
A precious ring,
A ring that I must use
In dear employment:
Therefore hence, be gone:
But if thou, jealous, dost return to pry
In what I further shall intend to do,
By heaven, I will tear thee joint by joint
And strew this hungry churchyard
With thy limbs:
The time and my intents are savage, wild,
More fierce and more inexorable far
Than empty tigers or the roaring sea.

BALTHASAR
I will be gone, sir, and not trouble you.

ROMEO
So shalt thou show me friendship.
Take thou that:
[ROMEO *gives* BALTHASAR *money*]
Live, and be prosperous
And farewell, good fellow.

BALTHASAR
For all this same, I'll hide me hereabout:
His looks I fear, and his intents I doubt.

[BALTHASAR *hides*]

ROMEO
Thou detestable maw, thou womb of death,
Gorged with the dearest morsel of the earth,
Thus I enforce thy rotten jaws to open,
And, in despite, I'll cram thee with more food!

[ROMEO *opens the tomb*]

[Enter ROMEO and BALTHASAR]

Romeo is in deadly earnest to enter the tomb where Juliet is laid to rest, first to behold her face and then to recover the ring he gave her,

"Is partly to behold my lady's face,
  But chiefly to take thence
  From her dead finger
  A precious ring,
  A ring that I must use
  In dear employment"

Romeo warns Balthasar not to pry or face deadly consequences,

"By heaven, I will tear thee joint by joint
And strew this hungry churchyard
With thy limbs"

Romeo is in a fierce mood, like,

"empty tigers or the roaring the sea"

In his fury he curses the tomb, accusing it of being a greedy mouth of death,

"Thou detestable maw, thou womb of death"

His use of the personification suggests his anger and fury and he is ready to take revenge, insisting that Death greedily ate up the most precious creature on earth,

"Gorged with the dearest morsel of the earth"

He uses the onomatopoeia,

"rotten jaws to open"

We can actually feel his fury
 in the onomatopoeia:

'Gorged' 'rotten' 'cram'

And he angrily says that he will give Death another body to devour,

"Thus I enforce thy rotten jaws to open,
  And, in despite, I'll cram thee with more food!"

PARIS
This is that banished haughty Montague,
That murdered my love's cousin,
With which grief, it is supposed,
The fair creature died,
And here is come
To do some villainous shame
To the dead bodies:
I will apprehend him.

[ROMEO *comes forward*]

Stop thy unhallowed toil, vile Montague!
Can vengeance
Be pursued further than death?
Condemned villain, I do apprehend thee:
Obey, and go with me, for thou must die.
ROMEO
I must indeed, and therefore, came I hither.
Good gentle youth,
Tempt not a desperate man,
Fly hence, and leave me:
Think upon these gone,
Let them affright thee.
I beseech thee, youth,
Put not another sin upon my head,
By urging me to fury: O, be gone!
By heaven, I love thee better than myself,
For I come hither armed against myself:
Stay not, be gone; live, and hereafter say,
A madman's mercy bade thee run away.
PARIS
I do defy thy conjuration,
And apprehend thee for a felon here.
ROMEO
Wilt thou provoke me?
Then have at thee, boy!

[*They fight*]

PAGE
O Lord, they fight! I will go call the watch.
[*Exit* PAGE]

PARIS
O, I am slain!
[HE *falls*]
If thou be merciful,
Open the tomb, lay me with Juliet.
[HE *dies*]

Paris sees Romeo and thinks that he has come to take revenge on the dead bodies, so he accosts Romeo and orders him to,

"Obey and go with me, for thou must die"

We should note that even in death Paris wants to take revenge.

Shakespeare is trying to show us how the Capulet's and the Montague's hate is spreading.

Romeo begs Paris not to fuel his anger anymore. He echoed the same sentiment that he uttered to Tybalt before killing him,

"By heaven, I love thee better than myself"

Paris was stubborn and he refused to listen to Romeo,

"I do defy thy conjuration"

They fight and Paris dies.

Romeo now realises who Paris is - the man who was supposed to marry Juliet.

PARIS and ROMEO with swords drawn

He is sad and he tells Paris that bad luck befell both of them for loving Juliet and he promises.

ROMEO

In faith, I will.
Let me peruse this face.
Mercutio's kinsman, noble County Paris!
What said my man, when my betossed soul
Did not attend him as we rode? I think
He told me Paris should have married Juliet:
Said he not so? Or did I dream it so?
Or am I mad, hearing him talk of Juliet,
To think it was so?
O, give me thy hand,
One writ with me in sour misfortune's book!
I'll bury thee in a triumphant grave.

[ROMEO *opens the tomb*]

A grave? O no! A lantern, slaughtered youth,
For here lies Juliet, and her beauty makes
This vault a feasting presence full of light.
Death, lie thou there, by a dead man interred.

[ROMEO *lays* PARIS *in the tomb*]

How oft when men are at the point of death
Have they been merry! Which their keeper's call
A lightning before death:
O, how may I call this a lightning?
O my love! my wife! Death,
That hath sucked the honey of thy breath,
Hath had no power yet upon thy beauty.
Thou art not conquered, beauty's ensign yet
Is crimson in thy lips and in thy cheeks,
And death's pale flag is not advanced there.
Tybalt, liest thou there in thy bloody sheet?
O, what more favour can I do to thee,
Than with that hand that cut thy youth in twain
To sunder his that was thine enemy?
Forgive me, cousin! Ah, dear Juliet,
Why art thou yet so fair? Shall I believe
That unsubstantial Death is amorous,
And that the lean abhorred monster keeps
Thee here in dark to be his paramour?
For fear of that, I still will stay with thee,
And never from this palace of dim night
Depart again: here, here will I remain
With worms that are thy chamber-maids,
O, here will I set up my everlasting rest,
And shake the yoke of inauspicious stars
From this world-wearied flesh.

"I'll bury thee in a triumphant grave"

Romeo sees Juliet in the tomb, and he says that it is not a grave, it's a lantern,

"A grave? Oh, no! A lantern"

We are going to draw a parallel here between Romeo's first meeting with Juliet at the ball and his last meeting at her death. In both cases he uses light imagery to describe her beauty.

"Oh, she doth teach the torches to burn bright" (Act 1 scene 5 line 42)

And now in death he says that Juliet's beauty lights up the vault,

"her beauty makes
This vault a feasting presence full of light"

The audience is now fully connected and emotionally involved because while he is burying Paris, Romeo says,

"Death lie thou there, by a dead man interred"

Romeo remarks that he is a dead man just like Paris. Before he dies Romeo delivers an emotional speech about Juliet's beauty. He maintained that although death had claimed Juliet, it didn't have the power and skills to destroy her beauty.

"Death,
That had sucked the honey of thy breath,
Hath had no power yet upon thy beauty"

He personifies death and accuses death of being a monster who trapped Juliet and kept her in the tomb because he loves her.

And wants her for his mistress.

"That unsubstantial death is amorous,
And that the lean abhorred monster keeps
Thee here in the dark to be his paramour?"

ROMEO (*continues*)
Eyes, look your last!
Arms, take your last embrace!
And, lips, O you the doors of breath,
Seal with a righteous kiss
A dateless bargain to engrossing Death!
Come bitter conduct, come, unsavoury guide!
Thou desperate pilot, now at once run on
The dashing rocks thy sea–sick weary bark!
Here's to my love!

[ROMEO *drinks*]

O true apothecary!
Thy drugs are quick.
Thus with a kiss I die.

[ROMEO *dies*]

[*Enter, at the other end of the churchyard,* FRIAR
LAURENCE, *with a lantern, crow, and spade*]

FRIAR LAURENCE
Saint Francis be my speed!
How oft tonight
Have my old feet stumbled at graves!
Who's there?
BALTHASAR
Here's one, a friend,
And one that knows you well.
FRIAR LAURENCE
Bliss be upon you!
Tell me, good my friend,
What torch is yond, that vainly lends his light
To grubs and eyeless skulls?
As I discern, it burneth
In the Capel's monument.
BALTHASAR
It doth so, holy sir,
And there's my master,
One that you love.
FRIAR LAURENCE
Who is it?
BALTHASAR
Romeo.

JULIET asleep attended by ROMEO

Romeo also apologies to Tybalt for causing his
untimely death. Romeo kisses Juliet and drinks the
poison.

"Thus with a kiss I die"

[ROMEO dies]

ROMEO drinks poison:
"Thus with a kiss I die"

[Enter FRIAR LAURENCE]

FRIAR LAURENCE at the tomb

FRIAR LAURENCE
How long hath he been there?

BALTHASAR
Full half an hour.

FRIAR LAURENCE
Go with me to the vault.

BALTHASAR
I dare not, sir
My master knows not but I am gone hence,
And fearfully did menace me with death,
If I did stay to look on his intents.

FRIAR LAURENCE
Stay, then; I'll go alone.
Fear comes upon me:
O, much I fear some ill unthrifty thing.

BALTHASAR
As I did sleep under this yew–tree here,
I dreamt my master and another fought,
And that my master slew him.

FRIAR LAURENCE
Romeo!

[FRIAR *advances*]

Alack, alack, what blood is this, which stains
The stony entrance of this sepulchre?
What mean these masterless, gory swords
To lie discoloured by this place of peace?

[FRIAR *enters the tomb*]

Romeo! O, pale! Who else?
What, Paris too?
And steeped in blood?
Ah, what an unkind hour
Is guilty of this lamentable chance!
The lady stirs.

[JULIET *wakes*]

JULIET
O comfortable friar!
Where is my lord?
I do remember well where I should be,
And there I am.
Where is my Romeo?

[*Noise within*]

Friar Laurence goes into the tomb with an ill-foreboding feeling.

"Oh, much I fear some ill unthrifty thing"

Friar Laurence discovers both Romeo and Paris' bodies whilst Juliet stirs from her sleep. She immediately asks for Romeo.

FRIAR inside the tomb: "The lady stirs"

Shakespeare continues the theme of being too late to save the situation: Romeo was too late to save Mercutio; too late to save Juliet; and the friar too late to save both Romeo and Juliet.

Shakespeare uses fate to perpetuate the tragedy of death: first Mercutio, then Tybalt, followed by Paris, and finally the star-crossed lovers, Romeo by poison followed by Juliet by dagger.

FRIAR and JULIET discover ROMEO dead

FRIAR LAURENCE
I hear some noise, Lady.
Come from that nest
Of death, contagion, and unnatural sleep:
A greater power than we can contradict
Hath thwarted our intents.
Come, come away.
Thy husband in thy bosom there lies dead
And Paris too.
Come, I'll dispose of thee
Among a sisterhood of holy nuns:
Stay not to question, for the watch is coming,
Come, go, good Juliet,
[*Noise again*]

I dare no longer stay.
JULIET
Go, get thee hence, for I will not away.

[*Exit* FRIAR LAURENCE]

What's here?
A cup, closed in my true love's hand?
Poison, I see, hath been his timeless end:
O churl! Drunk all,
And left no friendly drop to help me after?
I will kiss thy lips,
Haply some poison yet doth hang on them,
To make die with a restorative.
[JULIET *kisses* ROMEO]
Thy lips are warm!

[PAGE *enters graveyard with* WATCHMEN]

First Watchman
Lead, boy: which way?
JULIET
Yea, noise? Then I'll be brief.
O happy dagger!
[*Snatching* ROMEO's *dagger*]
This is thy sheath,
[*Stabs herself*]
There rest and let me die.

[JULIET *falls on* ROMEO's *body, and dies*]

They hear sounds and Friar Laurence urges her to leave but she refuses,

"Go, get thee hence, for I will not away"

She discovers that Romeo died from poisoning, and she kisses him in the hope that the residual poison from his lips will kill her.

She hears noises, and she quickly takes Romeo's dagger and kills herself.

JULIET says of ROMEO:
"Poison, I see, hath been his timeless end"

Shakespeare builds tension by changing remorse into tragedy when Juliet decides she cannot live without her husband Romeo resulting in her stabbing herself to be with him forever in death.

"O happy dagger!"

JULIET says in anguish over ROMEO's death body:
"O happy dagger!"
"and let me die"

[*Enter* WATCH *with* PAGE *of* PARIS]

PAGE
This is the place,
There, where the torch doth burn.
First Watchman
The ground is bloody,
Search about the churchyard:
Go, some of you, whoever you find attach.

[*Exeunt some* WATCHMEN]

Pitiful sight! Here lies the county slain,
And Juliet bleeding, warm, and newly dead,
Who here hath lain these two days buried?
Go, tell the Prince:
Run to the Capulets: Raise up the Montagues
Some others search:

[*Exeunt other* WATCHMEN]

We see the ground whereon these woes do lie
But the true ground of all these piteous woes
We cannot without circumstance descry.

[*Return some of the Watch with* BALTHASAR]

Second Watchman
Here's Romeo's man,
We found him in the churchyard.
First Watchman
Hold him in safety, till the prince come hither.

[*Return the Watch with* FRIAR LAURENCE]

Third Watchman
Here is a friar,
That trembles, sighs and weeps:
We took this mattock and spade from him,
As he was coming from this churchyard side.
First Watchman
A great suspicion: stay the friar too.

[*Enter the* PRINCE *and Attendants*]

PRINCE
What misadventure is so early up
that calls our person from our morning's rest?

[*Enter* CAPULET *and his* WIFE]

[Enter the WATCH with PAGE]

Shakespeare uses plain story-telling to move the tragedy forward to it conclusion.

By command of the Prince, the Watchman apprehend Friar Laurence:

"Here is a friar,
 That trembles, sighs and weeps"

The Capulets and then the Montagues arrive to learn the awful news. The friar tells all present how fate had intervened to cause the deaths of the star-crossed lovers. Finally, both families are reconciled in love and friendship.

[Enter PRINCE and Attendants]

PRINCE enquiring:
"What misadventure is so early up"

[Enter Lord and Lady CAPULET]

CAPULETS at the tomb

CAPULET
What should it be that they so shriek abroad?
LADY CAPULET
O, the people in the street cry 'Romeo',
Some 'Juliet', and some 'Paris'; and all run,
With open outcry toward our monument.
PRINCE
What fear is this which startles in our ears?
First Watchman
Sovereign, here lies the County Paris slain,
And Romeo dead,
And Juliet, dead before, warm and new killed.
PRINCE
Search, seek, and know
How this foul murder comes.
First Watchman
Here is a friar, and slaughtered Romeo's man
With instruments upon them,
Fit to open these dead men's tombs.
CAPULET
O heavens!
O wife, look how our daughter bleeds!
This dagger hath mistaken —
For lo, his house is empty
On the back of Montague, —
And it mis–sheathed in my daughter's bosom!
LADY CAPULET
O me! This sight of death is as a bell,
That warns my old age to a sepulchre.

[*Enter* MONTAGUE *and others*]

PRINCE
Come, Montague; for thou art early up,
To see thy son and heir more early down.
MONTAGUE
Alas, my liege, my wife is dead tonight,
Grief of my son's exile
Hath stopped her breath:
What further woe
Conspires against mine age?
PRINCE
Look, and thou shalt see.
MONTAGUE
O thou untaught!
What manners is in this,
To press before thy father to a grave?

Capulet sees Juliet bleeding,

"O Heavens!"
"O wife, look how our daughter bleeds"

He believes that Romeo killed her because his dagger was mis-sheath in Juliet's back.

[Enter MONTAGUE]

He declares that Romeo's banishment has killed his wife. He then sees Romeo's dead body. He is angry that Romeo had died before him.

"What manners is in this,
 To press before thy father to a grave?"

The prince wants to unravel the mystery behind these deaths.

Friar Laurence takes full responsibility for these deaths, and he is prepared to be punished for it.

MONTAGUES at the tomb

PRINCE
Seal up the mouth of outrage for a while,
Till we can clear these ambiguities,
And know their spring,
Their head, their true descent,
And then will I be general of your woes,
And lead you even to death:
Meantime forbear,
And let mischance be slave to patience.
Bring forth the parties of suspicion.

[WATCHMEN *bring forward*
FRIAR LAURENCE *and* BALTHASAR]

FRIAR LAURENCE
I am the greatest, able to do least,
Yet most suspected, as the time and place
Doth make against me of this direful murder,
And here I stand, both to impeach and purge
Myself condemned and myself excused.
PRINCE
Then say at once
What thou dost know in this.
FRIAR LAURENCE
I will be brief, for my short date of breath
Is not so long as is a tedious tale.
Romeo, there dead,
Was husband to that Juliet,
And she, there dead,
That Romeo's faithful wife, I married them
And their stolen marriage day
Was Tybalt's dooms day
Whose untimely death banished
The new–made bridegroom from the city,
For whom, and not for Tybalt, Juliet pined.
You, to remove that siege of grief from her,
Betrothed and would have married her
Perforce to County Paris:
Then comes she to me, and, with wild looks,
Bid me devise some mean
To rid her from this second marriage,
Or in my cell there would she kill herself.

[WATCHMEN bring forward

FRIAR LAURENCE and BALTHASAR]

Shakespeare uses the Friar Laurence's self-confession to recap to the audience the storyline in the play

"I will be brief, for my short date of breath
Is not so long as is a tedious tale"

FRIAR LAURENCE tells all: "I will be brief"

FRIAR LAURENCE (*continues*)
Then gave I her, so tutored by my art,
A sleeping potion,
Which so took effect as I intended,
For it wrought on her the form of death:
Meantime I writ to Romeo, that he should
Hither come as this dire night,
To help to take her from her borrowed grave,
Being the time the potion's force should cease
But he which bore my letter, Friar John,
Was stayed by accident, and yesternight
Returned my letter back.
Then all alone
At the prefixed hour of her waking,
Came I to take her from her kindred's vault;
Meaning to keep her closely at my cell,
Till I conveniently could send to Romeo:
But when I came,
Some minute ere the time of her awaking,
Here untimely lay the noble Paris
And true Romeo dead.
She wakes,
And I entreated her come forth,
And bear this work of heaven with patience:
But then a noise did scare me from the tomb,
And she, too desperate, would not go with me
But, as it seems, did violence on herself.
All this I know,
And to the marriage her nurse is privy:
And, if aught in this Miscarried by my fault,
Let my old life be sacrificed,
Some hour before his time,
Unto the rigour of severest law.

PRINCE
We still have known thee for a holy man
Where's Romeo's man?
What can he say in this?

BALTHASAR
I brought my master news of Juliet's death,
And then in post he came from Mantua
To this same place, to this same monument.
This letter he early bid me give his father,
And threatened me with death, going in vault,
If departed not and left him there.

He relays in explicit detail all the events that led to these tragedies, and he acknowledges that he unwittingly contributed to these deaths,

"Let my old life be sacrificed
Some hour before his time
Unto the rigour of severest law"

The prince maintains that Friar Lawrence was always a holy man and both Balthasar and Paris' page gave him details of all the events that led to their master's death.

PRINCE listening to **FRIAR LAURENCE, BALTHASAR, and the PAGE about events leading to JULIET and ROMEO's deaths**

PRINCE

Give me the letter
I will look on it
Where is the County's Page
That raised the watch?
[PAGE comes forward]
Sirrah, what made your master in this place?

PAGE

He came with flowers to strew his lady's grave,
And bid me stand aloof, and so I did.
Anon comes one with light to ope the tomb,
And by and by my master drew on him,
And then I ran away to call the watch.

PRINCE

This letter doth make good the Friar's words,
Their course of love, the tidings of her death:
And here he writes that he did buy a poison
Of a poor apothecary, and therewithal
Came to this vault to die and lie with Juliet.
Where be these enemies?
Capulet! Montague!
See what a scourge is laid upon your hate,
That heaven finds means
To kill your joys with love.
And I, for winking at your discords too
Have lost a brace of kinsmen:
All are punished.

CAPULET

O brother Montague, give me thy hand:
This is my daughter's jointure,
For no more can I demand.

MONTAGUE

But I can give thee more:
For I will raise her statue in pure gold,
That while Verona by that name is known,
There shall no figure at such rate be set
As that of true and faithful Juliet.

CAPULET

As rich shall Romeo's by his lady's lie,
Poor sacrifices of our enmity!

PRINCE

A glooming peace this morning with it brings,
The sun, for sorrow, will not show his head.
Go hence,
To have more talk of these sad things,
Some shall be pardoned, and some punished:
For never was a story of more woe
Than this of Juliet and her Romeo.

[*Exeunt*]

Balthasar even gave Romeo's letter to the Prince and the Prince confirms that the Friar was telling the truth.

"This letter doth make good the friar's words

The prince is furious, and he reprimands both Capulet's and Montague's for their hate.

"Where be these enemies?
Capulet! Montague!
See what scourge is laid upon your hate
That heaven finds means
To kill your joys with love!"

CAPULET and MONTAGUE reconciled

Capulet reaches out and asks for Montague's hand and Montague promises to erect a statue of pure gold of Juliet celebrating her beauty of truth and faithfulness. Capulet agrees that a statue of Romeo will be erected beside her.

"Poor sacrifices of our enmity"

The prince says that,

"A glooming peace this morning with it brings"

and continues with nature's judgement,

"The sun, for sorrow, will not show his head"

The prince concludes by saying that

"For never was a story of more woe
Than this of Juliet and her Romeo"

The **SUMMARY** of each **ACT** and each **SCENE** in the Shakespearean play, provides the storyline in a concise and detailed manner, ideal for exam revision.

The **SUMMARY** in each **SCENE** is constructed around the important quotes and phrases used in the **SCENE** for purposes of reinforcing the text, and memory retention.

The scene opens in a public place in the city of Verona, on Sunday at about nine in the morning.

Enter SAMPSON and GREGORY, servants of the house of CAPULET, armed with swords and bucklers (small round shields), boasting about what they will do to their arch enemy, the MONTAGUES, man or maid, should they meet.

Enter ABRAHAM, servant to Lord Montague, and BALTHASAR, servant to Romeo.

GREGORY tells SAMPSON to draw his sword, and they hatch a plan to start a fight with the two Montagues. SAMPSON bites his thumb, a sign of disrespect, and is challenged by ABRAHAM as to whether the insult is directed at him or not. Swords are drawn when ABRAHAM and SAMPSON dispute who serves the better Lord.

Enter BENVOLIO, nephew to Lord Montague.

BENVOLIO immediately orders the warring parties to cease fighting.

Enter TYBALT, nephew to Capulet's wife.

TYBALT hates peace hates the Montagues and tells BENVOLIO to look upon his death.

Enter three or four CITIZENS with clubs, who join the fray, and an OFFICER.

Enter Lord and Lady CAPULET, parents of Juliet, perturbed by the noise. Lord CAPULET is ready to join the fray with sword but is lampooned by Lady CAPULET.

Enter Lord and Lady MONTAGUE, parents of Romeo, perturbed by the noise. Lord MONTAGUE is ready to join the fray with sword but is told not to fight by Lady MONTAGUE.

Enter Prince ESCALUS with his followers.

The ESCALUS immediately stops the fight on pain of death, chastising all parties involved in the fray, and charging the CAPULET party to accompany him to old Freetown, for judgement, and later, in the afternoon, for the MONTAGUE party to do the same.

Exit all parties except Lord and Lady MONTAGUE, and BENVOLIO.

BENVOLIO explains to Lord MONTAGUE how the fray came about. However, Lady MONTAGUE is relieved that her son, Romeo, was not part of the fray, and she wished to know his whereabouts. BENVOLIO tells her of his concern for ROMEO and how her son avoided him by strolling away into the wood.

Lord MONTAGUE voices his concerns about ROMEO's sullen mood, explaining he neither knows nor can learn the cause of his sorrow, and that whatever the cause, neither he nor his friends can elicit the secret from ROMEO as to why.

Enter ROMEO, arriving from a distance.

Exit Lord and Lady MONTAGUE, on the advice of BENVOLIO.

ROMEO explains to BENVOLIO that he is still in love with ROSALINE although she is out of love with him, and muses to BENVOLIO about love's transgression, and unfair ways.

BENVOLIO consoles ROMEO but asks him to forget ROSALINE else spend the rest of his life endeavouring to do so.

[*End of ACT 1 scene 1* Summary]

The scene opens later in the day, in Capulet's house, in the city of Verona.

Enter Lord CAPULET, Kinsman PARIS, and Capulet's Serving man.

Lord CAPULET remarks to PARIS that penalty alike, it should not be hard for old man like himself and Lord MONTAGUE, to keep the peace.

PARIS agrees and empathises, but now asks Lord CAPULET if he can marry his daughter, JULIET. Lord CAPULET is wary about such a match, citing that JULIET is too young, not yet fourteen years, and would be ripe to be a bride two summers hence. PARIS counters that younger than she are happy mothers. Still not persuaded, Lord CAPULET advises PARIS to first woo her because she will need to consent to such a marry, and invites PARIS to an old-accustomed feast, so that he may compare JULIET to other young women. CAPULET then instructs his servant to venture forth into Verona to deliver the invitations.

Exit CAPULET and PARIS.

Unfortunately, the servant cannot read, and does not know what to do.

Enter BENVOLIO and ROMEO.

BENVOLIO tries to dissuade ROMEO from his infatuation with ROSALINE, saying when one fire burns out another is burning. But ROMEO retorts that he is shut up in a prison, kept without food, whipped, and tormented.

The servant injects, explaining that he needs to deliver invitations but cannot read, and hopes that they are not from the house of Montague, his masters' enemy. ROMEO obliges and read the invitations, even though he is from the house of Montague, but does not tell the servant.

ROMEO discovers that ROSALINE will attend the feast and is urged by BENVOLIO to attend so that he can show him that ROSALINE is like a crow in comparison to admired beauties of Verona who are like swans.

ROMEO is defiant and accepts BENVOLIO challenge to attend the feast, convinced that no beauties exist that can compare to his ROSALINE.

[*End of ACT 1 scene 2 Summary*]

The scene opens later in the day, within Capulet's house, in the city of Verona.

Enter Lady CAPULET, who asks NURSE to call forth her daughter JULIET.

Enter JULIET.

Lady CAPULET debates with NURSE the true age of JULIET which NURSE determines to be less than fourteen years by a fortnight and odd days but on Lammas Eve JULIET will fourteen years, ready to be married. NURSE relates how she weaned JULIET until the earthquake struck eleven ago, then used wormwood to unwean her. Lord and Lady CAPULET were then at Mantua. Since that time, eleven years ago, JULIET could run and waddle, and was mentored by NURSE's husband who is now no more. NURSE recalls how JULIET fell upon her face and acquired a bump as big as a young cockerel's stone. NURSE concludes by saying that JULIET wasn't the prettiest babe that ever she nursed and might live to see JULIET married.

Lady CAPULET interjects that marry is the very theme she came to talk about and asks JULIET how she stands on the dispositions to be married. Unlike her husband, Lady CAPULET is keen for her daughter not to wait but to get to marry now. JULIET responds by saying that marriage is an honour that she dreamed not of.

In further advocating the marriage, Lady CAPULET tells JULIET that valiant PARIS seeks her love, and wishes to marry her, disregarding ladies of esteem, younger than JULIET. Lady CAPULET continues telling JULIET that she was about the same age as these mothers when JULIET was born. NURSE concurs, citing that PARIS is a man of wax, perfect for JULIET, and both Lady CAPULET and NURSE agree that in Verona this summer, there hath not such a flower as PARIS. Lady CAPULET asks JULIET, this night at the feast, to look at PARIS, read his face, find delight writ there, examine every married lineament, find written in his eyes this precious book of love which only lacks a cover. JULIET is that cover, and so will share in all PARIS doth possess, and lose nothing in doing so.

Lady CAPULET becomes impatient, demanding JULIET to speak briefly as to whether she can like of PARIS' love. JULIET responds she will do as her mother suggests, as her consent gives strength to the marriage.

Enter the serving man to inform Lady CAPULET the guests have come, beseeched her and JULIET to follow. NURSE tells JULIET to go and seek happy nights to happy days.

[*End of ACT 1 scene 3* Summary]

The scene opens on Sunday evening, on a street, in the city of Verona, leading to Capulet's house.

Enter ROMEO, MERCUTIO and BENVOLIO, with five or six other MASQUERS and TOUCH-BEARERS, on their way to the feast at Capulet's house. The feast is a masquerade, where invited guests must dance and wear masks. So although the MONTAGUES are entering CAPULET territory, they are safe, hidden by their masks.

ROMEO is worried as to what excuse they will have for arriving at the feast, or should they just enter without apologising. BENVOLIO replies it is out of fashion to give explanations, nor have someone dress up as Cupid to frighten the ladies like a scarecrow, nor recite a memorised speech, but let them judge us however they please. We will give them a dance and then hit the road.

ROMEO pines for ROSALINE so does not want to dance but asks to be the one with carries the torch. MERCUTIO insists that he takes the role of Cupid and fly higher than the average man to find a new love, but ROMEO is unconvinced and says his soul is like lead, too heavy to dance and Cupid's arrow has pierced him too deeply, so he cannot leap any higher than his dull sadness but instead will sink under the heavy weight of love.

MERCUTIO counters ROMEO by saying if you sink then it is not right to drag down tender love. ROMEO questions whether love is really tender but thinks it is too rough, too rude, too rowdy, and it picks like a thorn. MERCUTIO concludes the debate by saying that he does not care how love plays, the mask will blush but not the man behind the mask.

BENVOLIO interrupts and tells the party they have arrived at the feast and should start dancing the minute they get inside.

ROMEO insists on taking the torch, watch playful people with light hearts dance, but will sit not dance. MERCUTIO remonstrates with ROMEO about his reluctance to participant in the feast but to use his common sense, instead of trusting his five senses.

ROMEO then reveals that he had a disturbing dream at night. In response, MERCUTIO says so did I, and ROMEO replies so what was yours, and in jest MERCUTIO answers that dreamers often lie. ROMEO with wit replies, they dream about the truth. MERCUTIO counters this with I see you've been with Queen MAB. Baffled BENVOLIO then asks who is Queen MAB?

MERCUTIO then given a detailed witty commentary on Queen MAB. She is the fairies' midwife, no bigger in size than a stone, riding around on a wagon drawn by tiny little atoms over men's noses as they lie sleeping. MERCUTIO continues describing the parts of plants and animals that make up her train, and how she rides every night through the minds of lovers and make them dream about love, or through lawyers' fingers and right away, they dream about their fees, or any other profession and make them lust for their desires. Queen MAB is the old hag who gives false dreams and brings bad luck. ROMEO interjects asking MERCUTIO to stop talking about things of no consequence.

MERCUTIO agrees and admits dreams are nothing but vain fantasy of an idle mind, more inconsistent than the wind. BENVOLIO reminds everyone that supper is done, and they will come too late to the feast if they don't stop talking.

ROMEO is still not sure if the feast will be the start of something bad, something that will lead to his own death, but whoever is in charge of his life, he is content for them to steer him whichever way they want.

BENVOLIO instructs everyone to strike, drum, and they continue on to the feast.

[*End of ACT 1 scene 4* Summary

The scene opens inside the hall in Capulet's house, late on Sunday evening.

Enter the MASQUERS, who march round the hall and stand to one side.

PETER and other SERVINGMEN approach with napkins.

PETER directs the other serving men in arranging the banquet furniture and food before departing from the hall.

Enter Lord CAPULET with his WIFE, his COUSIN, TYBALT, JULIET, and others of the house, meeting ROMEO, BENVOLIO, MERCUTIO, and other GUESTS and MASKERS.

Lord CAPULET welcomes all and expects all to dance even though they be shy but does not wear a mask himself as age is against him in charming young ladies. He instructs musicians to play music, knaves to turn over the tables and quench the fire, and for all to dance. He asks his COUSIN to sit and recall when last they wore masks, claiming you and I are too old to dance. The response is thirty years, but Lord CAPULET thinks it is more like twenty-five years and doubts his COUSIN's reckoning using Lucentio's wedding as a time marker.

ROMEO spots JULIET and asks a SERVINGMAN, who is the girl dancing with yonder knight, to which the reply is I know not, sir.

ROMEO remonstrates with himself on her beauty, how she doth teach the torches to burn bright, how she hangs upon the cheek of night like a rich jewel in an Ethiope's ear, her beauty shows a snowy drove dancing next to crows. ROMEO is captivated by JULIET's beauty, and retorts, did my heart love till now? And declares, for I never saw true beauty till this night.

TYBALT recognises ROMEO's voice, and instructs his Page to fetch his rapier, so that he can strike ROMEO dead, to satisfy the honour of his kin.

Lord CAPULET asks TYBALT what angers him so, to which, TYBALT replies, Uncle this is a MONTAGUE, our foe, who has come to scorn this feast.

Lord CAPULET disagrees citing how Verona brags of ROMEO as a virtuous and well-governed youth, and tells TYBALT to be content, not to challenge ROMEO, and not to disparage this house, but accept the judgement to be patient, to observe and not to frown and undo the gaiety of the feast.

TYBALT is adamant he will not endure ROMEO at the feast. In response, Lord CAPULET chastises TYBALT telling him I am Master here, you'll make a mutiny among the guests, and then tells him to go. TYBALT agrees to withdraw but says although ROMEO's intrusion shall now seem sweet, it will convert to bitterest gall when they meet again.

Exit TALBALT in a wilful seething rage.

Unaware of the altercation his presence has caused, ROMEO takes JULIET's hand, and delivers a religious sonnet on pilgrims holding hands leading to tender kiss. JULIET continues the sonnet by countering that "saints do kiss by palm to palm". The exchange continues with JULIET as the holy shrine waiting to be kissed by ROMEO as the pilgrim, until ROMEO says, "then move not, while my prayer's effect I take," and kisses her, remarking, "Thus from my lips by thine my sin is purged". JULIET requests ROMEO to "Give me my sin again". ROMEO kisses her a second time.

NURSE arrives to tell JULIET that her mother craves a word, and so she departs. ROMEO questions NURSE and learns that JULIET's mother is Lady CAPULET and says to himself "My life is my foe's debt".

BENVOLIO and ROMEO decide it is prudent to leave the feast, but are confronted by Lord CAPULET, who tries to entice them to stay and see out the feast, but to no avail as they both exit the feast.

Exit ROMEO, BENVOLIO, and everyone, except JULIET and NURSE.

JULIET asks NURSE to identify the gentlemen exiting the feast, in particular, her new love, declaring "If he be married, my grave is like to be my wedding bed", - a premonition perhaps! NURSE tells JULIET that her new love is ROMEO, a MONTAGUE, the son of her great enemy. JULIET declares "My only love sprung from my only hate!"

NURSE calls to JULIET to come away.

[*End of ACT 1 scene 5* Summary]

The scene opens in Capulet's orchard; to one side the outer wall with a lane beyond, to the other Capulet's house showing an upper window with balcony, very late on Sunday night.

Enter ROMEO, alone in the lane, who then climbs the outer wall, and jumps into the orchard.

Enter BENVOLIO with MERCUTIO in the lane. ROMEO listens behind the wall.

BENVOLIO calls out to his cousin ROMEO but receives no reply. MERCUTIO thinks ROMEO has gone home to bed, but BENVOLIO is convinced that ROMEO has leapt the orchard wall and asks MERCUTIO to call again.

MERCUTIO replies that he will conjure ROMEO like summoning a spirit, calling out for ROMEO to show himself in the likeness of a sigh, to speak but one rhyme, to cry "aye me!", to pronounce but love and dove, to speak to Venus and say the nickname of her blind son and heir, Young Abraham Cupid.

MERCUTIO continues by citing King Cophetua who hearth not, stirrers not, moveth not, and declaring ROMEO as an ape who is dead. He is determined to conjure ROMEO, and continues to call out, "I conjure thee by Rosaline's bright eyes", and then by other parts of her body, but to no avail.

BENVOLIO remarks if ROMEO has heard MERCUTIO, it will him angry, but MERCUTIO is adamant that his invocations are fair and honest. BENVOLIO continues, he must have hidden himself among these trees, and justifies this by saying "Blind is his love and best befits the dark".

MERCUTIO retorts "If love be blind, love cannot hit the mark", and continues with lewd innuendos. BENVOLIO replies that it is time to go, and concludes it is pointless to seek ROMEO if he does not want to be found.

Exit BENVOLIO and MERCUTIO

[*End of ACT 2 scene 1* Summary]

The scene opens in front of the upper window of Capulet's house with JULIET on the balcony and ROMEO below in the garden, very late on Sunday night.

[This is the famous balcony scene, where ROMEO below woes JULIET above]

ROMEO remarks to himself, having listened to the conversation of this friend, it is easy to jest about scars that never felt a wound.

JULIET appears on the balcony.

ROMEO see her and starts his soliloquy comparing JULIET to light through yonder window breaks, the sun who kills the envious moon, who is sick with grief, and although she be a maid to the moon, JULIET is 'far more fair', and should cast off the moon's vestal livery. ROMEO continues his soliloquy by wanting her to know of his love for her, and although she does not speak, her beauty speaks for her. If two of the fairest stars in all the heaven were to have business elsewhere, they would entreat her eyes to twinkle in their place till they returned. Her cheek would shame those stars as daylight doth a lamp, and her eye in heaven would through the airy regions stream so bright that birds would sing and think it were not night. ROMEO wishes that he were a glove upon JULIET's hand so he might touch her cheek!

JULIET thinking about her new love, says to herself, "Ay me!" but is unaware that ROMEO is beneath the balcony.

ROMEO remarks, "She speaks" and continues his soliloquy by saying to himself, "O speak again, bright angel, for thou art as glorious to this night as is a winged messenger of heaven" who makes mortal men fall on their backs to look up and gaze on angels walking on clouds and sailing in the air.

JULIET starts her soliloquy and ROMEO listens with intent. She begins by saying "O Romeo, Romeo! Wherefore art thou Romeo?" and asks him to deny his father and refuse his name or if not, she will no longer be a Capulet.

ROMEO is in a quandary as to hear more or to speak and declare his love.

JULIET continues her soliloquy, debating what's in a name, and is it that important. JULIET eloquently says, "That which we call a rose, by any other name would smell as sweet." She concludes whether he is called Romeo or not, he retains that dear perfection, and his name is no part of him, ROMEO can take all of her in exchange.

ROMEO decides to speak and calls out "I take thee at thy word. Call me but love, and I'll be new baptised. Henceforth I never will be Romeo".

JULIET is startled and replies "What man art thou that, thus be screened in night, so stumbles on my counsel?"

ROMEO tells JULIET that he hates because his name is her enemy. JULIET responds that she recognises the sound of his voice, and art thou not Romeo, and a Montague? In respond, ROMEO says he is neither of those things if she dislikes them.

JULIET wants ROMEO to tell her how he came and why? She is puzzled because the orchard walls are high and hard to climb, and the place is death, considering who he is, should any of her kinsmen find him here.

ROMEO is unperturbed and says he has night's cloak to hide him from their eyes, and should they find him, his life was better ended by their hate, than death prorogued, wanting of Juliet's love.

ROMEO explains love lent him counsel and lent him eyes to showed him the way to Juliet's place. JULIET responds by declaring farewell to compliment and asking Romeo dost thou love me? retorting she knows he will say Ay, and for him to pronounce it faithfully, or if he thinks she is too quickly won, she will prove more true than those who act coy and play hard to get. JULIET continues by saying she was unaware that he overheard her declaration of love, and not attribute this to trivial love, which by chance the dark night hath so discovered.

ROMEO is keen to swear his love, but JULIET tells him not to swear because it is too rash, too unadvised, too sudden, too like the lightning, which doth cease to be. JULIET wants Romeo to give love's faithful vow again, declaring her bounty is as boundless as the sea, her love as deep.

NURSE calls to Juliet.

JULIET tells Romeo she hears a noise inside, and for him to stay a moment until she returns. ROMEO is afraid all is but a dream, too sweet to be real.

Enter JULIET instructing Romeo, if his bent of love be honourable, to send word where and what time tomorrow they are to wed.

NURSE calls to Juliet who bids Romeo a thousand times good night, then exits again.

ROMEO is distraught and yearns Juliet to return, which she does, saying "Oh, for a falconer's voice, to lure this tassel - Romeo - back again, and although she must be quiet, she would make the Echo in a cave repeat "My Romeo" until its voice was more hoarse than hers.

ROMEO tells Juliet to send a messenger to him at nine tomorrow. Both are willing to stand forever least either of them forget the appointed time of nine, but eventually, JULIET remarks it's almost morning, she would have Romeo gone, and yet no further than a wanton's bird, but so loving-jealous of his liberty.

ROMEO declares he would be that wanton bird, and JULIET declares so would she. JULIET continues saying "Good night, good night! Parting is such sweet sorrow."

Exit JULIET.

ROMEO wishes he like JULIET were in sleep and peace, so he could spend the night with Juliet. ROMEO declares he will go to his ghostly friar's close cell, his help to crave and his story to tell.

Exit ROMEO

[*End of ACT 2 scene 2* Summary]

The scene opens near the cell where FRIAR LAURENCE resides.

Enter FRIAR LAURENCE into his cell carrying a basket. He begins his soliloquy about the Earth and the morn and how the sun comes up and burns away the dew and how the Earth is mother to nature's tomb when living things die and womb when they are reborn. He continues by saying in herbs, plants, stones there is a powerful grace which to the earth some special good doth give unless this grace turns to vice by being misapplied but vice sometime by action dignified be renewed to its original virtue.

Enter ROMEO near the Friar's cell speaking to himself about the rind of this small flower and how within this infant rind, poison hath residence and medicine power. To smell, it cheers; to taste, it kills. In man as well as herbs - grace and rude will. There is virtue and vice in all things.

Enter ROMEO into the Friar's cell and greets FRIAR LAURENCE.

FRIAR LAURENCE is concerned as to why Romeo, unlike old men with worries who never get any sleep, is up so early instead of being in bed, like most young men without a care, and concludes if not up roused by some distemperature, he hath not been in bed tonight.

ROMEO admits the latter, and when asked, tells Friar Laurence that he had been with Rosaline but had forgot that name and that name's woe. ROMEO explains that he had been feasting with his enemy where on a sudden love hath wounded him, and that both lover's remedies lie with the holy friar even though her family is his foe.

FRIAR LAURENCE tells Romeo to speak plain because riddling confession finds but riddling shift. ROMEO explains he love is the fair daughter of rich Capulet, and he will tell the friar later about when and where and how they met but begs the friar to marry them today. FRIAR LAURENCE is aghast, and asks is Rosaline, whom thou didst love so dear, so soon forsaken, and then remarks young men's love lies not truly in their hearts, but in their eyes. After further remarks on salty tears thrown away in waste, and the sun not yet thy sighs from heaven clears, the friar asks Romeo to pronounce that women may fall when there's no strength in men, in other words, women will not be faithful to unreliable men.

FRIAR LAURENCE agrees to assist in the marriage, for this alliance may so happy prove, but tells Romeo to be wisely and slow because they stumble that run fast.

[*End of ACT 2 scene 3* Summary]

The scene opens in a public place in Verona on Monday morning.

Enter BENVOLIO and MERCUTIO discussing Romeo's blind love for Rosaline and the challenge to Romeo's life by Tybalt, kinsman to old Capulet, sent by letter to Romeo's father's house.

MERCUTIO is convinced Romeo is metaphorically dead, stabbed with a white wrench's black eye, shot through the ear with a love song, the very pin of his heart cleft by blind Cupid's arrow, and asks rhetorically if Romeo is a man to encounter Tybalt.

MERCUTIO replies to Benvolio that Tybalt is more than Prince of Cats, he is the courageous captain of compliments, an expert duellist, but a man he hates because of Tybalt's foreign accent, dress, and mannerisms.

Enter ROMEO. MERCUTIO remarks to Benvolio, he is like a dried herring without its eggs, and is ready for Petrarch's poetry. Compared to Juliet, Laura was a kitchen slave, Dido a dowdy, Cleopatra a gypsy, Helen and Hero hildings and harlots.

MERCUTIO greets Romeo with a French salutation of 'bonjour!', and remarks to Romeo that he gave Benvolio and himself the slip, to which Romeo replies his business was great. MERCUTIO is not convinced and there follows a witty conversation between Romeo and himself on the art of love making.

Enter NURSE with servant PETER into the public place.

ROMEO is pleased to see Nurse, but MERCUTIO make derogatory remarks saying to Peter to tell Nurse to hide her face, for her fan's the fairer face. NURSE who does not know Romeo, inquires his whereabouts, to desire some confidence with him. Despite lewd objections from Mercutio and Benvolio, ROMEO agrees to follow Nurse.

Exit BENVOLIO and MERCUTIO with the latter singing a mocking romantic song to Nurse.

ROMEO apologises to Nurse for Mercutio's derogatory remarks, saying he is a gentleman that loves to hear himself talk.

NURSE is still angry and says if Mercutio speaks anything against her, she will take him down and twenty such Jacks, and if she cannot, she finds those that shall. NURSE berates PETER for standing there and not defending honour, but is rebuffed by PETER, who denies he saw no man use her at his pleasure, and if he had, his weapon should quickly have been out, if he sees occasion in a good quarrel and the law on his side.

NURSE tells ROMEO that her young lady JULIET bids her to seek him out but first wants to tell him, if he should lead Juliet into a fool's paradise, it would be an outrage for the gentlewomen is young, and if he should deal double with her, truly it would be an ill thing to be offered to any gentlewoman, and very weak dealing. ROMEO protests, and NURSE assures him she will tell Juliet as much knowing that she will be a joyful woman.

ROMEO bids NURSE to devise some means to come to shrift (confession) this afternoon and there she shall at Friar Laurence' cell be shrived (confessed) and married. NURSE at first refuses money offered by Romeo for her services, then accepts, and tells ROMEO that JULIET this afternoon shall be there.

ROMEO bids NURSE to stay. He instructs her to tell JULIET that behind the abbey wall, within this hour his man shall be with them, bringing cords made like a tackled stair, which must be used at night to climb over the abbey wall.

NURSE asks ROMEO is his man secret because two may keep counsel, putting one away, but ROMEO assures her that his man is as true as steel.

NURSE informs ROMEO there is a nobleman in town, one PARIS, that would happily lay claim to her, but JULIET, good soul, see him as a toad, although she angers her sometimes, and tells her that PARIS is the proper man.

They say their farewells. Exit all.

[*End of ACT 2 scene 4* Summary]

The scene opens in Capulet's orchard, at noon on Monday morning.

Enter JULIET and begins her soliloquy as she anxiously awaits NURSE's return, wondering whether Nurse can't find Romeo or is lame as it is three long hours, yet she has not come. Love's messengers should be thoughts, which ten times faster glide than the sun's beams, and had Nurse been youthful, she would be as swift in motion as a ball, bouncing words between the lovers, but old folk, many feign as they were dead, unwieldy, slow, heavy, and pale as lead.

Enter NURSE and PETER into the orchard. JULIET exclaims O God, she comes, what news, hast thou met with him, send Peter away.

Exit PETER who is instructed by NURSE to stay at the orchard gate.

JULIET is eager to extract the news NURSE has, but NURSE complains I am aweary, give me leave awhile, how my bones ache, what a jaunt, do you not see that I am out of breath? JULIET rebukes NURSE saying the excuse she makes in her delay is longer than the news itself and wants to know if the news is good or bad.

NURSE tells JULIET she has made a simple choice, and she knows not how to choose a man because although his features, face, leg, hand, foot, body are past compare, he is not the flower of courtesy but warrants him as gentle as a lamb. NURSE finishes by telling JULIET to go her own way, serve God, and finishes by asking JULIET if she had dined.

JULIET says emphatically No, no and wants to know about the marriage, but NURSE prevaricates claiming her head aches and is about to fall in twenty pieces, her back aches, cursing Juliet's heart for sending her to catch death by jaunting up and down to find Romeo.

NURSE tells JULIET that Romeo is like an honest gentleman, courteous, kind, handsome, virtuous, and asks JULIET has she leave to go to shrift (confession) today because there stays a husband to make her a wife, and she must climb a ladder when it is dark hence to Friar Laurence' cell go.

[*End of ACT 2 scene 5* Summary]

The scene opens at Friar Laurence' cell, late on Monday afternoon.

Enter FRIAR LAURENCE who recites so smile the heavens upon this holy act, and ROMEO who responds with Amen, amen.

ROMEO tells the FRIAR but come what sorrow can, it cannot countervail the exchange of joy that one short minute gives in her sight, and that once the FRIAR has closed their hands with holy words, then not even love-devouring death can stop him calling Juliet his.

FRIAR LAURENCE reminds ROMEO these violent delights have violent ends, and in their triumph die, therefore love moderately, as doth long love, not too swift and not too slow.

Enter JULIET, somewhat fast, and embraces ROMEO.

FRIAR LAURENCE remarks here, comes the lady, oh so light on foot will never wear out the everlasting flint pavement, will walk on the gossamers, spiderwebs, that idles in the wanton summer air and yet not fall. So light is vanity.

JULIET greets her ghostly confessor, FRIAR LAURENCE, who tells her that ROMEO will thank her for them both. JULIET reciprocates the thanks.

ROMEO addresses JULIET by saying if the measure of her joy be heaped like his, let rich music's tongue unfold the imagined happiness that both receive either by this dear encounter of marriage.

JULIET replies conceit is but a beggar, but within her true love has grown to such excess, she cannot sum up half her joy in words.

FRIAR LAURENCE tells both ROMEO and JULIET to come with him for they shall not stay alone till holy church incorporate two to one in marriage.

[*End of ACT 2 scene 6* Summary]

The scene opens in a public place in Verona, late on Monday afternoon.

Enter MERCUTIO with his page, BENVOLIO, and other men.

BENVOLIO tells MURCUTIO the day is hot, so they should retire, the Capulet's are elsewhere, and if they meet, there will be a brawl because hot days makes men's tempers fray. MERCUTIO responds with an analogy of a man who enters a bar, and claps his sword on the table, but waits to draw his sword on this second drink for no reason. The conservation continues about mood and how quarrels start caused by trivial events. MERCUTIO cites examples such as a quarrel with a man that hath a hair more or a hair less in his beard than thou hast, or a quarrel with a man for coughing in the street because he hath wakened thy dog that hath lain asleep in the sun, or with another, for tying his new shoes with old ribbon? MERCUTIO concludes by saying indignantly to BENVOLIO, "and yet thou wilt tutor me from quarrelling!"

Enter TYBALT and other Capulets, who are recognised by BENVOLIO.

TYBALT tells his followers to follow him because he wants to speak to BENVOLIO and MERCUTIO.

MERCUTIO tells TYBALT to couple his word with them with something like a physical blow, but TYBALT retorts with give him a reason to do so and continues to exploit the exchange of words with allusions to to them being minstrels before BENVOLIO tells TYBALT to either withdraw unto some private place, or reason coldly of their grievances, or else depart.

Enter ROMEO.

TYBALT recognises ROMEO and calls him a villain, but ROMEO retorts that he has reason to love him and will excuse the rage appertaining, telling TYBALT that he, ROMEO, is no villain, and, therefore, bids TYBALT farewell because he sees TYBALT know'st him not.

TYBALT is determined to start a fight and replies this shall not excuse the injuries caused by ROMEO's disrespect and invites ROMEO to turn and draw his sword. ROMEO retorts I do protest I never injured thee, but love thee better than thou canst devise, till thou shalt know the reason of my love, so good Capulet be satisfied.

MERCUTIO draws his sword, telling TYBALT to calm his dishonourable, vile submission, calling him a "ratcatcher" and asking him will he walk, or he, MERCUTIO, will take one of TYBALT's nine lives, and if not satisfied, beat the remaining eight from this rat-catcher, King of Cats. MERCUTIO tells TYBALT to make haste and pluck his sword out of his pilcher, scabbard, or his sword will be about TYBALT's ear instead.

ROMEO intervenes telling MERCUTIO to put his rapier up, but MERCUTIO tells TYBALT to start his passado, forward sword thrust.

MERCUTIO and TYBALT fight. ROMEO tells BENVOLIO to draw his sword and beat their weapons because there is no need to fight, and the PRINCE expressly hath forbidden bandying in Verona streets.

TYBALT under ROMEO's arm fatally wounds MERCUTIO and hurries away.

ROMEO tells MERCUTIO courage, man, the hurt cannot be much, but MERCUTIO disagrees saying ask for me tomorrow, and you shall find me a grave man. He continues with a plague o' both your houses, Capulet and Montague's, and to ROMEO "why the devil came you between us, I was hurt under your arm". MERCUTIO asks BENVOLIO to help him into some house or he will faint, saying they have made work's meat of me.

BENVOLIO helps MERCUTIO away, while ROMEO rebukes himself for MERCUTIO's demise, this gentleman, the prince's near ally, his own reputation stained with Tybalt's slander who been his kinsman that an hour, although TYBALT did not know it. And ROMEO regrets that O sweet JULIET, her beauty hath made him effeminate, and in his temper softened his bravery, which was as hard as steel.

BENVOLIO returns informing ROMEO brave MERCUTIO is dead, remarking that his gallant spirit hath aspired the clouds. ROMEO in remorse and turmoil replies, this day's black fate will determine future outcomes, this but begins the woe others must suffer.

TYBALT returns and ROMEO proclaims away to heaven, respective levity, and fire-eyed fury be my conduct now! Addressing TYBALT, ROMEO proclaims Mercutio soul is a little way above our heads, staying for Tybalt to keep him company, either you or I, or both, must go with him.

ROMEO and TYBALT fight, but TYBALT dies.

BENVOLIO tells ROMEO away, be gone, the citizens are up, and TYBALT slain, the PRINCE will "doom thee death".

Exit ROMEO claiming O, I am Fortune's fool.

Enter CITIZENS of the watch, asking, where is TYBALT that killed MERCUTIO, which way did that murderer ran. BENVOLIO tells them there lies that TYBALT. The CITIZEN of the watch tells TYBALT to get up, he is charged in the PRINCE's name, but there is no response, TYBALT is dead.

Enter the PRINCE, Lord and Lady MONTAGUE, Lord and Lady CAPULET, and others.

The PRINCE demands, where are the vile men of this fray. BENVOLIO responds by telling the PRINCE the unfortunate circumstances of this fatal bawl, pointing out there lies TYBALT slain by young ROMEO, that slew thy kinsman, brave MERCUTIO.

LADY CAPULET is in anguish on hearing the news, and pleads that the PRINCE, as thou art true, shed blood of Montague, as revenge for Capulet's bloodshed.

The PRINCE asks BENVOLIO who began this bloody fray, to which BENVOLIO explained in detail the sequence of events leading to first the death of MERCUTIO by TYBALT, then the death of TYBALT by ROMEO.

LADY CAPULET objects citing that BENVOLIO is a kinsman to MONTAGUES, and thus affection makes him false. She begs the PRINCE for justice and demands that ROMEO must not live.

LORD MONTAGUE intercedes saying that ROMEO was MERCUTIO friend, and did what the law would have done, end TYBALT life for committing murder.

The PRINCE decrees that ROMEO for that offence, immediately we do exile him hence, otherwise, when he is found, that hour is his last.

[*End of ACT 3 scene 1* Summary]

The scene opens in Capulet's house, on Monday evening.

Enter JULIET who begins her soliloquy impatient for cloudy night immediately, and for ROMEO to leap into her arms because at night lovers can see to do their amorous rites. JULIET continues by saying when she dies, take ROMEO and cut him out in little stars, and he will make the face of heaven so fine that all the world will be in love with night, and pay no worship to the garish sun. JULIET finally concludes O, I have bought the mansion of love, but not possessed it, and though I am sold, not yet enjoyed. So tedious is this day to an impatient child that hath new robes and may not wear them. JULIET calls to NURSE.

Enter NURSE with the rope ladder, but JULIET asks NURSE: why dost thou wring thy hands. NURSE responds that: we are undone, ROMEO is dead. JULIET retorts: can heaven be so envious? JULIET is unsure if ROMEO has killed himself or been killed. NURSE reveals that she is talking about JULIET's cousin TYBALT, and that ROMEO has been banished for killing TYBALT.

JULIET is distraught and describes ROMEO in many guises: O serpent heart hid with a flowering face, beautiful tyrant, fiend angelical, dove-feathered raven, wolfish-ravening lamb, a damned saint, an honourable villain, Oh, that deceit should dwell in such a gorgeous palace, namely, Romeo.

NURSE concurs remaking: there's no trust, no faith, no honesty in men, all perjured, all forsworn, all naughty, all dissemblers; shame come to Romeo! JULIET rebukes NURSE for such a wish, and herself to chide at him.

NURSE tells Juliet: will you speak well of him that killed your cousin? JULIET retorts: shall I speak ill of him that is my husband? JULIET then debates who is villain, ROMEO or TYBALT, and views ROMEO's banishment worse than death.

NURSE tells JULIET that her parents are weeping and wailing over TYBALT's corpse. JULIET responds by saying: wash they his wounds with tears? Mine shall be spent, when theirs are dry, for ROMEO's banishment.

JULIET instructs NURSE to find ROMEO and bid him come to take his last farewell.

[*End of ACT 3 scene 2* Summary]

The scene opens in FRIAR LAURENCE's cell, later on Monday evening.

Enter FRIAR LAURENCE and bids ROMEO to come forth, thou fearful man, thou art wedded to calamity. ROMEO enters from the friar's study at the back of the cell, anxious to know what news about his doom from the PRINCE.

FRIAR LAURENCE responds: A gentler judgment vanished from his lips, not body's death, but body's banishment. ROMEO is dismayed by the news: For exile hath more terror in his look, much more than death.

FRIAR tells ROMEO: Hence from Verona art thou banished; be patient, for the world is broad and wide. ROMEO counters: There is no world without Verona walls, but purgatory, torture, hell itself. FRIAR rebukes ROMEO telling him that banishment is dear mercy, but he does not see it.

ROMEO disagrees: 'Tis torture and not mercy; Heaven is here where Juliet lives, but Romeo may not. ROMEO is in turmoil and tells the FRIAR: Thou canst not speak of that thou dost not feel.

Enter NURSE after repeated knocks, to inquire about ROMEO's whereabouts. FRIAR tells NURSE: There on the ground, with his own tears made drunk. NURSE responds: Even so lies she, JULIET, blubbering and weeping.

ROMEO still in turmoil, feeling remorseful that he murdered one of JULIET's kinsman, TYBALT, consequently damaging her love for him, offers to stab himself, but NURSE intervenes, snatching the dagger away.

FRIAR LAURENCE addresses ROMEO telling him to pull himself together; act like a man; accept that you killed TYBALT; will you commit the sin of killing yourself; why complain about birth, heaven and earth; get up, your JULIET is alive; go be with your love, then escape to the city of Mantua, until the PRINCE pardons you. FRIAR LAURENCE instructs NURSE to tell JULIET: Romeo is coming.

[*End of ACT 3 scene 3* Summary]

The scene opens in Capulet's house, late on Monday night.

Enter Lord and Lady CAPULET together with PARIS.

LORD CAPULET tells PARIS that with the unfortunate death of TYBALT, whom JULIET loved dearly, there had been no time to approach his daughter about marriage, but the lateness of the hour, precludes JULIET coming down to see him.

PARIS concurs, telling Lord and Lady CAPULET: These times of woe afford no time to woo; Commend me to your daughter.

LADY CAPULET replies she will know JULIET's mind early tomorrow.

LORD CAPULET tells PARIS that he will vouch for his child's love, and she will be ruled in all respect by his direction.

LORD CAPULET tells his wife to go to JULIET and acquaint her of PARIS' love and bid her on Thursday she will be married to this noble earl.

He continues by saying we'll keep no great celebration, just invite a friend or two, so as not to show disrespect to the demise of TYBALT.

He then asks PARIS: what say you to Thursday? PARIS replies: My Lord, I would that Thursday were tomorrow.

[*End of ACT 3 scene 4* Summary]

The scene opens at JULIET's window, at dawn on Tuesday, after ROMEO and JULIET had spent the night together.

Enter ROMEO and JULIET, they stand by JULIET's balcony window.

JULIET thinks it is the nightingale, not the lark that pierced the ear, but ROMEO disagrees saying: It was the lark, the herald of the mourn; Night's candles are burnt out. But JULIET does not want ROMEO to be gone, but to stay a few more hours claiming: Yond light is not daylight; It is some meteor that the sun exhaled to be to thee this night a torchbearer, and light thee on the way to Mantua.

ROMEO tells JULIET: Let me be taken, let me be put to death. He continues by telling JULIET: yon Gray is not the morning's eye (light), 'Tis but the pale reflex of Cynthia's brow (the crescent moon); Let's talk, it is not day.

JULIET concurs, remarking: Some say the lark makes sweet division, this doth not so, for she divideth us. Eventually, now concerned for ROMEO safety, JULIET tells ROMEO: O now be gone! More light and more light it grows.

ROMEO reciprocates, "More light and light, more dark and dark our woes".

Enter NURSE hastily to tell JULIET that the day is broke and her mother is on her way.

ROMEO and JULIET kiss, he descends the balcony on the corded ladder, and exchange farewells, both feeling sad, pale and apprehensive about what the future holds. JULIET foresees ROMEO: As one dead in the bottom of a tomb.

Enter LADY CAPULET to tell JULIET to stop weeping for TYBALT, her cousin's death, claiming: Some grief shows much of love, but much grief shows still want of wit.

LADY CAPULET tells JULIET she must not weep for her friend ROMEO who is but a villain who slaughtered her cousin TYBALT. JULIET retorts ROMEO is no villain and says: God pardon him! I do, with all my heart. JULIET continues: Would none but I might venge my cousin's death!

LADY CAPULET retorts: We will have vengeance for it, fear thou not; Then weep no more; I'll send to one in Mantua, where that same banished runagate doth live; Shall give him such an unaccustomed dram that he soon keeps TYBALT company; And then, I hope, thou wilt be satisfied.

JULIET falsely acquiesces to her mother's vengeful hate and shows her willingness to assist in Romeo's death: I never shall be satisfied with ROMEO, till I behold him - dead; If you could find out but a man to bear a poison, I would temper it that ROMEO should upon receipt thereof soon sleep in quiet; To wreak the love I bore my cousin TYBALT upon his body that hath slaughtered him.

LADY CAPULET changes the topic of conversation by telling JULIET that her father has put her from her heaviness, by arranging for her to be the joyful bride to PARIS, the gallant young noble gentlemen, at Saint Peter's Church next Thursday morn.

JULIET is horrified replying: Now by Saint Peter's Church, and Peter too, he shall not make me a joyful bride; It shall be ROMEO, whom you know I hate, rather than PARIS.

LADY CAPULET responds: Here comes your father, tell him so yourself, and see how he will take it at your hands.

Enter NURSE and LORD CAPULET who begins his soliloquy: When the sun sets, the air drizzles dew; For still the eyes, which I may call the sea, do ebb and flow with tears; the bark thy body is, sailing in this salt food; the winds thy sighs, who, raging with thy tears, without a sudden calm will overset thy tempest-tossed body. LORD CAPULET concludes by asking his wife the response to the married proposal.

LADY CAPULET, in response, tells her husband: I would the fool were married to her grave! He replies by asking: Doth she not give us thank? Is she nor proud? Doth she not count her blessed, so worthy a gentleman to be her bride?

JULIET counters: Proud can I never be of what I hate, but thankful even for hate that is meant love.

Exit LORD CAPULET having warned his daughter that if she does not marry PARIS, he will disown and evict her.
Exit LADY CAPULET rejecting her daughter's plea to delay the marriage for a month, a week else make the bridal bed in that dim monument where TYBALT lies.

Exit NURSE having told JULIET that ROMEO is a dishclout compared to PARIS, and that the second marriage should make her happy unlike the first.

Exit JULIET who feels betrayed by NURSE for now rejecting ROMEO, and if all else fails, will take her own life. She now goes to FRIAR LAURENCE to seek help.

[*End of ACT 3 scene 5* Summary]

The scene opens at Friar Laurence' cell on Tuesday morning.

Enter FRIAR LAURENCE and PARIS discussing the marriage on Thursday.

PARIS tells FRIAR LAURENCE his father Capulet will have it so, and in haste, but the FRIAR questions whether PARIS knows JULIET's mind, and replies: uneven is the course, I like it not. PARIS responds by saying: Immoderately she weeps for Tybalt's death; for Venus (love) smiles not in a house of tears; her father counts it dangerous, and in his wisdom haste's our marriage.

FRIAR LAURENCE to himself regrets knowing the true reason why it should not be in haste, because he had already married JULIET to ROMEO.

Enter JULIET who exchanges pleasantries with PARIS who tries to get JULIET to confess her love for him but fails.

FRIAR LAURENCE intervenes and tells PARIS it is time for him to leave as he is ready to hear JULIET's confession.

Exit PARIS saying: God shield I should disturb devotion!

FRIAR LAURENCE tells JULIET he already knows her grief, it strains his wits as to what to do to prorogue (delay) her marriage on Thursday to PARIS.

JULIET is distraught threatening to kill herself with her knife if the FRIAR cannot give her some present counsel on how to prevent the marriage, otherwise her bloody knife will play the umpire, arbitrating in favour of death if he can no issue of true honour bring.

FRIAR LAURENCE responds to this desperate threat by telling JULIET: Hold, daughter, I do spy a kind of hope. The FRIAR tells her: If rather than to marry PARIS, thou hast the strength of will to stay thyself; then is it likely thou wilt undertake a thing like death to chide away this shame; An if thou darest, I'll give thee remedy.

JULIET becomes hopefully, saying: O, bid me leap, rather than marry PARIS, from off the battlements of yonder tower; Or bid me lurk where serpents are; chain me with roaring bears; Or bid me go into a new-made grave and hide me with a dead man in his shroud; And I will do it without fear or doubt to live an unstained wife to my sweet love (Romeo).

FRIAR LAURENCE responds and tells JULIET to: Hold, then; Go home, be merry; Give consent to marry Paris; Wednesday is tomorrow; Tomorrow night look that thou lie alone; Let not the NURSE lie with thee in thy chamber.

The FRIAR then shows her a vial.

He continues to tell her: Take thou this vial, being then in bed, and this distilled liquor drink thou off; When presently through all thy veins shall run, a cold and drowsy humour; No warmth, no breath shall testify thou livest; And in this borrowed likeness of shrunk death, thou shalt continue two and forty hours, and then awake as from a pleasant sleep.

He continues by telling JULIET: Now when the bridegroom in the morning comes, to rouse thee from thy bed, there art thou dead; Thou shalt be borne to that ancient vault where all the kindred of the Capulet lie.

The FRIAR completes the plan by telling her: In the meantime, shall ROMEO by my letters know our drift, and hither shall he come; And he and I will watch thy waking, and that very night shall ROMEO bear thee hence to Mantua.

The FRIAR concludes: And this shall free thee from this present shame, if no inconstant toy or womanish fear abate thy valour in the acting it.

JULIET responds with keenness: Give me, give me! O tell not me of fear!

JULIET takes the vial and says: Love give me strength, and strength shall help afford.

[*End of ACT 4 scene 1* Summary]

The scene opens in Capulet's house later on Tuesday evening.

Enter Lord and Lady CAPULET, Nurse, and two Serving men.

LORD CAPULET instructs one Serving man to invite all the guests on the list, and the second Serving man to hire twenty cunning (skilled) cooks. When CAPULET inquires how he know he will get cunning cooks, the Serving man tells him that the cunning cook will lick his fingers to check the taste.

Exit the Serving men.

Nurse tells LORD CAPULET that JULIET has gone to FRIAR LAURENCE who replies by saying: Well, he may chance to do some good on her.

Enter JULIET who replies to her father's question, telling him she has returned from a place: Where I have learnt me to repent the sin of disobedient opposition to you and your behests. JULIET falls to her knees and continues: And am enjoined by holy LAURENCE to fall prostrate here to beg your pardon; Pardon, I beseech you! Henceforward I am ever ruled by you.

LORD CAPULET responds by saying: Send for the county (PARIS); Go tell him of this; I'll have this knot (marriage) knit up tomorrow morning (Wednesday).

JULIET tells her father she had met the youthful Lord at FRIAR LAURENCE's cell, giving him what becomes (proper) love, I might, not stepping o'er the bounds of modesty.

In responds, LORD CAPULET tells his daughter to stand up, and remarks; Now, afore God, this reverend holy friar! Our whole city is much bound to him.

JULIET asks NURSE to help her sort such needful ornaments (garments) fit for the wedding. LADY CAPULET interjects: No, not till Thursday; There is time enough. But LORD CAPULET is adamant not to lose the opportunity of an early marriage, insists: Go, Nurse; Go with her; We'll to church tomorrow.

Exit JULIET and Nurse. Exit LADY CAPULET after remarking to her husband: We shall be short in our provision.

LORD CAPULET concludes: My heart is wondrous light since this same wayward girl is so reclaimed.

[*End of ACT 4 scene 2* Summary]

The scene opens in JULIET's bedroom, the bed curtains still closed, on Tuesday night.

Enter JULIET and NURSE.

JULIET asks NURSE to leave her to herself tonight, for she needs to say many orisons (prayers) to move the heavens to smile upon her state, which as well NURSE knows, is cross (troubled) and full of sin.

Enter LADY CAPULET who asks her daughter is she busy, and does she need help.

JULIET requests now to be left alone and let NURSE this night sit up with mother.

Exit LADY CAPULET and NURSE leaving JULIET to express her inner hopes and fears in a soliloquy.

JULIET begins her soliloquy by expressing her doubts about what she intends to do next: I have a faint cold fear thrills through my veins that almost freezes up the heat of life; I'll call them back to comfort me; My dismal scene I needs must act alone.

JULIET continues with apprehension: Come, vial; What if this mixture does not work at all?

JULIET continues with suspicion: What if it be a poison, which the FRIAR subtly hath ministered to have me dead, lest in this marriage he should be dishonoured because he married me before to ROMEO?

JULIET counters this suspicion: And yet, methinks, it should not, for he hath still been tried a holy man.

JULIET continues with the terror of being in a tomb: Shall I not, then, be stifled in the vault, to whose foul mouth no health-some air breathes in; The horrible conceit of death and night, together with the terror of the place; Where bloody TYBALT, yet but green in earth, lies festering in his shroud.

JULIET concludes her soliloquy with: At some hours in the night spirit's resort; So early waking, what with loathsome smells; Methinks I see my cousin's ghost seeking out ROMEO, that did spit his body upon a rapier's point; ROMEO! Here's drink, I drink to thee.

[JULIET *drinks and fall down on the bed hidden by the bed curtains*]

[*End of ACT 4 scene 3* Summary]

The scene opens in the Hall of Capulet's house at three o'clock on Wednesday morning, on the day of the wedding.

Enter LADY CAPULET and NURSE into the banqueting hall.

LADY CAPULET tells NURSE to take these keys and fetch more spices. NURSE makes known that they call for dates and quinces in the pastry.

Enter LORD CAPULET calling to all present to: Come on, stir, stir, stir! 'Tis three o'clock. Look to the baked meats, good Angelica; Spare not for the cost.
NURSE responds by telling the LORD; Go, you cot-quean (housewife), go; Get you to bed, faith; You'll be sick tomorrow for this night's watching.

CAPULET disagrees: No, not a whit, what; I have watched ere now all night for lesser cause, and ne'er been sick.

LADY CAPULET remarks she knows her husband has been a mouse-hunt (ladies man) in his time, but she will make sure he does not stay up any later now. Exit LADY CAPULET and NURSE.

CAPULET replies in jest: A jealous hood (woman), a jealous hood!

Enter four Serving men with spits and logs and baskets.

CAPULET inquires: Now fellow, what is there? The First Serving man replies: Things for the cook, sir, but I know not what. CAPULET tells him to make haste, make haste. To the Second Serving man, CAPULET instructs: Fetch drier logs; Call Peter; He will show thee where they are. The Second Serving man replies: I have a head, sir, that will find out logs, and never trouble PETER for the matter. Exit both Serving men.

CAPULET jests: Thou shalt be loggerhead. He remarks: Good faith, 'tis day; The county (PARIS) will be here with music straight. He calls for NURSE and his WIFE.

Enter NURSE.

CAPULET tells her: Go waken JULIET; Go and trim her up; I'll go and chat with PARIS; Make haste; The bridegroom he is come already.

[*End of ACT 4 scene 4* Summary]

The scene opens in JULIET's bedroom, the curtains still closed about the bed, on Wednesday morning, the day of the wedding.

Enter NURSE who tries to wake JULIET says to herself: I bet she's fast asleep; Tomorrow night, I bet, Count PARIS won't let you get much rest. NURSE suddenly observes that JULIET is still dressed in her clothes and realises JULIET is dead, and stricken by panic, calls out to LORD and LADY CAPULET.

Enter LADY CAPULET who on seeing her daughter cries out: My child, my only life; Revive, look up, or I will die with thee!

Enter LORD CAPULET who requests: For shame, bring JULIET forth; Her Lord (PARIS) is come. First NURSE, then LADY CAPULET announce JULIET's death.

LORD CAPULET in shock and remorse, utters she's cold; Her blood is settled, and her joints are stiff; Death lies on her like an untimely frost upon the sweetest flower of all the field.

NURSE responds with: O lamentable day! LADY CAPULET with: O woeful time.

LORD CAPULET concludes: Death, that hath taken her hence to make me wail, ties up my tongue and will not let me speak.

Enter FRIAR LAURENCE, County PARIS, and Musicians.

When asked by the FRIAR is the bride ready to go to church, LORD CAPULET replies mournfully: Ready to go, but never to return; Hath death lain with thy wife; There she lies, flower as she was, deflowered by him.

He continues by saying: Death is my son-in-law; Death is my heir; My daughter he hath wedded; all is Death's.

PARIS cannot believe the news saying: Have I thought long to see this morning's face, and doth it give me such a sight as this?

LADY CAPULET and NURSE both lament the accursed, unhappy, wretched, hateful day! Never was seen so black a day as this. O woeful day!

PARIS begins his soliloquy on Death's cruel heart: Beguiled, divorced, wronged, spited, slain! Most detestable Death, by thee beguiled, by cruel, cruel thee quite overthrown!; Not life, but love in death.

LORD CAPULET still distraught, riles against Dead: Despised, distressed, hated, martyred, killed! Why cam'st thou now to murder, murder, our solemnity; Dead art thou; Alack (curse), my child is dead, and with my child my joys are buried!

FRIAR LAURENCE interjects to bring understanding and compassion to this sorrowful event. He tells all that heaven has JULIET and she is now in a better place. He continues by telling all that they could not prevent her from dead, but heaven will give her eternal life. He criticises all for promoting their heaven on JULIET by getting her to marry into wealth and power.

The FRIAR tells all: And weep ye now, seeing she is advanced above the clouds, as high as heaven itself? He continues by saying: In this love, you love your child so ill, that you run mad, seeing that she is well (in heaven).

To mitigate the tragedy, he comments that it is best to marry well and die young than to be married for a long time.

The FRIAR continues to tell all: Dry up your tears; And in her best array (clothes), bear her to church. His concludes by saying: For though fond nature bids us all lament, yet nature's tears are reason's merriment.

LORD CAPULET in a solemn mood recites his mournful soliloquy:

All things that we ordained festival, turn from this office to black funeral,
Our instruments to melancholy bells,
Our wedding cheer to a sad burial feast,
Our solemn hymns to sullen dirges change,
Our bridal flower serve for a buried corse (corpse),
And all things change them to the contrary.

FRIAR LAURENCE directs all to prepare to follow this fair corse unto her grave, claiming the heavens do lour (anger) upon for some ill, move them no more by crossing their high will (judgement).

Exit LORD and LADY CAPULET, PARIS, and FRIAR LAURENCE, after casting rosemary on JULIET and shutting the curtains.
NURSE concurs with the First Musician for them to put up their pipes for this a pitiful case of sadness.

Exit NURSE and Enter PETER who tells the three Musician to play 'Heart's ease' because his heart is full of woe. After much dispute and wit as to what should be played, the First Musician finally calls PETER a pestilential knave. The Second Musician tells all: Hang him, Jack; Come, we'll in here, tarry (wait) for the mourners and stay dinner.

[*End of ACT 4 scene 5* Summary]

The scene opens on a street in Mantua on Wednesday morning.

Enter ROMEO who begins his soliloquy.

ROMEO starts by saying to himself: If I may trust the flattering truth of sleep, My dreams presage some joyful news at hand; I dreamt my lady came and found me dead; And breathed such life with kisses in my lips that I revived

and was an emperor. ROMEO concludes: How sweet is love itself possessed when but love's shadows are so rich in joy!

Enter ROMEO's man BALTHASAR.

ROMEO is impatient to know the news from Verona, asking: Dost thou not bring me letters from the FRIAR? How doth my lady? Is my father well? How fares my JULIET? For nothing can be ill if she be well.

BALTHASAR tells ROMEO the sad news, saying: Her body sleeps in Capulets' monument; And her immortal part with angels' lives.

ROMEO replies: Then I defy you, stars!

He tells BALTHASAR to give him ink and paper; hire post (immediately)

Horses, as he will hence tonight ride to Verona. ROMEO rejects BALTHASAR protestations, saying: No matter; Get thee gone.

Exit BALTHASAR.

ROMEO begins a new soliloquy about his grief and intent: Well, JULIET, I will lie with thee tonight; O mischief, thou art swift to enter in the thoughts of desperate men! I do remember an apothecary (pharmacist), and hereabouts he dwells.

ROMEO describes the Apothecary in tattered clothes, with overwhelming (eye-)brows, merger were his looks, sharp misery had worn him to the bones. In his shop a tortoise hung, an alligator stuffed, and other skins of ill-shaped fishes, and above his shelves a beggarly account of empty boxes, green earthen pots, bladders, and musty seeds, remnants of packthread, and old cakes of roses were thinly scattered, to make up a show. Noting this penury, ROMEO reasoned that if a man did need a poison now, this Apothecary would sell it to him. Eventually, ROMEO finds the shop.

Enter APOTHECARY.

ROMEO enters the shop, tells the APOTHECARY he can see thou art poor, and offers forty ducats for a dram of fast acting poison as will disperse itself through all the veins that the life-weary taker may fall dead, as violently as gunpowder fired from the inside of a cannon.

The APOTHECARY informs ROMEO: Such mortal drugs I have, but Mantua's law is death to any he that utters (sells) them.

ROMEO counters: Famine is in thy cheeks; Contempt and beggary hangs upon thy back; The world affords no law to make thee rich; Then be not poor but break it and take this (the forty ducats).

APOTHECARY accepts saying: My poverty, but not my will, consents.

ROMEO replies: I pay thy poverty and not thy will.

The APOTHECARY gives ROMEO the poison and tells him to put it in any liquid he will drink, and, if he had the strength of twenty men, it would dispatch him straight away.

ROMEO gives the APOTHECARY money justifying the purchase by saying: There is thy gold, worse poison to men's souls, doing more murder in this loathsome world, than these poor compounds that thou mayst not sell.

ROMEO continues by telling the APOTHECARY to buy food and get flesh on himself.

Finally, ROMEO ends by saying: Come, cordial and not poison, go with me to JULIET's grave, for there must I use thee.

[*End of ACT 5 scene 1* Summary]

The scene opens in FRIAR LAURENCE's cell on Wednesday night.

Enter FRIAR JOHN who calls out to FRIAR LAURENCE.

Enter FRIAR LAURENCE who asks: What says ROMEO?

FRIAR JOHN explains that he was unable to deliver FRIAR LAURENCE's letter to ROMEO because while going to find a barefoot brother, there in Verona, and finding him, the searches of the town, suspecting that they both were in a house where the infectious pestilence did reign, sealed up the doors and would not let them forth. So it was not possible to get to Mantua to hand the letter to ROMEO.

FRIAR JOHN returns the letter to FRIAR LAURENCE who is concerned that without reading the letter, ROMEO will not know of JULIET's ruse to fake death, and therefore cause much danger. He instructs FRIAR JOHN to go hence, get an iron crow (crowbar) and bring it straight to his cell.

Exit FRIAR JOHN.

FRIAR LAURENCE says to himself: Now must I to the monument (tomb) alone; Within this three hours will fair JULIET wake; She will beshrew (curse) me much that ROMEO hath had no notice of these accidents (happenings); But I will write again to Mantua, and keep her at my cell till ROMEO come; Poor living corse (JULIET), closed in a dead man's tomb!

[*End of ACT 5 scene 2* Summary]

The scene opens in the churchyard where stands the Capulet's monument, late on Wednesday night.

Enter PARIS with his PAGE, who bears flowers and a torch.

PARIS instructs the PAGE to put out his torch, give it to him, then hide under yon yew trees, holding his ear close to the hollow ground to hear any foot upon the churchyard tread, and whistle as a signal that thou hear'st something approach.

PARIS tells the PAGE to give him the flowers and do as he bid. The PAGE remarks: I am almost afraid to stand alone here in the churchyard, yet I will adventure.

PARIS scatters flowers at JULIET closed tomb, and in verse says:
    Sweet flower, with flowers thy bridal bed I strew
    O woe! Thy canopy is dust and stones
    Which with sweet water nightly I will dew
    Or, wanting that, with tears distilled by moans
    The obsequies that I for thee will keep
    Nightly shall be to strew thy grave and weep

Suddenly the PAGE whistles, and PARIS remarks: What cursed foot wanders this way tonight to cross my obsequies and true love's rite? PARIS moves away from the tomb.

Enter ROMEO and BALTHASAR, who bears a torch, a mattock (pickaxe), and a wrenching iron (crowbar).

ROMEO instructs BALTHASAR to give him the mattock and the wrenching iron, and to take this letter, early in the morning, to his father.
ROMEO takes the torch from BALTHASAR, charging him upon his life not to interrupt whatever he hears or sees, but to stay away.

He tells BALTHASAR that why he descends into this bed of death (the tomb) is in part to behold his lady's face, but chiefly to take thence from her dead finger a precious ring, which he must use for an important purpose.

He then tells BALTHASAR to be gone, and not to pry, otherwise he will tear him joint by joint, and strew this hungry churchyard with his limbs because the time and his intents are savage, wild, more fierce and more inexorable fat than empty tigers or the roaring sea.

ROMEO gives BALTHASAR money and tells him to live and be prosperous, but BALTHASAR taking no heed of ROMEO's threat, decides to hide nearby saying: His looks I fear, and his intents I doubt.

ROMEO begins to open the tomb with the mattock and wrenching iron, ranting at the tomb:
    Thou detestable maw, thou womb of death;
    Gorged with the dearest morsel of the earth;
    Thus I enforce thy rotten jaws to open.

PARIS observing from a distance, remarks:
    This is that banished haughty Montague;
    That murdered my love's cousin;
    with which grief, it is supposed the fair creature died;
    And here is come to do some villainous shame to the dead bodies;
    I will apprehend him.

PARIS reveals himself to ROMEO saying:
    Stop thy unhallowed toil, vile Montague!
    I do apprehend thee;
    Obey and go with me, for thou must die.

ROMEO responds by telling PARIS:
    Good gentle youth, tempt not a desperate man;
    Fly hence and leave me;
    Put not another sin upon my head by urging me to fury;
    By heaven, I love thee better than myself;
    Stay not, be gone, live;
    And hereafter say a madman's mercy bid thee run away.

PARIS defies ROMEO and they fight, ending with PARIS mortally wounded, declaring:
    O, I am slain!
    If thou be merciful;
    Open the tomb, lay me with JULIET.

ROMEO begins his soliloquy recounting how his friend MERCUTIO told him that his kinsman PARIS should have married JULIET but is unsure whether he heard it, or dreamt it, or was experiencing a moment of insanity.

Although dead, ROMEO says to PARIS:
   O give me thy hand;
   in sour misfortune's book;
   I'll bury thee in a triumphant grave.

ROMEO opens the tomb to reveal JULIET inside, then continues his soliloquy

ROMEO in lament says:
   A grave? Oh, no!
   A lantern, slaughtered youth;
   For here lies JULIET;
   Her beauty makes this vault a feasting presence full of light;
   Death, lie thou there, by a dead man interred.

ROMEO lays PARIS in the tomb.

ROMEO continues his soliloquy on how death is experienced:
   How oft when men are at the point of death have they been merry;

Then how death cannot defeat beauty:
   O my love, my wife!
   Death, that hath sucked the honey of thy breath;
   Hath had no power yet upon thy beauty.

ROMEO next turns his attention to TYBALT in his bloody sheet, lying next to JULIET, saying that he can do TYBALT no better favour than to kill himself by the very hand that killed TYBALT.

ROMEO continues by addressing JULIET:
   Ah, dear JULIET, why art thou yet so fair?
   Shall I believe that unsubstantial death is amorous; And that
   the lean abhorred monster (death)
   Keeps thee here in dark to be his paramour (mistress)?

ROMEO determined that JULIET will not be death's mistress, declares:
   For fear of that, I still will stay with thee;
   And never from this palace of dim night depart again;
   Here, here will I remain with worms that are thy chamber maids.

ROMEO continues:
    Oh, here will I set up my everlasting rest;
    And shake the yoke of inauspicious stars;
    From this world-wearied flesh;
    Eyes, look your last;
    Arms, take your last embrace;
    Lips, the doors of breath, seal with a righteous kiss; A dateless
    to engrossing death.

ROMEO kisses JULIET, takes out the poison to drink, saying:
    Come, bitter conduct, come, unsavoury guide
    Thou desperate pilot, now at once run on
    The dashing rocks thy seasick, weary bark
    Here's to my love!

ROMEO drinks the poison, saying:
    O true apothecary
    Thy drugs are quick
    Thus with a kiss I die.

Enter FRIAR LAURENCE with lantern, crowbar, and spade. He stumbles upon BALTHASAR who identifies himself as a friend that knows the FRIAR well, and that ROMEO had Ben inside the Capulet's monument a full half an hour.

When asked by the FRIAR to go to the vault, BALTHASAR replies he dare not because his master, ROMEO, did menace him with death if he did stay to look on his intents.

The FRIAR tells him to stay, he will go alone, even though fear comes upon him, some ill unthrifty thing.

BALTHASAR occurs saying: I did sleep under this yew tree here; I dreamt my master and another fought; And that my master slew him.

The FRIAR approaches the tomb (vault/monument/sepulchre) saying to himself: Alack (sorrow), alack, what blood is this which stains the stony entrance of this sepulchre? What mean these masterless and gory swords to lie discoloured by this place of peace?

He enters the tomb remarking: ROMEO! O, pale! Who else? What, PARIS too? And steeped in blood?; Ah, what an unkind hour is guilty of this lamentable chance!; The lady stirs.

JULIET wakes up, who asks the FRIAR where is her ROMEO?

The FRIAR tells JULIET: come, come away from that nest of death, contagion, and unnatural sleep; Thy husband in thy bosom there lies dead; And PARIS too; I'll dispose of thee among a sisterhood of holy nuns; I dare no longer stay.

JULIET is adamant: Go, get thee hence, for I will not away.

Exit FRIAR LAURENCE from the tomb.

JULIET continues: What's here? A cup, closed in my true love's hand? Poison, I see, hath been his timeless end; and left no friendly drop to help me after? JULIET kisses ROMEO.

Enter the PAGE with WATCHMEN into the churchyard.

JULIET on hearing noise in the churchyard, snatches ROMEO's dagger, saying: O happy dagger; This is thy sheath (her body), then stabs herself. Finally, saying before she died: There rest, and let me die.

The FIRST WATCHMAN remarks: the ground is bloody. He then tells the other WATCHMEN to search about the churchyard; Go, some of you; whoe'er you find, attach (arrest).

Exit some WATCHMEN to do his bidding.

The FIRST WATCHMAN recounts: Pitiful sight! Here lies the County (PARIS) slain; And JULIET bleeding, warm and newly dead; Who here hath lain this two days buried. He then instructs other WATCHMEN: Go tell the PRINCE; Run to the CAPULETS; Raise up the MONTAGUES; some others search.

Exit other WATCHMEN.

The FIRST WATCHMAN continues his observations: We see the ground where on these woes do lie; But the true ground of all these piteous woes, we cannot without circumstances descry.

Enter some WATCHMEN with BALTHASAR, who is to be held until the PRINCE comes hither.

Enter another WATCHMAN with FRIAR LAURENCE, who is to be held because he had mattock and spade and was coming from this churchyard.

Enter the PRINCE and ATTENDANTS.

The PRINCE remarks: What misadventure is so early up, that calls our person from our morning rest?

Enter CAPULET and his WIFE, who tells the PRINCE and all present how people in the street cry 'ROMEO', some 'JULIET', and some 'PARIS', and all run with open outcry towards the monument.

The PRINCE in reply, demands: What fear is this which startles in our ears. The FIRST WATCHMAN answers: Sovereign, here lies the County PARIS slain; And ROMEO dead; And JULIET, dead before, warm and new killed.

The PRINCE then demands: Search, seek, and know how this foul murder comes. The FIRST WATCHMAN replies: Here is a friar, and slaughtered ROMEO's man, with instruments upon them fit to open these dead men's tombs.

LORD CAPULET in turmoil cries out that his daughter bleeds, and the knife (dagger) should in ROMEO's sheath instead of in his daughter's bosom. LADY CAPULET is just as distraught saying: This sight of death is as a bell that warns my old age to a sepulchre (tomb).

Enter LORD MONTAGUE, who replies to the PRINCE's remark on his early rising: Alas, my liege, my wife is dead tonight; Grief of my son's exile hath stopped her breath; What further woe conspires against mine age?

The PRINCE tells LORD MONTAGUE to look, and thou shalt see. MONTAGUE is aghast to see his son dead saying: What manners is in this, to press before thy father to a grave?

The PRINCE continues telling MONTAGUE to seal up the mouth of outrage for a while, till we can clear these ambiguities, and then will he judge, but in the meantime be a slave to patience, so bring forth the parties of suspicion.

FRIAR LAURENCE is brought forth and declares he is the greatest, able to do least, yet most suspected as the evidence is against him of this direful murder but stands ready to impeach and purge. Himself, his has already condemned and excused.

The FRIAR tells the PRINCE he will be brief in telling this tedious tale because his life is near its end:

    ROMEO, who lies there dead, was husband to that JULIET;
    I married them - their stolen marriage day was TYBALT doomsday;
    Whose untimely death (by ROMEO's sword);
    Banished the new-made bridegroom (ROMEO) from the city (Verona);
    For whom (ROMEO), and not TYBALT, JULIET pined;
    Then comes she to me - to rid her from this second marriage (to PARIS); Or in my cell there would she kill herself;
    Then gave I her a sleeping potion - for it wrought on her the form of death;
    Meanwhile I writ to ROMEO - to help to take her from her borrowed grave;
    FRIAR JOHN was stayed by accident - returned my letter back;
    At the prefixed hour of her waking, came I to take her from her vault;
    Here untimely lay the noble PARIS and true ROMEO dead;
    She wakes - but then a noise did scare me from the tomb;
    And she would not go - but did violence on herself;
    All this I know, and to the marriage her NURSE is privy.

FRIAR LAURENCE acknowledges: if aught in this miscarried by my fault, let my old life be sacrificed - unto the rigor of severest law.

The PRINCE replies: We still have thee for a holy man. He then demands: Where's ROMEO's man? What can he say in this?

BALTHASAR tells the PRINCE saying:
    I brought my master news of JULIET's death;
    And then in post he came from Mantua;
    To this same place, to this monument;
    This letter he early bid me give his father;
    And threatened me with death, going in the vault;
    If I departed not and left him there.

The PRINCE replies: Give me the letter; I will look at. He then demands: Where is the country's PAGE, that raised the watch?; Sirrah - What made your master in this place?

The PAGE replies:
    He came with flowers to strew his lady's grave;
    And bid me stand aloof, and so I did;
    Anon comes one (FRIAR LAURENCE) with light to open the tomb;
    And by and by my master drew (his sword) on him;
    And then I ran away to call the watch.

The PRINCE having listened and read the letter, replies:
  This letter doth make good the FRIAR's words;
  Their course of love, the tidings of her death;
  He (ROMEO) did buy a poison;
  Came to this vault to die and lie with JULIET.

The PRINCE in anger continues:
  Where be these enemies? - CAPULET! MONTAGUE!;
  See what a scourge is laid upon your hate;
  That heaven finds means to kill your joys with love!;
  And I - have lost a brace of kinsmen (MERCUTIO and PARIS).

CAPULET asks for MONTAGUE's hand in friendship, and gives his daughter's jointure (dowry) as an acceptance of his daughter's marriage to ROMEO.

MONTAGUE reciprocates by saying he will raise her statue in pure gold, that while Verona by that name is known, there shall no figure at such rate be set as that of true and faithful JULIET.

In conclusion, CAPULET adds: As rich shall ROMEO's by his lady's lie; Poor sacrifices of our enmity!

The PRINCE adds his conclusions:
  A glooming peace this morning with it brings;
  The sun for sorrow will not show his head;
  Go hence, to have more talk of these sad things;
  Some shall be pardoned, and some punished;

The PRINCE remarks:
  For never was a story of more woe
  Than this of JULIET (Capulet daughter) and her ROMEO (Montague son).

[*End of ACT 5 scene 3* Summary]

ROMEO - House of Montague

Romeo is the central character in the play and his actions help to move the plot along. He sends the audience on a roller-coaster ride.

He is the love-sick son of the Montagues. He has a very changeable character because at the start of the play he is overwhelmed with grief about his unrequited love for Rosaline and as soon as he meets Juliet he forgets about Rosaline and falls deeply in love with Juliet. We can characterise him as one who acts with his heart instead of his head, hence a certain impulsiveness reign in him.

He marries very quickly, kills very quickly and dies very quickly. He is also a very daring young man, and this is seen when he scales the walls of Juliet's Garden at the peril of death. He acts with much passion and his actions endears him to the audience. When he loves, he loves deeply and gives it his all - even his life. His shocking behaviour in killing both Tybalt and Paris is certainly a case of 'do or die'. He urged them not to provoke him and even declared his love for them, but they wouldn't relent so his behaviour is somewhat excused albeit wrong. He is also very kind and sensitive, and we see this in his liaison with the poor Apothecary whom he purchased the poison from.

Romeo is also headstrong and threatening because Balthasar got really scared when he ordered him to stay away from the tomb and he obediently adhered to his commands. He is a devoted cousin and friend but treats people with love and respect as seen in his communications with Benvolio, Mercutio, Friar Laurence, and the poor Apothecary. His sacrifices contribute to bringing about both his parents and the Capulet's union and an end to their feud.

Just like Romeo, she is the main character whose actions help to move the plot along. Her determination and strength of character endears her to the audience. Her independence and boldness leave the audience reeling.

Juliet is beautiful, young and energetic and takes matters into her own hands and tries to solve it. She can be categorised as being the romantic heroine of the play. Her unbounded love for Romeo and her actions are sometimes erratic and impulsive. She marries him very quickly and didn't think about its dire consequences. Not only was it bigamy if she married Paris but it ultimately led to both hers and Romeo's deaths, not to mention Paris'. Her behaviour does not fit into the normal norms of Elizabethan era where women had no voice and were ruled by the males in their family. Being a patriarchal society, Juliet's father controlled her life, claiming that she belonged to him, forcing her to marry Paris.

Juliet has taken some bold steps for a fourteen-year-old - she defies her parents and marries Romeo and allows him into her room to consummate their marriage.

She is brazen enough to take the potion irrespective of whether it kills her or not.

She was even prepared to stay in that gory, eerie tomb with all those rotting corpses. Her courage and her stubbornness overwhelmed the audience because she demonstrated an enormous amount of bravery in the end when she stabs herself and dies.

This headstrong, alluring character teaches us a lesson that

> 'love supersedes hate'

and that

> 'love conquers all'.

Hence unwittingly contributing to the union of her parents and that of the Montague's at the cost of her own life.

Friar Laurence is a very, very controversial character and some of his actions are debatable. He is warm and compassionate towards both Romeo and Juliet and it's obvious that they respect him and hold him in high esteem. The fact that they so trustingly and wholeheartedly entrusted their lives to the friar is proof of this. He is familiar with herbal concoctions and is very skilled at marrying nature with birth and death. He said that,

"Nature's mother, is her womb"

His is very perceptive because he could immediately detect Romeo's troubled mood,

"He argues a distempered read"

He works tirelessly to help Romeo and Juliet and he agrees to marry them in the hope that their families will re-unite. Sadly though, his good intentions go awry, and this unleashed a string of unfortunate incidents which culminates in the death of Romeo and Juliet.

The friar is always seen as godly and wise, but his actions are debatable. One can argue that since he is a man of God, not only must he adhere to the teachings of God not to lie, but he also set a bad example for the young lovers when he asked Romeo and Juliet to lie and pretend.

Furthermore, he shouldn't marry them without their parents' consent. He has orchestrated a devious and deceptive plot and he pretended that everything normal when Juliet was 'dead' in her room. He also told her parents that they are being punished and that they must not annoy God any further.

On the other hand, we just cannot criticise him, he had to do it because Juliet threatened suicide if he didn't find a solution to her problem. He gave her the potion which induced her into a death-like state.

He was also involved in Romeo's plan to visit Juliet in her room before his banishment. He also sheltered Romeo after he killed Tybalt and was banished. He tried in vain to send a message to Romeo in Mantua about his plans, unfortunately fate played a cruel trick, and the plague prevented the letter from being delivered which had serious consequences.

The friar worked tirelessly to solve Romeo and Juliet's problems. He went personally to the tomb to bring Juliet back to his cell until Romeo arrives. To his horror, he discovers Romeo's dead body and Juliet arousing from her sleep. She is distraught on awakening to find her husband Romeo next to her, now dead.

The friar heard sounds and he begged Juliet to hide with him, but she refused. We may argue that if he had not left her and hid, then maybe she would be alive. In the end the friar acknowledges his mistakes and was prepared to accept any punishment given to him because he felt personally responsible for the deaths of Romeo and Juliet.

The prince held the friar in high regard and investigated all the claims that the friar had made. He even read Romeo's letter from Balthasar and the Prince concluded that the friar was telling the truth, so he pardoned him. Although the Friar acted irresponsibly at times, we are ready to forgive him because he acted out of sheer love and compassion.

He is the headstrong, determined patriarch of the Capulet family. He rules with an iron fist as seen in his conversations with Juliet when she refused to marry Paris. There was a cold detachment between father and daughter because Juliet addressed him in rather formal terms, 'Lord' and 'father'. He yells,

> "wife my hands itch"

implying that he was going to use physical force against Juliet for defying his orders. We can juxtapose his harsh, cold and detached behaviour towards Juliet, his verbal abuse of her,

> "Out you green sickness, carrion!
> Out, you baggage! You tallow face!"

His behaviour here shocks the audience. Yet Capulet displayed a totally different character at the feast. He severely reprimands Tybalt for insisting that Romeo be removed from the ball because he infiltrated the function. Ironically, he shows much admiration and respect for Romeo.

Capulet was the dominating head of the family like most men in the Elizabethan patriarchal society. Lady Capulet's behaviour suggested that she was scared of her husband when Juliet asked her to tell Capulet that she didn't want to marry Paris. She ignores her daughter's pleas and tells Juliet to tell her father herself.

Lord Capulet's tendency for violence is also shown at the beginning when he asks for his sword to use against the Montague's when there was a disturbance on the street. Hilariously his wife says that he needs crutches and not a sword- referring to his old age and his inability to fight. He is also very distant and detached just like his wife regarding Juliet's feelings and her needs. This detachment is highlighted when he thinks that Juliet is weeping so profusely for Tybalt.

We can also surmise that Capulet, although hard on the exterior has a very endearing and profound love for Juliet. His emotive outburst when she died is heart-wrenching and we tend to empathise with his pain. We must also not forget his sudden change of heart when he learns that Juliet has changed her mind and has agreed to marry Paris. He was ecstatic- he gave in to her request for clothes, he didn't sleep on the night before the wedding, and he told the servants not to 'spare a dime' and to be lavish in the preparation of the wedding feast. In the end, his kind gesture to erect a statue of Romeo absolves Capulet of any unruly behaviour and we tend to sympathise with his pain of losing Juliet.

Lady Capulet strikes us as being cold and detached from Juliet needs and fragile emotions. Right at the outset, we are shocked to learn that the nurse was more of a mother to Juliet than lady Capulet was. Lady Capulet didn't even know the exact date of Juliet's birth, but the nurse could quote Juliet's exact day and date of her birth. The nurse also suckled Juliet as a baby, hence developing a close bond with her.

Lady Capulet ignored Juliet's pleas when she asked her mother to tell her father that she didn't want to marry Paris. She very blatantly told Juliet to tell her father herself.

Lady Capulet was very excited about the match between Juliet and Paris. The union between Juliet and Paris was more like a business contract because Lady Capulet describes Paris as,

"The gallant, young and noble gentleman"

Lady Capulet was also out of touch with Juliet's true feelings because just like Capulet, she too thought that Juliet was mourning for Tybalt.

"Evermore weeping for your cousin's death"

Lady Capulet was also emotionless because she says that Juliet's show of sadness and compassion is very silly.

"But much of grief shows still some want of wit"

Lady Capulet strikes us being vengeful and full of hate because she tries to console Juliet by seeking revenge on Romeo.

"We will have vengeance for it, fear thou not"

Lady Capulet tells her husband that Juliet doesn't want to marry Paris and she adds,

"I would the fool were married to her grave!"

She definitely foreshadows Juliet's fate because later Juliet does get 'married' to her grave. However, we have to juxtapose her reaction now to that of her remorse and sadness when Juliet dies.

Lady Capulet did not intervene furiously like the nurse in defending Juliet when she was harassed by her father for not wanting to marry Paris. All she said was,

> "Fie, Fie! What are you mad"

Yet the nurse was more vocal, and she stood up to Capulet who was very angry with her. The nurse yelled,

> "God in heaven bless her!
> You are to blame, my Lord to rate her so."

Juliet threatened to kill herself when she begged her mother to delay the marriage,

> "if you do not, make the bridal bed,
> in that dim monument where Tybalt lies"

This threat did not move her as a mother because in the end Juliet did carry out this threat and killed herself. Lady Capulet said,

> "Talk not to me, for I'll not speak a word. Do as thou wilt,
> for I have done with thee"

Juliet addressed her mother in very formal manner as 'Madam' or 'Ladyship' hence we see a distant relationship between mother and daughter.

Lady Capulet was very active in the wedding preparations, ready and eager to please her husband. Because of Juliet's acquiescence to marry Paris the next day, we see a different, more cordial tone to Lady Capulet's earlier brash tone when she later visits Juliet's bedroom

> "What, are you busy, ho? Need you my help?"

When Juliet dies, Lady Capulet was more interested in her own mortality and didn't react as deeply distraught as the nurse did when she saw Juliet 'dead' in her room.

The Nurse is a vital, energetic character who is central to moving the plot along.

Shakespeare presents her as a spunky, bawdy, humorous character who helps to cut the tension of a very serious and dramatic play.

Her joviality is rather endearing to the audience, and she is a huge influence on Juliet's life. Her unbounded love for Juliet is really admirable.

She constantly defends Juliet and understands her desires and her dilemmas. She takes Juliet's message to Romeo, and she is accosted and humiliated by Mercutio. When she comes back, she presents the audience with much humour when she beats around the bush' before she finally gives Romeo's message to Juliet.

She also goes faithfully to Friar Lawrence's cell and tells Juliet of Romeo's planned visit. She even produces the rope that Romeo would use to climb up to Juliet's chamber.

Nurse also breast-fed Juliet and even knows the exact date when she was born. She displays a deep-seated and profound affection for Juliet. Her bawdy jokes about Juliet's love life is quite entertaining.

"Go girl. Seek happy nights to happy days"

Sometimes Nurse's role can be controversial. Being the trusted intermediary, Nurse is compelled to make decisions about Juliet's life and doesn't always get it right. Unbeknown to Juliet, Nurse was acting in her own interests. Juliet became horrified when Nurse changed her viewpoint by undermining Romeo and praising Paris. Juliet was in utter shock and she called the nurse,

"O most wicked fiend"

Yet earlier on, Juliet addresses Nurse as:

'my dear nurse'; 'good nurse'.

Likewise, in a similar fashion, Nurse addresses Juliet in endearing terms as:

'lamb'; 'ladybird'; 'love'.

But lady Capulet does not address Juliet with this kind of love and affection.

Now Juliet decides to dump her trusted confidant and solve her own problems

We will draw a parallel between the Nurse's reaction to Juliet's 'death' in her room to that of her mother's when Juliet dies at the end. Lady Capulet shows her grief in just two lines which lacks total emotion, and these two lines are about herself,

"O me!
 This sight of death is as a bell,
 that warns my old age to a sepulchre."

Meaning that this death reminds me of my own mortality and that I will also die soon. Now when we juxtapose the Nurse's grief when she discovers Juliet 'dead'

In Juliet's room, we see that Nurse uses short, snappy sentences, repetition, exclamation marks and dark imagery to express her grief.

"O woe! O woeful, woeful, woeful, day!
 O day, O day, O day, O hateful day!"

We can feel the Nurse's deep pain and sadness from all these exclamations.

FATE

Another dominant theme of the play is fate. The play, right from the outset to the very end, experiences the wicked games the hand of fate plays in the lives of Romeo and Juliet. The chorus warns the audience that Romeo and Juliet are

'star-crossed lovers'

During the Elizabethan era people believed that the 'stars' controlled their fate and Shakespeare makes constant reference to the 'stars' throughout the play. Romeo especially makes reference to the stars because when he sees Juliet dead, he gives out a cry of agony and he curses the stars,

"Then I defy you stars"

He Firmly believes that the stars had shaped his fate and now the stars are responsible for Juliet's death. Even their meeting was an act of fate and their love doomed from the beginning because their families were sworn enemies.

Another example of the cruel hand of fate, which is the most important one is when Friar Lawrence's well-intended plans went awry, and his letter was not delivered to Romeo hence causing many problems which ultimately led to Romeo and Juliet's death. Romeo was unaware of the potion that Juliet drank because he didn't receive the letter, drinks the poison and kills himself which leads Juliet to wake up and kill herself.

It seemed as though fate governed every aspect of their lives and destroyed it in the end. Romeo at the beginning runs into Peter and Romeo reads the guest list and sees that Rosaline's name was on the list so he decided to go to the ball. Had he not bumped into Peter with the guest list, he wouldn't have gone to the ball and met Juliet.

Once again, we see the hand of fate leading them along.

It's important to note that Romeo had some sort of strange premonition when he went to the ball. He said that he feels like danger is,

"Hanging in the stars"

The friar also warns Romeo that people who act impulsively have destructive ends.

"These violent delights have violent ends"

When Romeo and Juliet have dreams and visualise finding each other dead in the tomb. The Prologue in Act 1 identifies Romeo and Juliet as being born into the feud,

"From forth the fatal loins of these two foes"

The use of the adjective 'fatal' suggests that Fate had controlled the lives of their children and their lives had to be sacrificed to bring about peace to these two hateful, warring families.

Romeo and Juliet are fundamentally the greatest love story ever written. The theme of Love dominates the play with its bursting, overwhelming passions that almost borders on insanity. Love is seen as an overwhelming, powerful force that sends Romeo and Juliet to the realms of ecstasy. Its dominant force allows Romeo and Juliet to make impulsive, irrational decisions that ends up in disaster.

At the beginning Romeo is very depressed about his unrequited love for Rosaline which is obviously superficial love because he forgot about his love for Rosaline as soon as he met Juliet. Their wild passion for each other sends the audience on a roller-coaster ride because this forbidden love overshadowed all human understanding and logic.

Romeo and Juliet defy their parents and get married without their consent and break all social barriers and norms because their families are enemies. This all-consuming love catapults them into heights that defies all reasoning: Juliet taking the potion, Juliet sleeping among the dead, rotten, worm-infested tomb, Romeo buying poison and killing himself, and Juliet stabbing herself with the dagger - all in the name of love.

When Romeo meets Juliet, he associates her to the heavens, and he uses light imagery to describe his passionate love for her and her beauty.

> "O she doth teach the torches to burn bright."

And Juliet is the 'sun' and her eyes are the 'stars.' He associates his love to being 'heavenly' and 'pure.' We should also look at parental love. Juliet's parents were very detached from her emotions throughout the play but in the end their true love for her spilled out when they expressed their grief at her death.

The Nurse's unwavering, deep love for Juliet is that pure unconditional love that Juliet experienced. One can connote that at the end Shakespeare deliberately left the nurse out in the final scene when Juliet died because maybe the nurse would have been genuinely devastated and would have showed it in her endless wailing.

When we look at Romeo's mother's relationship with him, there seems to be a deep, genuine love and concern on lady Montague's part. At the beginning of the play, she was very happy that Romeo did not get involved in the brawl. She also died of heartbreak when she heard that Romeo was banished.

Hence in the end, despite its tragic events, we learn that "Love conquers all"

Q1   How does Shakespeare present the ways in which Tybalt's hatred
of the Capulets in fluences the outcome of the play?   **[40]***
Refer to this **Extract** from Act 1 Scene 5 and elsewhere in the play.

*In this **Extract**, Tybalt has just spotted Romeo at the Capulets' party
and expresses his anger to Capulet.*

Extract

TYBALT	*'Tis he, that villain Romeo.*
CAPULET	*Content thee, gentle coz, let him alone.*
....	
TYBALT	*It fits, when such a villain is a guest.*
....	
CAPULET	*He shall be endured:*
....	
TYBALT	*Why, uncle, 'tis a shame.*
CAPULET	*Go to, go to;*
....	
TYBALT	*Patience perforce with wilful choler meeting*
....	

OR

To what extent do you think Shakespeare presents Juliet's response
to love as impulsive and dangerous?
Explore at least two moments from the play to support your ideas.

[40]*

Q2   [1.1] What does the extract show an audience about Juliet's
thoughts and feelings at this point in the play?
Refer closely to details from the extract to support your answer.

[20 minutes 15 marks]

[1.2] How does Shakespeare present love in Romeo and Juliet?
Refer to characters and events from the play in your answer.

[40 minutes 15 marks]

Extract
Romeo and Juliet – from Act 4nScene 3, lines 24 to 88
In this extract, Juliet doubts the intention of the Friar

Q3(a) Explore how Shakespeare presents the character of Lord Capulet in this extract.
Refer closely to the **Extract** in your answer.

(b) In this **Extract**, Lord Capulet demonstrates his power as head of the Capulet family.
Explain the importance of power elsewhere in the play.
In your answer, you must consider:
- how power is presented
- the effects power has within the play.

You must refer to the context of the play in your answer.

Extract
Romeo and Juliet – from Act 1 Scene 5, lines 60 to 88
In this extract, Tybalt is complaining about Romeo being at the Capulet party.

[Total 40 marks]

Q4 Starting with this moment in the play, explore how Shakespeare
presents relationships between adults and young people in 'Romeo
and Juliet'.
Write about:
- how Shakespeare presents relationships between adults and young
  people at this moment in the play
- how Shakespeare presents relationships between adults and young
  people in the play as a whole.

*Read the following **Extract** from Act 3 Scene 5 of Romeo and Juliet and then
answer the question that follows.*
*At this point in the play, Juliet has just been told that she must marry
Paris.*

Extract
CAPULET
- How now, wife,
Have you delivered to her our decree?
LADY CAPULET
Ay, sir, but she will none, she gives you thanks.
I would the fool were married to her grave.
CAPULET
Soft, take me with you, take me with you, wife.
....
JULIET
Not proud you have, but thankful that you have:
....
CAPULET
How how, how how, chopt-logic? What is this?

[30 marks] AO4 [4 marks]

Q5 Discuss how Shakespeare presents the character of Lady Capulet in the play.

[Total 40 marks]

Q6 Discuss the relationship between Romeo and Juliet in the play.

[Total 40 marks]

Q7 Discuss how Shakespeare presents the character of Friar Laurence in the play.

[Total 40 marks]

Q8 Discuss how Shakespeare presents the character of Tybalt in the play.

[Total 40 marks]

Q9 Discuss the relationship between Juliet and her Nurse in the play.

[Total 40 marks]

Q10 Discuss the theme of 'Fate' in the play.

[Total 40 marks]

Q11 Discuss the theme of 'Love' in the play.

[Total 40 marks]

Q12 Discuss how Shakespeare presents the character of Mercutio in the play.

[Total 40 marks]

Q13 Discuss the role of Prince Escalus in administering justice in the play.

[Total 40 marks]

Q14 Discuss the role of the servants to promote and support the feud between the Capulets and the Montagues.

[Total 40 marks]

Q15 Discuss how Shakespeare presents the character of Romeo in the play.

[Total 40 marks]

Q16 Discuss how Shakespeare presents the character of Juliet in the play.

[Total 40 marks]

AUTHOR

AUTHOR

Evelyn Samuel was born in South Africa, educated at the University of Durban-Westville, gaining a BA in English, Speech and Drama. She then went on to gain a Higher Education Diploma at the University of South Africa, and then onto the UK where her knowledge and skills were applied in educating students to achieve top grades in English Language and Literature up to A-level. Evelyn gained her Qualified Teacher Status in 2006, but in her pursuit to explore new horizons, continued her education gaining Diplomas in teaching English as a Foreign Language' to International Students, 'Writing Stories for Children', and most recently, gaining a Diploma in 'Travel Journalism'. Apart from teaching and writing, Evelyn's interests include travel to exotic places, cycling, dance, cuisine, and exploring new horizons.

www.EveSuperEasyBooks.com
EveSuperEasyBooks@gmail,com

STUDY GUIDE

Evelyn provides an in depth **SUPER SUPER EASY** interpretation of one of Shakespeare's most popular plays, first performed circa 1597 at the Curtain theatre, a forerunner and neighbour to the famous Globe theatre built in 1599. This guide is a must for those students determined to achieve a top grade in English Literature at any level from Key Stage 3 to GCSE to A-level.

STORY LINE

Shakespeare's Romeo and Juliet is the story of two young people who fall in love but find themselves on opposite sides of a feud between their two families. The Capulets expect their daughter Juliet to marry her suitor, Paris. However, Juliet cannot bear to marry anyone but Romeo of the House of Montague, so they get married in secret with the help of Juliet's Nurse and Friar Laurence. Unfortunately, because of the ongoing feud, Tybalt of the House of Capulet challenges Romeo to a fight. Instead, Mercutio, a close friend of Romeo, enraged at Romeo's refusal to fight accepts the challenge and is accidentally killed by Tybalt when Romeo intervenes to stop the fight. Romeo reacts by seeking revenge, fights Tybalt and kills him. In judgement, Prince Escalus banishes Romeo from Verona. Romeo is distraught, as he cannot be now with Juliet, his newlywed wife. In a desperate attempt to reunite with Romeo, Juliet seeks help from Friar Laurence who persuades her to fake her own death as a ruse to escape her next-day, would-be bigamous marriage to her suitor Paris, chosen by her parents Lord and Lady Capulet. Tragically, Romeo is not aware of the ruse, as a letter sent by Friar Laurence explaining the ruse, fails to reach him in time. Romeo arrives to find Juliet dead, or so he thinks. Distraught, he drinks poison and dies next to the drugged Juliet. When Juliet awakes, she is devastated to discover Romeo's dead body beside her. Consequently, she stabs herself, so that, as in life, she would be with her true love Romeo in death.

Printed in the USA
CPSIA information can be obtained
at www.ICGtesting.com
LVHW071939251123
764815LV00013B/70